GETTING
Praised
Raised AND
Recognized

MURIEL SOLOMON

PRENTICE HALL
Englewood Cliffs, New Jersey 07632

Prentice-Hall International (UK) Limited, *London*
Prentice-Hall of Australia Pty. Limited, *Sydney*
Prentice-Hall Canada, Inc., *Toronto*
Prentice-Hall Hispanoamericana, S.A., *Mexico*
Prentice-Hall of India Private Limited, *New Dehli*
Prentice-Hall of Japan, Inc., *Tokyo*
Simon & Schuster Asia Pte. Ltd., *Singapore*
Editora Prentice-Hall do Brasil, Ltda., *Rio de Janeiro*

10 9 8 7 6 5 4 3 2 1

To Steven, Amy, Brian, and Catherine

Solomon, Muriel.
　　Getting Praised, Raised, and Recognized / Muriel Solomon.
　　　　p. cm.
　　Includes index.
　　ISBN 0-13-355157-1. -- ISBN 0-13-355165-2 (pbk.)
　　1. Career development. 2. Self-presentation. 3. Self-realization.
　　4. Interpersonal relations. I. Title.
HF5381.S6462 1993
650.1--dc20   92-35568
                                                    CIP

PRENTICE HALL
Professional Publishing
Englewood Cliffs, NJ 07632
Simon & Schuster. A Paramount Communications Company

INTRODUCTION

You can't afford to be ignored, but opportunities to stand out from the crowd seldom drop in your lap. This book is about getting the notice you need—creating your own breaks, detecting the right circumstances, and saying the right words.

Whether you're shy, verbose, or moderately talkative, however, you share a common problem. Yesterday you felt secure if you did your work and got along well with others. Today you can no longer bank on good performance alone. You have to think beyond your particular job and prove your worth to the whole organization.

Receiving recognition spells survival. This means letting go of misdirected modesty. Reveal your competence because the top brass have antennae that pick up signals when you're considered valuable to the company. Your job and your future hinge on that *perceived* value. So forget reality as you see it and deal with *their* presumptions.

But if no one's paying attention, how can you demonstrate your merit after you've been ignored, gored, or unrewarded? You embark on a tested plan to alter interpretations that click into place whenever people see and hear you or read about you.

In *Getting Praised, Raised, and Recognized,* you'll find uncomplicated, nitty-gritty, sure-fire strategies, logical steps, and word-for-word scripts. Use them to overcome your particular trouble spots and to

- grab and keep attention, becoming more visible and audible;
- take initiative in making your job more important;
- spell out direction for your professional development;
- receive the credit and respect you've earned;
- advance what others perceive as their self-interests;
- build a bigger support base inside and outside the office;
- understand your options when dealing with discrimination;
- establish a more relaxed, congenial working atmosphere.

In the marketplace, these are saleable skills.

Each of the book's four parts examines a separate goal: to be seen in the best possible light as (1) a winner, (2) a skillful and innovative performer, (3) a rising star, and (4) a valued part of the company. The contents page identifies suggested treatment for more than 100 specific symptoms of being undervalued.

Opportunities to change perceptions are there for the taking, yet remarkably, few people are takers. Either you don't know how or you won't risk the wrong approach. But to improve results, you have to take the plunge, stop the spin you're in, and turn the situation around to your advantage.

The strategies you'll read aren't difficult but do require putting your tongue in park until you start your brain. Rarely do perplexing situations demand instant replies. You'll usually have time to grab this quick reference book from your desk drawer. I hope the information will serve you well in getting the notice, recognition, and rewards you deserve.

Muriel Solomon

CONTENTS

PART I

REWARDS

BEING PERCEIVED AS A WINNER

Sometimes you're too smart for your own good. Being too open and too successful also makes you too threatening. Once bosses worry that you might replace them, or that your glory might diminish their reputation, they may hold you back. Learn a cardinal rule from politicians: *Never outshine your boss.* If you do, someone less qualified gets the prize you deserve.

And that's just one of myriad ways you can lose out. Another is to think of yourself as a loser. Your opinion becomes transparent and contagious. Soon others get the same idea.

Hanging on to your job and moving up depend on delicate maneuvering to protect the way you come across. You can reverse a negative outcome by projecting the image of a winner: someone everyone wants to follow who's also a team player doing what's best for boss and company.

Continually position yourself, especially when you're feeling misled, manipulated, or embarrassed. Straightforward but tactful responses are effective during good-faith bargaining.

1

SAFEGUARDING YOUR SIDETRACKED INTERESTS

Your cowardly boss slides a migraine decision off his desk onto yours with "You do this so well." That's using flattery to set you up to take the rap. Or, after you've mounted a great track record and the boss eliminates your position by reorganizing or makes conditions so uncomfortable that a lesser-paying job sounds inviting, recognize the camouflage to hold you back or ease you out.

You also may become the sacrificial lamb because of a change in conditions. An embarrassed boss can't face you after having to renege on a promise or reshuffle limited resources. A greedy boss is so intent on pursuing her own needs, she's oblivious to yours.

Ensnared by such antics, you can still come out feeling good and looking in control as you protect your own interests.

1.1 HIDDEN AGENDAS
Handling Intentionally Misleading Bosses

You suspect your boss of a cover-up. He's disguising the real reason for cutting a hefty chunk out of your budget. His explanation is faulty because your results *do* justify the costs, and this cut jeopardizes your program's success. The boss knows this as well as you do, but his tone says, "This is a done deed, don't argue with me."

You feel uneasy. You sense that you're hearing only a part of the story. Maybe he considers you a threat and he's trying to push you out. Maybe he wants you to be the fall guy if the project fails. The list of motive "maybes" is as endless as the string of methods: hedging doubletalk, seesaw decisions, contradictory statements, to name a few. What's the boss's hidden agenda? And how can you come out of this without permanent scars?

Strategy

Freeze! Delay your response until you get some straight answers to learn what else is involved here. Dig out the concrete from the heap of ambiguous, abstract talk.

Steps

1. Ask questions instead of countering with legitimate arguments. While correcting the boss is a tremendous temptation, that's not disclosing *why* he's acting this way. If possible, excuse yourself to continue the discussion a little later, after you've had time to give his decision some thought.

2. Suggest alternatives. Once you're able to make a good guess, you can probably come up with ideas to meet your boss's needs as well as your own.

Script

Boss, I understand your budgetary concerns, but I'm confused about our objectives. Do we still have the same ones or have they been changed? (Originally, budget and objectives were aligned, and if you cut the former you have to adjust the latter.)

Look, Tom, I'm sure you know what I meant.

No, boss, I'm not sure. Is there something you're not telling me? Some other problem we should be discussing? (Gently probe for the hidden reason.)

Well, Tom, to be perfectly frank, I'm getting pressure from upstairs that, in today's shifting market, the project's costs could be lowered if we hired an outside group to . . .(Bingo! The boss is protecting his own job while yours tosses in the wind. He needs more solid ammunition to withstand the pressure.)

Boss, would it help you (you've put yourself on the boss's side, not against him) *if I were to prepare a schedule of comparative costs . . . ? What if we were to change the targets to include . . .?* (You've now made yourself and your boss a team to help meet company priorities.)

Summary

If your suggestions are accepted, fine. But that's not your main objective. You want the boss to see that your concern extends beyond your own welfare to include the best interests of your boss and the organization. Your future brightens as the boss realizes you are more valuable as an ally than as a scapegoat. So even if you lose this particular match, you've positioned yourself to win later on.

1.2 SNOOKERED
Knowing Your Vulnerability Reduces Deception

Some bosses constantly manipulate you because you keep falling for their tricks. You jump every time the boss butters you up with excessive, unearned praise. Or you produce an unreasonable amount of work because she keeps telling you, "I know you won't let me down." Or he clams up with a sulky stare until you agree to do what you were told. Or her praises, followed by "however, you shoulda" send you scrambling to redo the assignment over and over again. Or you avoid clearing the air because you're afraid any hint of disagreement may keep you from advancing.

While emotional vulnerability buttons come in a variety of shapes, some bosses have figured out just the one to touch to make you jump through the hoop. When you wake up, you feel put upon, at times exploited and trapped. Without jeopardizing your job, how can you get the boss to level with you and treat you fairly? How can you look like a winner when you feel like a victim?

Strategy

Plan ahead and rehearse your response. By knowing "if they say this, I'll say that," you avoid reacting automatically when someone pulls the emotional trigger that hits your susceptibility spot.

Steps

1. Identify the hard-to-resist ploy. Whether it's flattery, guilt, pride or fear of confrontation, recognize the emotional appeal *as it's being made.* Program your brain to sound the alarm, and lock your lips until you figure out what to do.

2. Practice your responses at home. Literally, figure out exactly what you will say next time you want to offer an alternative or turn down the boss. Say it out loud, hear yourself say it. If you need more rehearsal, record your voice and play back the tape to improve your replies.

3. Delay a few moments to consider the request. Review your options, the pros and cons, the consequences. If the request seems reasonable, accept with a simple okay. If not, question it or come up with a substitute way to handle the matter. If this is a phone request, hang up and say you'll call right back.

Script

Boss, I appreciate your kind comments, but I think we have to examine the distribution routine a little closer. Perhaps we could . . . (Be gracious about phony praises, but shift immediately to the facts. Talk about what's needed. Help your boss stand on grounds that are firmer than those built on flattery.)

(With a smile and a laugh) *Aw, c'mon, boss, you wouldn't be trying to make me feel guilty, would you?"* (In other words, "Boss, I'm on to your game.")

Boss, are you annoyed about something? Have I offended you? If so, I apologize, but please tell me what it is so that I can correct it. (Force an end to the silent treatment. If hostility is there, get it out in the open where you can deal with it.)

Let me play back what I thought you wanted (let's clear the air) *because I don't want to waste any more of your time. Please stop me when I get off the track.*

Summary

Some bosses who sense your insecurity will try to take advantage of you. Whether you choose to laugh off or pleasantly confront a manipulative attempt or let them know that you know what they're doing, act like a winner. Refuse to let others con you. As they press your vulnerability button, surprise them with a controlled response.

1.3 LEGAL ROBBERY

When Another Project Gets "Your" Resources

At your lean-staffed agency, you and Ellen, another project director, have been sharing a secretary and a receptionist/typist. At this morning's staff meeting you learned Ellen talked the boss into having "your" receptionist/typist work exclusively for her project in order to pursue an additional revenue source.

Flabbergasted, you expressed surprise and asked to discuss the matter later. Now, in anticipation, you're staring down a double-barrel problem. First, the switch leaves you short-staffed and second, you fear you've lost prestige in the office. Your adversary considers you too weak to fight back. Let her keep that thought—for now.

Strategy

Act as though you are going along with their plan. Then, to undo or modify the sealed deal, unobtrusively bargain to recoup part of your losses.

Steps

1. Swiftly gather background information before the discussion. Use basic who, what, when, where, why, and how queries. Determine if the commitment is temporary or long term. Adjust your thinking to current reality.

2. Assess your damage. If you'll need to cut down on quality or quantity, can you omit parts of your current operation until you regain some resources?

3. Declare yourself part of the act. Then come in the back door. Ask questions instead of accusing the plotters.

Script

Well, boss, it's good news that we have another potential source of revenue. (A pleasant, professional, nonconfrontational manner keeps a boss comfortable rather than defensive.)

Am I correct in assuming this new venture will require . . .? (soft, inquiring, interested tone) *I understand why you'd want to shift staff, but how do we meet the problem of . . .? What if we were to suspend the xyz part of my operation temporarily until we see some increased profit* (you can't maintain quality without the transferred typist), *then I could help Ellen by supplying . . .* (pointing up your value to them by volunteering your expertise).

Good, our secretary is so used to working with me that this task shouldn't take much more of her time. (You gave up 50 percent of the receptionist/typist's time, but have managed to get more than half of the more valuable secretary's time.)

Summary

On balance, you may lose a little of the resources. But you win by preventing the quality of your work and your reputation from going down the drain. Furthermore, by standing up for yourself, the boss and your colleagues will no longer take you for granted, expecting you to go along silently with whatever plot they happen to hatch. You've elevated their perceptions of you.

1.4 WELSHERS
Dealing with Bosses Who Habitually Renege

Your boss has promised you (a promotion) (an assignment) (an office with a window) (you name it). And what did you get instead? Excuses or silence on the subject.

Many people make promises they forget. Frankly, your interests aren't automatically their top concern just because something is vital to you. Most bosses are glad to comply when reminded. Some keep the faith and forget to tell you.

But others make the promise expressly to avoid a hassle and have no intention of following through. Your blood pressure is rising because you feel mistreated, and you're afraid to call the boss on his unkept word. You even begin to doubt your own memory: "The boss *did* say that he'd recommend my proposal to the board. Sure, he did! Either the boss is getting senile or he just doesn't give a damn about me and the contributions I make."

In the face of insincere or forgotten promises, how can you maintain your self-respect and project self-confidence?

Strategy

Maintain your composure by *assuming* the incident is the result of a misunderstanding. Accusing the boss of reneging will get you nowhere now and hurt your chances to change future outcomes. Then clarify the boss's position and your own.

Steps

1. Eliminate the possibility of preoccupation or absentmindedness. By questioning the boss, you reveal your interest, lower your anxiety, and avoid embarrassing charges when mere forgetfulness was the culprit.

2. Agree on facts and semantics. Assumptions aren't facts. Distinguish between what is actually so and what you inferred. Discuss and spell out vague or ambiguous terms. Give the boss a chance to correct your misconceptions.

3. Synthesize your views. Blend your thinking, suggesting future action that would be mutually beneficial.

Script

Boss, I'd like to call your attention to an oversight. (Your cool, composed, eye-on-the-ball, professional manner keeps the boss from getting defensive.) *I know you're a man of your word,* (attributing the highest motive) *and so you've probably just been too busy to take my proposal . . .*

Boss, I'm a little confused. I'd appreciate your clarifying something for me . . . (and after the explanation) *Let me recap our discussion to be sure I have it straight.*

(After you're convinced the boss reneged on his promise on purpose) *Boss, what was the problem here? Why were we* (softer than the finger-pointing "why were you") *unable to . . .? Yes, I see your problem, and I hope you can see mine. . . .Well, in that case, perhaps we could establish a concise written rule that crystalizes the policy for all of us.*

Summary

Calmly state your concerns as a conscientious member of the team. Then direct the discussion toward working with your boss so that you both arrive at the same solution. If you roll over dead, you look like a wimp. If you confront, tactfully and pleasantly, you look like a winner.

1.5 I.O.U.s

Bartering's Better Than Giving Away Favors

Beware of the wheeler-dealer, the "do this for me now, I'll do that for you later" type. For example, your boss said, "Work on this project for a couple of months, and I'll back you for a raise next budget period, okay?" It was a request, not a threat, yet you feared the boss would make life miserable if you didn't comply. So you did the extra work, and the raise never came.

Make it a rule to do the favor *only* if it makes you feel good and glow with importance over helping your boss or organization. But don't do it because you want the boss to "owe you one," expecting a long-range promise to be honored. Where is the ironclad, gold-rimmed guarantee that the boss will pay up? Furthermore, the boss might resent feeling indebted to you and give you the cold shoulder from then on.

When you're asked to do a favor that inconveniences you, tie your acceptance to old-fashioned bartering.

Strategy

Request something in exchange for the favor. It needn't be of equal value, even a token will suffice. But this is necessary to protect your self-respect and to keep others from taking advantage of you.

Steps

1. Be prepared with a list of your own favors. Think ahead about the changes you'd like made or what would make your work easier. When the opportunity arises, you're ready with bartering chits.

2. Establish the barter immediately. Right after the boss issues the request, graciously accept, then tactfully suggest how you can be repaid.

Script

Boss, I'll be glad to help out on the project while Jack is away. (establishing you're a team player) *However, I might not have time to complete my other work.* (The boss has created the problem, and you're tossing it right back.) *Could we put those density reports we discussed on hold, temporarily, until Jack returns?* (Now you're offering a solution, a fair exchange.)

That's okay, boss (friendly, cooperative attitude). *I have no problem coming in Saturday mornings, but I would appreciate your adjusting my weekday schedule. It would help me to leave at 4 instead of at 5* P.M. (Appeal to the boss's sense of fair play; you have every right to expect to be compensated in some way for your overtime.)

Summary

Few people truly appreciate your giving them something for nothing. It's human nature to place more value on what we pay for than on what we get gratis and to show more respect to the person who charges us than to the one who doesn't. Therefore, if you're going to grant a favor, get at least something symbolic in return for your efforts.

1.6 OUTSIDER

When Someone Else Is Hired for "Your" Job

You're feeling cheated, hurt, disappointed, puzzled, and insecure. Your administrative ability is rated topnotch. You always meet your goals and your budget. So why is the company bringing in an out-of-towner to replace your retiring boss instead of moving you up? Why weren't you promoted?

Perhaps the board wants a public relations advantage, an appointee with a recognized reputation. Maybe the one hired has political clout. On the other hand, maybe you're regarded as lacking a particular skill or talent.

You may, for instance, be an excellent implementing manager, but appear thin on creativity and motivation. If you dutifully follow the company line, without question or suggestion, nobody knows your vision for improving the company. Do some honest soul-searching. Then ask your boss why you were overlooked and adjust your actions accordingly.

Strategy

Learn what you need to do to get on the bandwagon. Discover the direction in which the company is headed and concentrate on helpful ways the company can improve and grow. Create opportunities to express your conclusions to your boss.

Steps

1. Think up and test ideas to carry out the company's new emphasis. Start with the company's stated objectives. Read everything relevant you can get your hands on: reports, newsletters, news stories, journal articles. Record in-depth discussions on radio and TV. Make notes when important people talk about trends and patterns in your industry. Then work up new approaches you can try out in your own unit. If needed, take courses or attend seminars to strengthen your weak areas.

2. Break out of the mold. Separate yourself from your peers who are also fine performers. Tactfully broadcast your successes. Relate accomplishments of your particular unit to the larger picture. Inoffensively tell how you get things done, suggesting how the plan can be applied to other parts of the company. Rehearse your responses to anticipated challenging questions.

3. Reach new contacts and establish important pacts. Working within the framework of your rules, discuss with your boss the advantages of forming new alliances.

Script

I really hope you can be frank with me, boss. I have to know how I placed in the competition so that I can work on areas where I need to improve. (Stop torturing yourself and get facts you can work on.) *And what is the company looking for at this time?*

I'd like to share with you some information about a plan we've been testing in my division. My spirited crew is very excited about the results. We've increased production and dropped absenteeism to an all-time low, so there may be some parts you'd like to adapt . . . (Soft-pedal the boasting.)

It seems to me we're going downhill with our traditional thinking and we need to try some different approaches to get past this difficult period. I've talked to several key people on the outside and . . .

Summary

Consider your being overlooked a beginning instead of the end. If you didn't get the job you think you deserve, it's time to let other people know how good you really are. People can't know what you're thinking if you keep still. Talk about your vision for the company—your job isn't simply making widgets, you're helping to establish a nationwide clamor for your products. Tell the boss you want the next promotion and you're willing to work very hard to get it.

1.7 LEAPFROG
Being Bypassed Again on a Meaty Assignment

You know you are extremely competent and capable, but you're afraid that you're coming across as a loser. You can't understand why you were overlooked to represent the department at the forthcoming conference. You work harder and produce better results than Terry, who was chosen instead of you.

The first thing to consider: Exactly what is it on which you're working so hard? Are your energy and time expended on tasks the boss considers mediocre priority? Or are you so busy doing a good job that you didn't realize you were stepping on toes? Is it possible that the boss perceives you as a threat and doesn't want to give you any more exposure?

Why guess? Whether you need to apologize, share credit, or start working on whatever the company considers most important, you are going to have to have a talk with your boss.

Strategy

Shed the loser feeling by making positive plans. Shine some light on the invisible net of poor perceptions that's entrapped you. Only then can you pinpoint the changes you want to make in the way you've been acting.

Steps

1. Identify your own unique talent that your boss has previously found especially useful. Recall past conversations and evaluations. Decide how you can use this talent again to show your boss that you're ready for more important assignments.

2. Ask your boss for feedback. Accept any criticism without alibis or excuses. Discuss how you intend to correct any problems that surface, setting up a progress report schedule if appropriate. Give honest credit for your boss's help when you document your accomplishments.

3. Become more knowledgeable or proficient in any area where the boss or company wants to focus. Be more alert to the boss's priorities and prepare to shift your energy and emphasis there. Research, memorize vital stats, prepare notes, and rehearse so that you can talk extemporaneously on trends, developments, or the latest laws or regulations.

Script

Boss, you've mentioned my coordinating ability a few times. I was wondering, would it be helpful if I were to set up a meeting of representatives from _____ *?* (Creating tasks that the boss regards as valuable makes your stock go up.)

I'd appreciate your telling me frankly why I wasn't picked so that I can work on being chosen next time. . . . I can see how that could disturb you. Why don't we alter the routine a little to avoid a repetition . . . (Don't argue, even if it's not your fault. Shift to a better way of doing something.)

According to this month's journal, the companies studied achieved a 25 percent reduction by . . . (Show you're on top of the latest news and interested in the whole company, not just your unit.)

Summary

When you're repeatedly bypassed on the best assignments and feel your work is as good or better than those chosen, go right to the horse's mouth and ask your boss why. Accept your responsibility, and then shift any criticism of you, personally, to the system and how it can be improved. Find new ways to display your talent and knowledge.

1.8 APPROPRIATORS

When Bosses Use Your Ideas as Their Own

The boss expressed no opinion at all when you presented your cost-cutting plan. Not for or against, just "Hmmm." Later, he told the group about *his* plan, never mentioning that it came from you.

Relax. You'll feel better after you realize this shows that your thinking and your boss's are simpatico. If only subconsciously, the boss associates you with having good ideas. Even if you are not specifically and appropriately thanked, it's like money in the bank. You're earning the boss's interest in you.

Sometimes bosses absorb your thoughts through osmosis, and subconsciously blend them with their own. Unfortunately, other people do deliberately pick your brain and have never learned to give or share credit. Nevertheless, remember that the boss believes your thinking is on target. So walk tall—you are a valuable asset! Just repackage your contributions.

Strategy

Change the way you've been feeding the boss ideas. Devise a plan to get your talent acknowledged.

Steps

1. Separate your ideas into two categories—those you do and those you don't want credit for. Changes in rules and procedures benefit you more if bosses believe they originated them. Keep on planting these suggestions, and giving them time to grow within the boss's mind. Without nagging, persistently allude to them.

2. Supply innovative ideas and plans at committee or staff meetings. Aim to improve high-priority matters. Or submit a proposal to the boss, in writing, with copies to other personnel affected.

Script

Boss, when you mentioned that we should reduce delivery costs, did you mean that we should centralize this function . . .? (If disrupting a routine may be unpopular, let the idea come from the top instead of from you. If the change smacks of an opportunity, go after it.)

My proposal is that we can increase our sales by contacting . . . (Think your suggestions through carefully in advance so that you're prepared to answer every anticipated objection.)

Summary

Be encouraged if the boss is "stealing" your ideas and using them as the boss's own. That's reassurance that your thinking is on track and very much needed. Now go the next step. Present your ideas when others are present, defending your position. You'll be looked at as a winner.

To safeguard your sidetracked interests, stop feeling like a victim or waiting for people to come to you or change their troublesome ways. Go after the support you need and the fair treatment you deserve. Learn to bargain for those concerns that are important to you and you'll often hit paydirt.

2

NEGOTIATING FOR THE ACTION YOU WANT

You don't have to be a magician to pull a reward out of your hatbox of complaints. You just need a plan. When you're angry about the direction of your career, or the cut in your travel allotment, or the piddling pay for a lengthened workweek, your boss doesn't know what you're thinking if you don't tell. And if your goal is to effect some changes, you need to negotiate.

Think of negotiating as exchanging. You're willing to give up something in order to get something else. The boss is used to this give and take, so you needn't feel intimidated. But you do have to be prepared.

You can't plot a good, positive plan working on an emotional, negative thought. So convert the negative to a positive, as in "I'm furious at the way the boss keeps dumping rush jobs on my desk at 4 P.M." to "We need a better plan for processing late developments."

Once you're clear on the idea, gather facts, define and prioritize your goals, and devise a game plan.

2.1 MUZZLED
Listening and Letting Others Speak First

When fact-gathering leaves you with more questions than answers, don't settle for "I assume that." If you're uncertain about the boss's feelings, ask to discuss the matter. Then hush up and listen as you probe for pertinent information.

Hearing the boss spell out what's important before you put your cards on the table gives you an immediate advantage. You know what interests and needs to emphasize when it's your turn to talk.

People can't process a lot of information at once. If you'll limit yourself to two or three clear, concise, specific points that you relate directly to the concerns they just expressed, their heads will snap to attention. Listen also for a common thread that runs through both your views.

Strategy

Pull together divergent opinions. You and your boss need to know each other's thinking, and it's quite possible the boss has not been aware of yours. Once you make this known, try to break the impasse. Look for an alternative that allows you both to escape through the horns of the dilemma.

Steps

1. Clarify meanings. The same word can have different interpretations. "Many" times computes as a dozen times to you, three or four to someone else. Listen for ambiguous terms. If you sense a disguised message, ask more questions. Also you can unmask concealed feelings by watching body language.

2. Make mental notes of repetition. When you hear an idea reiterated in a variety of ways ("backlog," "behind schedule," "need a faster way,"), you know your boss feels strongly about it.

3. Remain unemotional and businesslike. Stick to issues and neither side gets defensive, each respecting the right to its own views. Come across calm, confident, and cooperative. If you think you're being intimidated, tactfully respond with the facts to avoid threatening an insecure boss.

4. Recap points the boss made. Differentiate between issues you're willing to go along with as part of the team and those where you disagree.

5. Offer a compromise. Suggest how each of you could give in a little to get something you want.

Script

Excuse me, boss, but what do you mean when you say "urgent"? (Clarify—one person's pickle is another's relish.) *Could you give me some sample situations where that would apply?*

You mentioned the department's reputation a few times. I certainly want to protect it, too. (common goals) *The stumbling block seems to be the effect of the timing* (narrowing down the problem). *Is that right?*

I understand your concern about the front office, but I feel differently about the procedure. I can go along with getting the response ready before leaving at night, if you can agree to wait until the next day for the full report. How do you feel about that? (win-win solution)

Summary

Listen to learn what's important to the other person before you tell what you want. As you improve your listening skills, you'll pick up clues that can help dissolve your differences. When you appear reasonable, low-key but focused on important issues, that style marks you a winner to be watched.

2.2 PRETENDING
Seeing Issues Through Another Guy's Eyes

Naturally, you see things differently from the way your boss does. At different levels, you have separate and distinct vantage points. But if you could pretend for a few moments that you are the boss, you might discern what your boss considers important. Playing the boss's role, ask yourself: "What are my chief concerns?" "Who can give me the help I need?" "Who may be working against me and how can I win them over?"

Before you sit down to bargain, go through files and ask questions around the office about the boss's values and objectives and the opposition your boss faces. Keep digging until you can understand the boss's emotions and outlook.

Become so entrenched in the boss's needs that as you sketch out your approach, you temporarily put aside your personal objectives. Let yourself feel a *genuine and sincere concern* for your boss. This concern will come through in your remarks because you'll choose words that relate to the boss's aims and interests. Now you're talking the boss's language.

Strategy

Win over the boss with simple, forceful information and a positive psychological tone. To grab and keep anyone's attention, accept the fact that we are all self-centered enough to want to discuss our own personal interests.

Steps

1. Organize and rehearse your ideas. Write them down, analyze for clarity and continuity, and sharpen the points. Listen to yourself on a tape recorder, noting places to expect opposition. Reword to minimize this reaction.

2. Appreciate the boss's time constraints. Give only the information needed for a decision—and no more. Don't try to set the stage with a long preamble. Don't drop hints. Get right to point, telling the boss what's needed and why. If you try to control the buildup, the boss is likely to become impatient, jump to the wrong conclusion, or get defensive. And watch your timing. Avoid this discussion when you sense your boss is under much stress.

3. Don't show your whole hand at the start. State factually what you'd like to have happen, but don't tell everything you're willing to concede to get it—not yet.

4. Show sensitivity in your presentation. Interpret your ideas through the boss's lenses. Word suggestions so that any concessions you're asking wouldn't prove embarrassing or cause the boss a loss of prestige and self-esteem. Ask yourself what you would want said to you if you were sitting in the boss's chair.

Script

Boss, I'm here with a suggestion that might help you (good, maybe a solution instead of another headache). *I know you've been ordered to cut costs and you feel bad that everybody's upset about your new travel directive, requiring us to stay over so that the company pays a cheaper plane fare. I find this a terrible inconvenience, and I'd like to ask you to consider—*

(Boss, embarrassed, cuts you off.) *I'm really sorry, Bob, we can't make changes because it's against company policy to—*

Boss (interrupting), *I appreciate the awkward position you're in. You're being forced to make unpopular cuts, you can't appear to lag behind other directors, and you feel you have no choice.* (Persistent, having expected her response, you restructure to open the door.) *Could we discuss a couple of options that may be available? I feel strongly about . . . could we talk about another way that would be more acceptable to all of us?*

Summary

To get the boss to buy, stop trying to sell. Instead, see the boss through the boss's eyes. With that kind of insight, even if the boss doesn't go along with the entire proposal, you can probably get a good portion of it accepted.

2.3 WHAT'S IN IT FOR ME
How to Link Both of Your Aims

Whatever benefits your boss desires—more recognition, increased profit, additional time—explain why your suggestion will help achieve it. To get what you want, show your boss how to get what he wants.

Next, explain the importance of your objective. You need more authority as project director to negotiate the level where key decisions are made. You want your efforts publicized to help you get a promotion. You want more meaningful work, increased responsibility, greater creativity.

Then show how two separate interests can dovetail. Shift the focus from packaging and pushing your objectives to discovering and working toward *mutual interests*.

Strategy

Demonstrate the way each of you can win something you regard as important. Leave room to work out a compromise.

Steps

1. Understand relationships. Know how your role relates to the boss's, and how you both relate to the department, division, company. Does your boss have the power to make the change you want? If you have to go higher, figure out how to team up, with your boss opening the doors.

2. Establish rapport and goodwill. In putting forth common goals, avoid a defensive reaction by immediately showing your understanding of the boss's feeling. Ask why the boss takes a certain stand, the purpose of a new regulation, what needs to be accomplished.

3. State your expectations. Tell the most you hope to get (you want to establish a new unit) without saying the least you'd be satisfied with (expanding your role so that you can ask for a raise next time). Try to learn the minimum the boss will accept (which activities absolutely must be covered).

4. Examine jointly what would have to happen to accomplish both your aims. Until the boss warms up to the idea and to get things moving, suggest minor small steps. Practice giving in on less important goals, when doing so will help you reach your main goal.

Script

Boss, I'm here to ask you to change my title (getting right to the point). *I realize that puts you in the middle of bureaucratic red tape* (I know I'm inconveniencing you), *but I truly believe we'd both benefit.*

How is that? (You've snagged his attention.)

Customers prefer to deal with people with more impressive titles, a title that better reflects the actual work. The net result will be more sales which I know is your top priority.

You make a good point, Peter, but this is no time to ask for a raise.

Look, I'm not denying that I want a raise and I don't want to substitute a glorified title for a raise, but we can talk about raises after I show you that I can increase my sales. (The immediate goal is the title change; a later goal is the raise for which you're now building a base.) *Frankly, the title would mean a lot to me. Having a more impressive resumé would boost my ego. But I do think changing my title will also help you have a smoother and more profitable operation by making it easier for people to contact me.*

Summary

Seek the common ground where your two interests merge. Link your goals, taking mutual advantage. When you can show that giving you what you want is a way for others to get what they want, you're headed for the winner's circle.

2.4 TRIAL RUN
Arranging a What-Have-You-Got-to-Lose Test

You know the important aspect of your work that you can do better than anyone else. Focus on this one essential competency. Hone your skill until you're convinced you're the greatest. What you do very well today, you want to do exceedingly well tomorrow.

Now ponder how you can apply your skill to a new idea. First convince yourself, then you can ask your boss to take a chance on you.

While the benefits you anticipate should be high, the risk you request your boss to take must be low: minimal costs, time, effort, staff. A well-defined period for the test and conditions such that you logically can go back to the old way at the end of that period. Meeting those prerequisites, you're ready to request a trial run.

Strategy

Make an offer the boss can't refuse. Emphasize the slight risk for a large benefit; in other words, what have you got to lose?

Steps

1. Do some research. Learn some history. Why are things done this way today? Which procedures appear to be flexible and which ones are etched in stone? What would be gained by your innovation?

2. Demonstrate your belief in yourself. When the boss realizes how committed you are, this commitment itself becomes potentially persuasive.

3. Strike while the iron's hot. When an idea is floating around and an event occurs that makes the time suddenly right, move quickly. Others may come up with a similar plan. If you have to stay up half the night, get your thoughts organized and have them on the boss's desk before someone else beats you to the punch.

Script

Boss, I know I can organize this better than anyone else. I am committed to making this work. (Earnest self-confidence begets confidence.) *Without the expense of the usual market research, my unit can test the reaction. Instead of mere statistical projections, you'll have actual comments from real, live people. At the very least, we will have learned what is and isn't workable, although I'm sure we'll get much more.* (Enthusiasm is catching.) *We'll have the value of word-of-mouth publicity, with the message that we really care about our customers.*

Fern, I like the idea, but frankly, I'm reluctant to change anyone's position until I'm convinced it will work out.

I understand, boss, and I agree with you. Would six weeks be a fair testing time? If you're not satisfied by the end of the six-weeks test, I'll go back to the old routine. (Now move toward a firm agreement.) *I'm just asking for the chance, boss. If I meet the objectives we've discussed, if my good results please you and you start seeing the benefits in six weeks, then I can expect that permanent change in my position we agreed on. Do I have it right?*

Summary

Every organization needs innovative thinking. If you can make the change appear well worth the risk, you become increasingly valuable to the boss and the company.

2.5 BREATHING ROOM
Bargaining for Control over Your Own Work

Your desire for both security *and* freedom creates mixed emotions. Although comforted by the safety net of established routine, you also want to feel you have at least a little influence over what happens to you on the job. Even if the changes you're able to initiate are minor, participating in discussions helps you keep your dignity.

But the problem is deeper than morale if you dare to disagree with your boss about your right to call some of the shots. Your future may be at stake. This apprehensive, inflexible boss who makes all judgment calls for you feels threatened. She's afraid to operate without total power. Too insecure to consider other opinions, your wounded boss might attack and hurt your standing.

It's time to negotiate, minimizing the hazards of speaking up by talking with utmost tact. Gain the boss's trust because the one loss you can't afford is a squashed self-esteem.

Strategy

Blame the system. If the boss instituted that system, blame present conditions that are interfering with how it's working now, and how the boss and the company will benefit from your handling certain tasks on your own.

Steps

1. Use tactful confrontation, not ultimatums. By shouting, "Back off, I know what I'm doing" or threatening to quit, you lose the fight even if you win the round. Repercussions will come later. Instead, allay the boss's fears.

2. Signal that you know your own worth. That is your strength. Tell why contributing your ideas is important to the boss and to you. By quietly, persistently, asking for something you regard as reasonable and vital, you transmit an *unspoken* message: "If my minimum requirements aren't met, I may be willing to walk."

3. Jointly work out a new system. Together, define which decisions are within the parameter of your assignments and which ones will require approval before proceeding. If the boss pops up with a counterproposal you didn't expect and you're uncertain how to react, just say "I need a little while to think about that."

Script

Boss, I appreciate how much you value accuracy and I certainly agree that we can't operate without safeguards. I'd just like to report to you a few incidents that indicate our system needs a little revamping (keeping the criticism impersonal and positive). *I'm asking that you consider making some changes.*

I know how hard you're working for us to meet our quotas, boss, but getting approval at each stage is a bottleneck. I've proved my ability and I feel I have earned the right to make the decision in certain cases. (We both know you depend on me to do excellent work.) *It's important to me, for my own integrity, to feel I'm contributing to the company's success.* (It's my mission to help the company.)

Here is a list of work requiring your okay. Could we start with the decisions you have to make because you're the only one with sufficient information . . .

Summary

Expressing your opinion is important both for your own self-respect and to get respect from your boss, establishing rapport between the two of you. Without this opportunity your dissatisfaction rises at the rate your self-esteem drops. Minimize your risk by allaying the boss's fears. Even if you don't get all you want, you'll live to fight another day. And you'll be viewed as somebody who tries to improve the company.

2.6 SIMON LEGREE

Conferring with the Slavedriver Boss

To meet the economic crunch, your company began downsizing. Several colleagues were laid off during the reduction. You survived the cut, but now you're trapped. You're being required to take over work previously done by two of your friends.

You find yourself laboring long hours into the night just to keep up. You don't dare slack off. And if you complain, you may find yourself in the next batch of layoffs. But you don't know how much longer you can take the exhaustion, anxiety, pressure, and stress without cracking up or becoming physically ill.

You know you have to speak to your boss. You keep putting it off because, understandably, you're just plain scared.

Strategy

Whoa, back up. This is really not your problem. Toss it back to the boss. You're the victim of circumstances that were probably beyond the boss's control, but only the boss has the authority to lessen tension and relieve stress by reducing the work required.

Steps

1. First, be sure you're not being compulsive. See if, on your own, you can free up some hours. Are you holding on to any tasks you should be delegating? Are you being a perfectionist, redoing less important work? Do you refrain from telling colleagues this is not a good time to talk? Are you utilizing time savers—working from lists, deciding, not putting off matters, attending to urgent tasks without getting sidetracked, sticking to time blocks for phone calls, reducing paperwork and files by tossing out materials you don't really need.

2. Decide the number of hours you can reasonably work without becoming ill. You're no good to yourself or your company when you work beyond your endurance level. You can't contribute to achieving mutual goals if you're too exhausted to perform.

3. Control your fear of being fired. You'll no longer feel paralyzed if you start to act. Resolve right now that if the company stubbornly demands you work more hours than you can take emotionally and physically, you'll look for another job or another kind of work. Begin instantly to update your resumé and start a job search. Maybe this is the time to pursue that other type of work you've been thinking about.

4. Ask your boss to redefine your job. Without a hint of criticism, in a calm, friendly tone, state the problem. Ask your boss, in the light of so many changes, to establish current priorities. Break down your work into segments showing the hours and percentage of time required for each chunk. Then let the boss decide where you're most needed.

5. Discuss alternative benefits. If the boss talks about your taking on many new responsibilities, negotiate for a change of title and salary after a successful trial period. If you are being asked to work more hours without more pay, discuss benefits you'd like in return.

Script

Boss, I'd like to call your attention to a problem we've been experiencing since the layoffs, the difficulty in getting the work done on time. (This is no surprise, the boss has been expecting you.) *Since we're operating under a new structure, what are the company's current goals, and how does my job relate to them?*

Here's a list of time estimates for my present tasks. These take 140 percent of the regular work week, so I have to know which tasks get priority. Do you want other people to take over the ones left undone, or should they be put on hold for now? (You're forcing your boss to face up to the hard decisions that are the boss's to make.)

Boss, although you're tough and demanding, you've always been fair. If I'm going to put in a lot of extra hours, I'm going to need some changes in my schedule. Can we talk about flex time or more personal days off, or the right to take the company car home to give me more time? (We're both reasonable and I expect some form of compensation.)

Summary

As long as you remain silent, the boss assumes you find the extra demands difficult but doable. Until you speak up, your boss can't know the agony you're going through. Furthermore, you don't have authority to redistribute the workload—that's a decision an executive gets paid to make. With tact and dignity, demand that your boss correct an injustice. Your desire to negotiate a workable plan marks you as someone the company wants to hold on to.

2.7 SPECIAL SKILLS
Stating Your Case to Get More Training

Plan ahead. There's no way to accurately predict what will occur in the job market. Whatever happens to the economy, you're wise to keep sharpening your skills. Should budget cuts cause a hiring freeze or if there's a downturn in your industry, you want to be ahead of your competition.

One way is by educating yourself-in new areas. If your company has to reorganize or consolidate, your long years of loyalty won't guarantee security but good transferable skills might.

You hope you can convince your boss it's in the best interest of the organization to provide you additional training. In times when benefits are being curtailed, however, many companies are reluctant to spend money on staff development. So if your original request is refused, go another route.

Strategy

Investigate all possibilities open to you to increase your special skills. Then go for the best deal you can negotiate.

Steps

1. Determine where you are now and where you need to go. What skills do you already have of interest to other employers? Proficiency in management technology, for example, is a transferable skill. Learn from people in related fields what other skills you must master to increase your value there. Read reference books, professional journals, and newsletters to discern trends, along with the requirements and new skills needed.

2. Explain your training needs in terms of benefit to the company. You may feel mentally sluggish without continued development, but to interest your boss, tie your needs to those of the company. Write out these anticipated benefits, pinpointing what the new knowledge you're requesting will allow you to do.

3. Propose to foot part of the bill. If the company won't pay all the costs, show how important you believe the training to be by offering to spend your time, energy, and some of the money required. At the least, get the company to agree to giving you time off to attend the training.

4. Invest in yourself. If you feel your career track requires additional training to make you more valuable in the job market, for example, becoming literate in computers, then bite the bullet and budget the costs to pay your own way. Check with community colleges, adult education classes, vocational schools. Look into local courses, professional conferences and seminars you can attend on your own time.

Script

We need to apply the state of the art. By helping me develop in this area, I can turn the new skill into more company profit. This will allow us to come up with a better and cheaper way to do the same thing. (Stress value to the company.)

(Following a refusal) *I'm so sure we need this course, I'm willing to pay my own transportation and hotel bill, if the company will pay the tuition.* (How much more sincere can you be?)

There's an all-day seminar described in this brochure that I believe
would prove valuable for us. I'd like your permission to take the day
off to attend (a fair exchange, everyone gains).

Summary

The right kind of knowledge is power. Pinpoint the additional training
you need. If the company won't foot the entire bill, negotiate for part of it.
If your boss says that's still out of the question, it can be worth the cost to
buy the training yourself.

2.8 USURPERS
Retrieving Decisions a Boss Delegated to You

Your boss suffers from paternalitis, a swelling of the manager's role.
He has to solve your problem before you're even aware you have one. The
symptoms start as soon as he reluctantly delegates duties, because he
believes he can do each job better than anyone else. Fearing he'll hear about
a problem too late for remedial action, he keeps a tight rein.

Understand the boss's concern. There is some risk because, although
some authority is delegated, the boss still bears ultimate responsibility for
your actions. Unsure of everyone else, he's careful never to draw the lines
of delegation too clearly. The boss reasons that you will need his help and
experience. Instead of revoking the delegated authority, he usurps it.

When talk between delegator and delegatee is too infrequent or
ineffective, everybody gets a little jumpy. Delegated rights are important to
your career. To hold on to them, negotiate.

Strategy

Get the backseat driver to back you up instead of steering over your
shoulder. Politely insist on the respect you deserve. Although you may feel
as if you're walking on eggshells, if you're careful not to undercut the
boss's authority you can regain the control delegated to you.

Steps

1. Discuss the boss's concerns. Most managers delegate to get assistance and to gain extra time for assuming more challenging tasks. The

best ones also want to help their people develop, and they know that giving additional responsibility and authority is a motivator. Usurpers need to be reminded that this course of action is also to their advantage since a chain is only as strong as its weakest link.

2. *Set up an accountability process.* If you screw up, your boss is held responsible. Allay this fear by keeping your boss reasonably and properly informed. Agree on a system—perhaps a combination of firsthand observation, periodic written and oral reports, and a mechanical measure of your productivity.

3. *Demonstrate your leadership as problems arise.* Don't come whining when there's difficulty. Instead, tell the boss precisely what you want and discuss the best way to get it. Act confident and authoritative, as though you know what you're doing. If you need help in a specific area, say so.

Script

Boss, you put me in charge because you felt I could do the work and to give you more time. But you're still working on the project every day. I feel hog-tied when I must make pertinent decisions such as allocating resources. I understand your concern about maintaining our high quality and I'm sure you want me to use my own good judgment . . . (putting forth the concerns you both feel).

If I were you, I'm sure I'd have the same worries. (Let me put them to rest.) *If I run into anything I can't handle, I'll let you know early enough to take remedial action. You'll still have the control you need. Let's set up a way you can catch me before I stray too far afield.*

Boss, during this rush period, if these orders are going to be filled on time, we are going to need more machines. (This is the problem; this is the answer; I need your approval.) *I have a couple of ideas, but what do you think would be the best way to avoid . . .*

Summary

When you're given an assignment, with the necessary responsibility and authority to get the job done, refuse politely to check every step with your boss before you take action. Persuade the boss to loosen the reins by negotiating a good communication system: The boss gets information when needed; you get freedom to move. Good negotiating is going after what you want by accenting the positive. Restate your objection as an objective. Know your boss's aims and fears before you start talking, then focus on the point where your two goals meet. Rubbing two good minds together creates a spark. Work through each point until each of you gets something you regard as important. More than avoiding complaints, negotiating gains your boss's confidence and lets you look like a winner. However, you can avoid many problems if the boss's expectations and yours are clearly spelled out from the start.

3

BEING PERFECTLY CLEAR ABOUT EVERYONE'S EXPECTATIONS

Crossed signals, unfulfilled hopes, hurt and angry feelings, inconsistent and unreasonable presumptions—these are results of poorly communicated expectations. Yours and your boss's.

To prevent disappointment and to be perceived a winner, take the initiative. Before you start, put on the table whatever you and your boss anticipate. Understand *precisely* what the boss hopes will happen as a result of some action you'll take on a given assignment. And just as important, speak up, reciting your expectations with crystal clarity. Then, without danger of deluding yourself, your plans will be firmly rooted in reality.

The resulting perception—that you get things done—acts as a magnet to others who'll want to work with you. As long as you're tactful and respectful, you can say what you think without feeling compelled to utter what you *assume* the boss expects to hear. The real risk is in remaining mute and adding to the confusion.

3.1 GOOD GAMBLE
Improving the Odds by Betting on Yourself

You have power to control only your own thoughts and actions. You can't will others to do things for you. Since no one else is as concerned about your career as you are, it's up to you to make yourself do what you know you *can* do. For instance, you're the only one who can write the contracts. Capitalize on your ability and become more valuable by training others to do this.

Take some risks, because you're in a rut if you're perfect all the time. Allow yourself to make mistakes by trying something new. Bosses are frustrated when bright staff people follow directions but take no initiative. Once you comprehend your boss's expectations, stay within the bounds of company policy, but take the ball and run with it. To be considered for advancement, you need experiences through which you can improve.

Have faith in your common sense and creative ideas. If you spend too much time getting every little step approved, you appear indecisive or evasive. The boss doesn't expect or appreciate your playing it so safe. Until you're willing to try and willing to fail, you can't grow in your job or your value.

Strategy

Invest your time and energy in learning. The only surefire return you can expect comes from banking on yourself.

Steps

1. Clarify your responsibilities with your boss. Recognize a stroke of good luck when the boss suggests your taking on a task you've never attempted before. Golden opportunities don't come on silver platters. Perched on the right track, you'll be run over by the doers if you just sit there. Take the first step by showing your excitement and asking questions. Queries also help the boss delineate what's really needed.

2. Stop expecting perfection. Getting yourself to accept the challenge is the hardest step you'll have to take. You owe it to yourself to at least consider taking it. If you stay parked in the same slot because you do the job so well, you're blocking your own drive. Overcome your insecurity by finding out exactly what's involved and where you can get help.

3. Minimize your losses. Define your skills—no one's going to do this for you. Once you know your strengths, identify required areas in which you're weak. If you don't take available courses, it's a cop out. Negotiate with the boss and get in writing what your new standing would be after you complete essential training.

Script

Yes, boss, I'd be very interested in coordinating the conference (instantly ready to swing into action). *Approximately how many delegates will attend? How soon will it be held? Do you want me to put together a planning group or have you already done that?* (Leap at the chance to make new contacts or improve a skill.)

Boss, if I continue to stay in the office the whole time, I'll never be ready to go out in the field. How about splitting my duties half and half until I'm prepared to solo? At the end of one year, if I meet your requirements, will my rank be changed to that of field officer? (Make sure what you do moves you in the direction you want to go.)

Summary

Until you take a chance, you'll never know what your real capabilities, interests, and satisfactions may be. What's a snap today robs tomorrow of challenge. In addition, if you want others to show faith in you, you must first show faith in yourself. You can't expect to be regarded as ready to move up until you show you're willing to step out of your rut and learn something new.

3.2 ALIBIS

Dealing with Excuses for Unmet Expectations

The assignment wasn't made clear and now the boss is accusing you of not following through as expected. Fearing the consequences, the normal reaction is to defend yourself with a flood of excuses. Don't. Take a deep breath and find out what you're dealing with. Is this a simple misunderstanding (the report is there, buried on the boss's desk) or serious criticism (you failed to turn in something the boss has been waiting for).

Even if you were wrongly accused, (it was actually your subordinate who messed things up), forget the excuses. And don't interrupt or counterpunch. Avoid alibis if you *were* at fault (the devil made me do it) (everybody does it) (you mean that's against the rules?). Instead, ask for evidence or suggestions so that you and your boss can deal with the situation constructively. When expectations aren't met, you're not there to win a debate but to resolve a problem.

Strategy

Calmly untangle the knotty problem. In a pleasant and friendly manner, suggest how the situation can be changed or corrected.

Steps

1. Sort out the problem and separate the issues. Deal with one issue at a time, being specific and unambiguous. Your polite, unemotional tone will invite mutual respect.

2. Instantly acknowledge any part you played in creating the problem. Don't try to weasel out of it. If your subordinate did something wrong, you are still responsible. Admit "our" mistake and apologize.

3. Quickly shift the focus. Move away from blaming anyone to improving the system that allowed this problem to happen. Involve the boss in a discussion about needed changes. Stress what you expect to occur as a result of this talk.

4. Stop feeling victimized. You and your boss have different expectations that must be clarified. What appears to you as criticism may actually be the boss's attempt to help you improve. Hear what the boss is saying about what matters most. You may, for instance, be concentrating so much on content, you're sloppy about spelling and grammar—carelessness that could hold you back. Be sure you haven't been fooling yourself to avoid dealing with a problem. Find another road around the stumbling block if you've been rationalizing.

Script

Yes, boss, I'm very sorry that my division has not been able to accomplish that yet. Frankly, I didn't realize the urgency and I'll get right on it. From now on, do you think it might be helpful if, instead of "as soon as possible" we put a definite deadline with these kinds of assignments? (First, suggest how you'll deal with the immediate problem, then how to avoid repetition.)

If we are going to do a better job reducing errors, we are going to need an additional piece of equipment. . . . (Be firm about what is needed to meet expectations.)

In restating your view, would I be correct in saying you expected . . . (clarification, please) *In that case, we would have to shift. . . .* (Let's improve procedure.)

Summary

The best way to deal with excuses is to avoid having to make them. Before you begin, be perfectly clear about what the boss expects from you. Speak up in that initial talk, expressing what you need or expect in order to carry out the assignment. Everyone makes mistakes. If you are in error, admit it quickly, apologize, and turn to ways to correct the situation.

3.3 NO SURPRISES
Separating Fact from Fiction

A major problem has emerged. Don't let your boss hear about it first from someone else. The boss expects you to come through with whatever you agreed on and to be kept informed. Even if it's a good surprise, the boss has to know immediately, to be prepared to respond when asked about the matter.

Sometimes, however, what you or your boss hear about isn't happening at all. Some people purposely spread rumors to gain attention, appear more important, or deliberately harm others. Again, alert your boss, because rumors spread like wildfires. State how you've sifted through information and which facts, if any, have been verified.

Other times, the root of the rumor is actually the boss—a czar who tries to control every bit of information meted out to employee-subjects. Workers talk, and when they don't have the facts they fill in the blanks themselves. What began as "I think that" gets repeated so often it becomes gospel. Explosive rumors cause serious slowdowns. When the story you're told is potentially damaging, establish rumor control.

Strategy

Expose the facts and reduce the speculation. Everybody working in the organization has a right to expect correct information.

Steps

1. Don't let a rumor monger swear you to secrecy. You can't resolve a problem unless you can discuss it.

2. Trace the rumor. Probe for as many facts as you can. Interrogate each carrier. Ask a lot of questions. Sift through the answers to determine aspects that can be verified. Determine the necessity for action.

3. Suggest authentic newscasts. Offset the natural tendency of employees to imagine and supply missing parts of the puzzle. People get anxious when they don't know what to expect. Tell them.

Script

How did you hear about this, Craig? Well, do you know who told Pat? (Are we dealing with a first-hand or a tenth-hand interpretation?) *Did Pat tell you if the information came from any official source—perhaps some report or memo?* (Try to determine the danger of acting—or not acting—on this rumor right away.)

Boss, I know you were waiting until Friday to announce the changes. But word has leaked out, and some ridiculous rumors are being believed. I think everyone wants to hear the facts directly from you.

In addition, I'd like to suggest we color code our bulletin boards, each with a red-alert section with daily official updates and that we establish telephone hotlines to reduce the damage that rumors can cause when people aren't given correct, current information. (The grapevine works overtime—feed it the facts.)

Summary

The rule for a rumor is trace it, then face it. You want your boss to level with you, and you have to level with your people. You can't stop rumors from starting, but you can control the spread of misinformation by providing ways to instantly communicate the latest available facts. Everybody has the right to expect the truth.

3.4 MIND READER

Deciphering Intent from Your Ambigious Boss

You'd like to fulfill your boss's expectations if you could only figure out what they are. Sometimes the orders you get are inconsistent or unreasonable or incomplete. You need to know what's wanted generally, but you also need to know the deadlines, budget limits, quantity required, and other specifics.

Maybe the boss thinks you own a crystal ball, but you know you're not clairvoyant. You puzzle how to get someone who's quiet and uncommunicative to speak an extra word and give you some feedback. You and the rest of the staff really need that. The lack of plain communication is having a demoralizing effect.

On the other hand, it's possible that the confusion is intentional. An insecure or indecisive boss may be sending mixed messages to stall or avoid being blamed for a bad decision. The ambiguity is bedded in half-truths meant to manipulate or deceive.

In either event, you're caught in a murky situation that's screaming for clarification.

Strategy

Ask pointed questions. Seek to distill clear directions from the muddied water.

Steps

1. Clarify your assignment in advance. Do this in person because memos only make the water more murky. Query the boss about his or her expectations. Feel free to express yours.

2. Grab the lead when the boss creates a leadership vacuum. Instead of getting boiling mad or stewing that the boss raised your hopes and let you down, offer a better procedure.

3. Push for a written or modified policy guide. Large companies often have too many rules; small ones, too few or none at all. Many differences in expectations occur because basic policies aren't carefully explained, or procedures conflict with one another. Spell out the rules, such as hours to work, time off or personal days, holidays, vacations, pension plans, crisis procedures.

Script

Do you want an in-depth report or a summary? I estimate the assignment will take five weeks to complete. By what date do you need the information? (No guesswork here, you both agree.)

I don't think I've expressed to you how important it is to me to move up. I want to plan realistically, so it would help me to know how well you think I'm doing my job and the ways I can improve. (Ask for feedback if the boss doesn't provide it.)

Boss, I'd like to volunteer to be on a committee that would simplify the tons of executive orders we have. If we could work up clear and concise guidelines, don't you think that would avoid a lot of misconceptions?

Summary

If your boss expects you to report to work when it's your most religious holiday, or to increase quantity and still maintain the same quality, or to perform a task without proper equipment, or to take on more tasks than you can reasonably handle, you have no choice but to clarify these unreasonable or inconsistent expectations. You'll be a hero around the office because everyone benefits if you help to establish distinct, unmistakable policy.

3.5 SELF PROTECTION ─────────────────────

Documenting Agreements with Your Boss

Sometimes in giving out a new assignment, bosses themselves aren't clear about the results they want. If the objectives sound fuzzy to you or orders vary from the usual routine, ask a lot of questions. By answering your queries, the boss will be better able to focus on what is really needed. Also, this conversation gives you a chance to play a part in shaping your new role.

But beware of long-distance commitments. Bosses want the ideas they come up with to work. To assure success, a boss will promise, for example, to relieve you of some tasks in a few weeks, or if you bring in a certain number of new contacts, you'll get a specified bonus.

Unfortunately, after you start work on the new project, the boss has a memory lapse or is transferred to another city. If there is no evidence of your agreement, you are left high and dry.

Strategy

Protect yourself. Put your agreement in writing right away.

Steps

1. Use questions to get a clear view of your assignment. Voicing enthusiasm, check your assumptions—what's expected specifically of you and what you'll be getting in return. If you're not pleased with the response, again utilize the question to express disagreement.

2. Prepare a written summary of your discussion. Do this immediately upon getting back to your desk. This is especially important if the boss is bending the rules and making an exception to company policy. Send the original to the boss, as part of a thank you note, keep a copy for yourself, and send a copy to anyone else involved.

Script

Boss, that sounds really challenging. Tell me more about what you have in mind for me. . . . Don't you think there might be some opposition if we were to move that fast? (Okay to play devil's advocate, but soften your criticism with a question.) *Will I be working at my same job classification or another more descriptive title? Would I be correct in assuming this will affect my current salary?* (Tell me precisely what I should expect.)

(Memo to the boss) *Thank you again for giving me this exciting opportunity to make an important contribution. To recap what we discussed: my role will be to . . . and our objectives are . . . If, as we agreed, by the end of two months, I am able to meet those objectives, I will be given a 15 percent salary increase and the title of assistant development officer.*

Summary

You have a right to expect commitments to be honored, but don't hold your breath. Documentation helps. Whether you have to remind the old boss or inform a new boss, protect yourself with evidence of your agreement.

3.6 ABOUT THAT RAISE ─────────────────

Improving Chances When You Risk Asking

The big question, before you even think about going to your boss, is: Do you have a right to expect a raise? (other than an automatic, across the board increase). Yes, you're working hard, but are you working hard at whatever the company considers top priority?

Reviewing your accomplishments: Have you helped move the company ahead of competitors or improve its service to clients? Have your responsibilities expanded since your last increase? Have you produced an extraordinary number of vital widgets? What's happening in your company and in the job market? Did you find out from studying pay trends that you've been underpaid?

These are some of the questions you'll consider in building an impressive case. Your aim is twofold—show the boss you're worth more than you're being paid, and be ready with responses to the boss's reasons for not granting your request. Up the odds in your favor by knowing what to expect.

Strategy

Prepare a presentation based on your value to the company, present and future. Rehearse at home, adjust your remarks after studying your tape recordings, and role play with a friend.

Steps

1. Quantify your accomplishments. Keep a log as you go along (it could take the form of brief progress reports to your boss). That makes it easy to document highlights. Emphasize your value now and, from your steadily improved performance, why the company should expect more from you in the future. Assure yourself, then assure your boss that you're valuable because you help the company meet its goals.

2. State the increase you expect. This is no time to be namby-pamby; however, a percentage increase often works better than a dollar figure. Prepare a payrate chart of current local and national salary ranges for your type of work. Gather data from peers, personnel department, want ads, employment agencies, and your business or professional association.

3. Separate your raise from the company's profits. Your company needs you. When profits are down, a company desperately needs its best workers. You deserve a raise, but you may be better off with another form of reward. Consider requesting an incentive bonus if you meet a certain goal, to tie increased pay to your efforts instead of to company profits.

4. Rehearse your presentation. In a strong, firm, unemotional voice, rattle off numerically the stated objectives you've met—reduced costs, increased production, and so on. Prepare answers to anticipated arguments (times are difficult, we're downsizing, your raise would create a domino effect), and be ready for the stall (yes, you deserve the raise, but not now, maybe later).

Script

Boss, all year you've been stressing the importance of making new contacts (company priority). *I've increased mine by 36 percent, with the potential of expanding to . . .* (current figures and future estimates).

According to this pay rate chart, my current salary is below the national range . . . I feel a 15 percent increase would be a fair adjustment.

I know these are difficult times, boss. That's why it's even more important to keep your good workers like me motivated, workers you can depend on to give you the outcome you're looking for. (With fewer employees, now you especially need me to fill a void.)

Well, I do understand your situation and I'm sure you can understand my concern to advance my career. Since you agree I deserve the raise but the budget is so tight that you can't swing it now, how about an incentive bonus—if I accomplish ___(goal) by July first, I'll receive a ($__or__percent) bonus? (Or negotiate other items besides cash, such as adjusting your schedule, getting an extra week's vacation, a promotion down the road.)

Summary

Know what to expect and prepare for objections before you ask for a raise. When your expectations are reasonable, it's well worth the risk of facing rejection. Now that the boss knows you're anxious to move up, you'll be watched more closely. If the boss revealed some areas in which you need to improve, you know where to work harder.

3.7 LATERAL MOVE
Assessing Pros and Cons of a Transfer

The Labor Department tells us more workers are unhappy than are happy in their work. You complain about the hours, pressure, lack of challenge, constant confrontations, and anxiety over being fired from a job you don't like in the first place. You feel confused, abused, underutilized, and dead-ended, but you're scared to budge because you desperately need financial and emotional security.

Today there's no job guarantee for even long-time loyal workers, but you can improve your chances and prepare for contingencies. Don't wait in paralyzed fear for the company to lower the boom. Before you see telltale signs, start today on your resume update and job search. This action alone gives you back some control over your life and reduces the risk of stress-related physical problems.

If your boss tells you that your work is great but there's no way to move up, consider moving over to another division, or moving out to another company where there's good potential for advancement. Sometimes it's worth taking a temporary pay cut to move in a desired direction, receive important training, be nearer the top level, and anticipate higher long-range revenue.

Strategy

Get unstuck. Whether you decide to hang on, move up, or move out, lay out your options and develop a plan.

Steps

1. Update your skills. You may want to stay the same, but company objectives change. Keeping your job can hinge on your continually updating your skills. Take courses, get training, go to conferences, attend seminars. If you bury your head in the sand, you're dead and don't know it.

2. Identify what is really bothering you about your job. Do you type all day when you're really an artist? Is your boss unreasonable? Are you worth more than you're paid? Are your skills underutilized? Are you unchallenged, with no way to move up? Identify the problem or you may pack it up, unwrapped, and take it with you to the next job.

3. List the good features of your current job. You're able to use your talents? Feel well qualified? The boss is equally abusive to everyone—it's not a personal attack? Salary and fringe are fair? The company has a good grievance system? There are training opportunities? You're assured a role in the company's future? After compiling the list, you may decide you don't need to change your job as much as you need to change your attitude.

4. React to warning signs. Why were you removed from an important policy-making committee? Transferred to a lower job at the same salary? Pushed to turn in work well ahead of time? Talk to your boss to find out if you're dealing with real or imagined trouble. If there is a problem, try to work together with your boss to deal with it. Then immediately start on a job search to generate more options than are in your present status. Add to your personal support system and share important job information. List your skills that can be transferred from one type of job to another.

5. Look at newly created jobs and smaller units. Some contented workers never would have changed if their old jobs hadn't been threatened. People are going on their own into retail sales, financial and personal services, and agencies to help laid-off workers. A smaller division or company may be better for you if you could assume more duties and not be held down to strictly defined job classifications.

6. Control your emotions and don't quit in anger. That's too high a price to pay. Keep plugging away, work out a stategy to get along until you're ready to move along.

Script

Boss, I thought I was doing a good job, but I'm getting signals I don't know how to read. Is there anything about my performance you want to tell me? (Clear the air and ask for a chance to correct.)

I appreciate your leveling with me. Since you have been pleased with my work, would you help me transfer to another division where I'd have more opportunity? Whom would you suggest I contact? (Your boss probably knows the score and who has openings and may be willing to pick up the phone right at that moment to say a few kind words.)

Summary

Staying or moving is a difficult decision. After you weigh the pros and cons and examine your options, the main question is: What choice brings you closer to your personal goals? The first step is to be perfectly clear about your own career expectations.

3.8 JOB INTERVIEW
A Guide for Looking Like a Winner

You heard about an opening in another department or another company. The job seems right for you. The hurdle is how to stand out from other applicants, appearing imaginative without being gimmicky. Your aim is to present yourself as being uniquely qualified to offer the employer what no other person can. What can you expect and how can you improve your chances?

1. Look at your resumé. Did you have 200 copies printed to cover every eventuality? Then yours is like hundreds of others crossing the employer's desk. You want better odds than that. Gain an advantage by preparing a one-page summary that snags the eye and the curiosity. A general resumé reflects multiple skills, background, experience and studies, but it won't help you land a *particular* position. What will help is limiting and focusing. Everything you say must *support* your contention that you're the best person for this one specific job.

Be definite about your job objective. Not "I want to help people," but "I want to counsel the handicapped in seeking job opportunities." State only relevant skills. "As a former teacher and social worker, and one skilled in communicating . . . "

Forget about listing what you did; tell how well you did it. "These efforts resulted in a 23 percent increase in sales over two years." Speak skill language: "Responsible for administering the division's $1,000,000 annual budget and providing direction to its 500 employees." Revealing a little of your personal side, such as "Other Experience: Gourmet Cook," provides the interviewer an icebreaker.

2. Rework your letter to obtain an interview. Start with the point of contact. "Our mutual friend, Burt Friendly, told me you're looking for . . . Your office may need someone with my particular background and experience." Summarize your understanding of the position requirements, showing how your accomplishments, experience, and training dovetail with six or so of the main criteria.

State your personal qualifications. "If you're looking for dependability, consistently high quality work . . . " Explain why you're anxious to work for this particular company or department. End with a request for an interview.

Wait a week and then call for the interview. If you get a date and time from the secretary, fine, it's all you need. If the employer hasn't the vaguest idea who you are, say "Good morning, Mr. Prospect. I'm Julia Seeker. As I pointed out in the resumé I recently sent you, I believe I am well qualified to handle the position you've advertised. When may I come in to talk to you about it?" Keep it brief—this call is *solely* to land the interview. Limit what you say to create the desire for Mr. Prospect to meet you in person.

3. *Train for your interview.* You've got too much riding on it to be saddled with self-doubt. but with plenty of practice runs around the track, you can come through like a thoroughbred.

Prepare, prepare, prepare. Learn all you can at the library from the company's annual reports and trade or professional publications. Pick up brochures at the company office. Try to chat with a few employees and customers.

(To someone who works for the company) *Do you think you're headed toward expansion or consolidation? Are you aware of any particular problems the company might be having?*

If you're preparing work samples, be extremely critical, choosing just a few representing your very best work. Practice showing the samples.

(Hand each piece separately to underscore an achievement) *This brochure I designed resulted in a 48 percent increase in phone inquiries.*

Decide in advance what you'll wear and how you'll get there. Call the day before to confirm the time.

Rehearse sharp answers to pointed questions. You can anticipate the most common queries. Having ready a good response makes you appear confident and articulate. Initially, write your answers without worrying about style. Then make them shorter and snappier to sound more like normal conversation. Read your answers aloud until they sound good to you. You want to brag casually, modestly, and inoffensively.

Interviewers *want* to hear your achievements. Don't make them plow through a pile of your own put-downs to find them. And a few other no-no's: Don't tell personal problems. "I need this job because I'm facing a tough custody battle." And don't belittle yourself. If your track record isn't too great, sell your enthusiasm and willingness to work diligently. When you can't do what is asked, couch the negative positively.

No, but I'd certainly like to learn the technique (shows your willingness to pay your dues before you advance).

Now practice in front of a mirror, listen to yourself on tape, and role-play with a friend.

4. Sample answers to common questions.

Q. *Tell me a little about yourself.*

A. (This is no time for your life history. Summarize where you've been as preparation for where you want to go.) *I've been very fortunate, always in jobs that were challenging. It was one of my greatest thrills to have earned the abcd teaching award. I want very much to use my experience and skills in helping frail elderly accomplish meaningful tasks.*

Q. Who takes care of your children?

A. (Don't get angry if you're a woman and you know a man would never be asked this question. Just dismiss it briefly.) *The children attend (a child center) (an after-school program). My husband works at home.*

Q. *Why are you interested in this job? Why do you want to work here?*

A. (Link your answer to your job goals and priorities.) *I read that this company emphasizes career development and that you plan to expand. I'm a hard worker and a quick study. I want to work where I'm encouraged to develop the potential I know I have.*

Q. *Why do you want to change jobs? Why are you leaving your present position?*

A. (Keep it positive.) *I feel the need for something more challenging. My unit was eliminated in the consolidation.*

Q. *Tell me what you found most satisfying about your recent job.*

A. (Talk results.) *I was free to develop my ideas and had the satisfaction of seeing my ideas work. For example, I produced a weeklong series of events, staged in 25 sites throughout the community, that drew record crowds and resulted in excellent free publicity for the company.*

Q. *What did you dislike about the job? What made you lose your temper?*

A. (Toss off something insignificant.) *I drove 32 miles a day from my home to the office. I'd have preferred to use that time more constructively.* (Show maturity by blaming a system, not a person.) *I seldom lose my temper, but it can be frustrating when an important paper gets lost in interoffice mail.* (Turn the negative into a positive.) *Actually, I enjoyed my job very much, but I had gone as far as I could. I need to learn something else that allows me to use more of my talents.*

Q. *How were you rated on your last evaluation?*

A. (Don't lie or embroider. Stress the positive and work in some minor criticism. Sound up-front by mentioning some area you're trying to improve.) *I was rated outstanding or above satisfactory in all categories. Although I'm an experienced administrator, in this last job I coordinated rather than supervised, and this gave me little opportunity to use and sharpen my personal development skills.*

Q. *What kinds of decisions are the hardest for you to make?*

A. (Accent your ability to resolve issues rather than admit a problem.) *Generally, I make decisions easily. Sometimes, there isn't time to gather all the data I need, and then I have to rely on my intelligence, experience, and instinct.*

Q. *Where do you want to be in the next five years?*

A. (Show you have definite career goals.) *I'd like to head a large division or small company. If I am fortunate to work here, I know I could hone all the skills I have, and that would be of mutual benefit to me and the company.*

Q. *What salary were you expecting?*

A. (Don't mention salary or talk benefits until you're offered the job—focus on your capabilities.) Sidestep with *I'm confident this is a good place to work and that you pay a fair salary.* (If you feel forced to name a figure, talk range.) *The going rate for my type of work is between . . .* (avoid selling your services too cheaply or pricing yourself out of contention).

Q. *Why do you think the company should hire you?*

A. (Talk about your desire to do an excellent job, why you have what they're looking for. Ask questions about the company. It's okay to refer to your notes.) *Before I respond, may I ask a little more about the postion we've been discussing. What do you consider the most important aspect of the work?* (Then get back to the question.) *I could be of great help to you with your expansion plans. Specifically, I've had considerable success with . . .*

Q. (For some positions, the interviewer wants detail to judge if you're an astute planner.) *You've had a chance to study our agency objectives. If selected our executive director, what would you do next year to achieve the fund-raising objectives?*

A. (Rattle off several doable, tangible, measurable objectives.) *I would double the revenue by increasing membership groups from 100 to 150, increasing by 25 percent paid advertising in the monthly newsletter, and producing and selling printed resource material to a minimum of 50 groups.* (Your figures may be a little off, but without a thorough study, your informed guess is probably close.)

5. *Ending the interview.* Keep good eye contact. Smile. Shake hands with a good strong handshake.

I certainly am interested in this job. Thank you very much for your time. When may I call you back?

Immediately after the interveiw send a brief thank-you note.

It was a pleasure talking to you today, and I want to thank you again for giving me so much of your time. Regarding the conference planning we discussed, you may be interested to know that last year I arranged a successful statewide three-day event for 250 participants (information or an ability important to the interviewer you forgot or couldn't work into the discussion). *Again, thanks for your consideration. I'm looking forward to talking to you next Thursday.*

Summary

Good luck always helps. But much of the good luck you create for yourself. You can anticipate most of what will occur during the interview. Being well prepared enables you to think fast on your feet.

4

FIGHTING YOUR FEAR OF SOUNDING FOOLISH

You can't keep your good ideas to yourself. To be seen as an idea person, a perceived winner, you have to take a risk and let others know your thinking and logic.

You know that, but you're immobilized by fears. You're afraid of criticism, rejection, failure, not coming across well, giving the wrong impression, and appearing boastful. Or you may feel shy finding yourself with new people and wanting more time to size up the situation before sounding off.

Even outgoing, self-confident professionals can get tongue-tied in a discussion with recognized experts in their field. Some leaders who appear to be in control all the time will confess to occasional decision lapses or mute moments out of fear of sounding foolish. But for most situations you can conquer this fear, or at least keep it from holding you back.

4.1 PSYCHING YOURSELF
When You're Petrified of Criticism

Self-berators try to beat their bosses to the punch, criticizing themselves so severely that no one else need find fault with them. But for many of you, the fear of criticism is paralyzing. Rather than act in your best interest, you try to play it safe, never getting up the gumption to try.

You're robbing yourself of a wide range of experiences vital for anyone who wants to hang on to a job. Experiences form patterns that are stored in your long-term memory bank. Those deposits allow a new situation to trigger the release of an old memory, giving you an instant, instinctive answer. Such quick decisions are actually based on previously learned lessons.

While you can't gather experiences without taking some risks, you can minimize the risk and overcome the fear with planning and practice. You'll begin to realize your fright was magnified and rooted in the unknown or uncertain. As you get across your knowledge, you gain control over your inhibitions.

Strategy

Determine to stick to the issues. Concentrate on what's needed. This will keep you so busy you'll forget your fears about your feelings. You'll stop worrying about somebody else's reaction because you will have anticipated and prepared for critical responses.

Steps

1. Plan ahead what you'll say to create acceptance. Research your subject to have answers ready for most legitimate objections. Stop exaggerating the impending doom or being overly concerned with minor, really insignificant details. A good idea stands on its own merit. Regard your efforts as successful if you accomplish whatever steps you set out to take.

2. While planning, ask opinions of those you expect to be critical. You and your nemesis both need room to save face as you modify your views. Extend courtesy by recognizing your critic as a reasonable person.

3. Convert critics with solid, authoritative evidence. Refer to journal articles, CEO speeches, recordings, case histories. Show you can debate issues without taking criticism as a personal affront. When you want changes, slow down. You can avoid much criticism if you suggest gradual modifications.

4. Role-play among friends. Practicing in a safe spot restores your confidence and reduces your fear because you're readied for likely reactions. While role-playing, pretend you're the persons you most admire.

How would they phrase problems and solutions? What manner, tone, body language? You *become* the way you act.

5. Show pride in your ideas. In an objective manner, talk about how good your work is. You reviewed it and came to that conclusion. Look people in the eye and maintain that eye contact to be convincing.

Script

(Tell yourself if you achieve certain steps, you'll consider the try successful.) *I'll request time at the next meeting for a one-minute talk on cost cutting; I'll rehearse until I can speak from one-word reminder notes; I'll evaluate my performance.*

(Massage fragile egos.) *Of course, Maria, you're entitled to your opinion. If I were running your department, I'd probably react the same way. However, consider that if we were to expand . . .*

(Acknowledge a critic's abilities.) *I do appreciate the experience you've had, Ted, but results from the latest studies would indicate it can be done in three months.*

(Hit with an unanticipated objection.) *You raise a good point, Jack. I'll have to think about that.*

(Express your enthusiasm.) *Cal, I'm feeling really good about this proposal. I've done my homework. I'm convinced we can do it.*

Summary

Preparation reduces the fear of criticism and your confidence grows with each try. But winning or losing isn't as important as gaining new experiences. You can feel good about failure if it taught you a lesson. Enjoy the excitement of something new. And just by calmly and factually standing up for your beliefs, you look like a winner.

4.2 CONQUERING FRIGHT ─────────────────────
When You're Scared Stiff of Rejection

These are times that not only try men's souls, but also demand you exercise your enterprise. Nevertheless, when you're afraid of being rejected, you protect yourself: you hold back on suggestions, you don't participate in discussions, and you don't submit unsolicited proposals. You fear saying the wrong thing or not expressing a thought adequately.

Hearing about so many mergers, downsizings and closings, nobody feels totally secure. While you can't control these decisions, you can *adjust* to the decisions that affect you. Take the initiative because top brass are looking for people who can think up alternatives. Furthermore, you have the right to request what you need to do a better job. There's no guarantee you'll get it, but you have the right to ask.

Now, if you can regard your request as part of *carrying out a mission,* your fear will fade. Of course you're trying to help yourself, but what you're suggesting will also benefit your subordinates, peers, boss, the department, or the whole company. Zoom in on the mission. Your zeal will subdue your anxiety.

Strategy

Change your pattern. Appreciate the benefits of taking a risk. All you lose is one chance, and you'll get plenty more. You will have learned for the next time that you're up at bat. The boss now sees you have potential that bears watching. You win even if you're rejected.

Steps

1. Watch who gets applauded and rewarded. Find out why. Learn their interests, read their writings, ask their views about where the company is headed. Then devise your own definite, tangible plan. Direct your message to decision-makers and opinion-molders. Come up with something the boss can really use and rejection is less likely.

2. Limit your pitch to a few major points. Concentration has more impact than a broad smattering. The attention span is short, so keep to the essentials and make one point at a time.

3. Expect to be accepted. Use body language that shouts your belief in yourself and your idea—shoulders back, smooth glide across the floor, acting strong even if your legs feel like rubber. Looking confident is better than carrying a rabbit's foot, but try treating yourself to one small expensive accessory, such as a tie or pin, to help carry yourself as though you already had more power.

4. Reinforce your confidence. When you receive an earned compliment from your boss or colleagues, add it to an audio tape. Play back this tape to inject yourself with confidence whenever you feel that old fear and then start procrastinating.

Script

The major benefit of a coordinated effort is reduced costs. And in doing so, we're also able to improve the quality and speed of our service. (Keep the focus narrow, meeting specified goals.)

This proposal would help each of our units receive the essential materials in advance of . . . (This idea assists all the troops.)

Summary

You'll overcome your fear of rejection when you appreciate the potential benefits from taking a risk. Accepted or rejected, coming forward with ideas increases your worth to the company. And when you make your suggestions or requests in the name of others who'll benefit, your belief, confidence, and enthusiasm shine through.

4.3 VOLUNTEERING
Trying Even if You're Afraid of Failure

If you allow your fear of failure to limit your attempts, you distort your view of reality. You need many different kinds of experiences to deepen your insight, improve your decision-making ability, and gain the rewards you deserve.

Examine your recent activities. Did you feel safe only with a familiar routine? Are you clinging to frayed hopes and antiquated goals? Have you stopped using your natural talents because you're afraid you'll fail at something new? If so, be heard or fall behind.

Your fear of being ridiculed may be lodged in an overly competitive attitude. "If this doesn't work, my reputation is ruined." "If I really tried, I could have been first on the list" (competitive and insecure simultaneously).

Whatever the basis, it's as important to deal with your imaginary fears as with your reasonable ones. Then you can veer from worrying about the impression you make on other people to thinking about the people themselves. That will enable you to volunteer for new experiences and gain new freedom and confidence.

Strategy

Control your fear by staring it in the face. You have to *admit to yourself* exactly what your real concern is before you can act upon it and effect changes.

Steps

1. Identify the worst-case scenario. Be honest and open with yourself. Nobody's listening. If you volunteer for a new venture, what do you think the failure really means? How much would you actually lose? Is your job or a promotion *truly* in jeopardy? (Which is rarely the case.) Are you just worried about being embarrassed and losing some admiration?

2. Focus on areas about yourself that you can change. Seize control over the direction in which your career is headed. We all have limitations. You can accept yours without feeling bad about them. Instead, welcome doing what's best for you. Decide specific ways you'll change how you act that, in turn, will cause others to change their reaction to you. Experiment with something new to see how well you like it.

3. Create your own opportunities. Be alert to catch what's needed. Then submit your ideas without waiting to be asked. Suggest formation of, and volunteer to serve on, a task force to study this pressing problem. Help plan a workshop or training program.

4. Volunteer for important committees, contact groups, or agencies. You'll assist the group, and your efforts will lift your own self-image. Study to become expert in one area, then volunteer to lecture. Or offer to give training classes in your own company with resulting favorable publicity in your newsletter.

Script

(Give yourself a pep talk.) *If I'm going to get better assignments, I have to be seen as more outgoing and come across as an idea person. I must decide in advance and prepare ways I'll volunteer my suggestions and services. Even if I don't always get accepted, I have much more to win than to lose.*

Boss, it seems to me that many of us who must talk to outside groups would benefit from additional training. Since we already have video equipment, what about setting up group sessions where each of us could be taped? An expert could lead the group in critiquing each performance. I'd be glad to make the arrangements.

Summary

Don't let anxiety drain your energy. Realize the reason you haven't been volunteering your ideas and efforts is the fear of being embarrassed if you fail. Prepare yourself to handle that contingency by reviewing how the benefits outweigh the risks of failure. Plan, and act on your plan. Each time mark your own report card, noting how well you did. Modify where needed and try, try again.

4.4 SOUNDING SAGACIOUS
Feeling Accepted During Discussions

You're always quiet at meetings and with groups. You don't speak up even though you have good suggestions for handling problems. You fade into the background because you're too shy to participate. Or you wonder how to phrase a question so that others won't think you're stupid, especially when everyone else seems to comprehend. Or you're afraid you'll sound boring or pushy. Or you fear you'll appear to have an inflated ego.

It's quite all right to be quiet if this is a conscious choice. You may want more information before voicing an opinion or perhaps you're just not interested in the topic. You know you can talk up when you want to, and you're not letting the fear of sounding foolish hold you back. But if you are allowing fear to dictate your life, that's not emotionally healthful.

Nor is it career-wise. Your value to the company increases if you help get issues resolved. Keep in mind meetings cost money. So in addition to helping the group move in a good direction, you can help reduce costs by offering good alternatives during the discussions.

Strategy

Look for information other people can use in reaching a decision. Utilize regular staff meetings to share information that other units, departments, or divisions would find relevant.

Steps

1. Study agendas in advance. Prepare your arguments ahead of time to support the position you'll take at the meeting. Determine the best way to make your point in less than one minute. Use available props, such as a blackboard or easel, to diagram the activity you're discussing. Pick and choose the times to talk. It's often best to come in at the end of the discussion. You can summarize and then end with your suggested action. If you've nothing new to add, you're more impressive saving your comments for times when your speaking will make a difference.

2. Practice displaying those traits you fear you lack. Afraid you sound too aggressive? Make your points while evidencing humility. Help your peers who are having trouble communicating their thoughts. Get practice being poised and articulate with additional informal sessions, gathering your group to discuss a problem.

3. Understand opposing views aren't meant as a personal affront. And you, in turn, can speak to the issues without stomping all over someone else's feelings. Respond with a smile or nod to show you're picking up meanings. People raise their voices to defend an idea, not to attack you personally. Don't fold and go mum—answer the charge. Prepare for free-flowing arguments. A small group is good training ground to reinforce your debating skill.

4. Ask open-ended, pointed questions. If something isn't clear to you, other participants will be grateful if you seek clarification. Questions can help get the discussion back on track and extract information necessary to make decisions. Questions also let you join the discussion when you're unfamiliar with the subject.

Script

We agree we're spending too much time at these meetings and need to set limits. According to my calculations, the average cost of our meetings is . . . (Be prepared with reports.)

That was a fascinating story, Len, I really could relate to it. Would I be correct in saying that you think we should eliminate that procedure because . . . (reaching out and helping your peer express a view). *I'm not sure I understand your point, Ann. Do you see a pattern emerging from those stats you compiled? What do you believe we should be preparing for?*

I found this chart helpful in compiling the required data. I made a copy for each of you. You can see if it works for you as well.

Summary

By expressing what is already inside you, you develop your good ideas instead of worrying about what you lack or trying to become something that's not in your nature to be. Also, being a good listener and asking good questions makes you a very important part of group discussion.

4.5 SMALL TALK
Overcoming Your Annoyance with Chitchat

Since small talk is simply amiable chatter, light—even idle—conversation, why is it a serious handicap for people who can't speak that language? They're usually perceived as unfriendly, aloof, icy, and sometimes hostile. Not a great recommendation.

Some won't speak small talk because it bores them, and chatting with those they regard as less than their intellectual equal might sound condescending. It takes grace to step down and be friendly. Many more are thoughtful, observant, and quiet until they have something important to say or a strong opinion to voice. Others want to appear more outgoing, but can't seem to find the right words. And some are just too shy to speak until spoken to.

Whatever is behind your reluctance, learn to engage in small talk because chitchat serves a serious purpose. It's an icebreaker. You need to warm up, and on new occasions to get acquainted, before you feel comfortable about plunging into serious subjects. If small talk doesn't come naturally to you, it's easy enough to learn.

Strategy

Plan several openers you can adapt for various situations. The key is to shift concern away from your feelings and express your interest in others.

Steps

1. Make the first move. Stop waiting for people to come to you. Go over and talk to them. Assume they've forgotten your name and introduce yourself again, then pose a question to get a conversation started.

2. Inquire about interests, hobbies, and jobs, or comment about your observations. Friendly curiosity is fine as long as you don't get too personal and start prying.

3. Toss out a minor problem or noncontroversial opinion. Practice small talk waiting for the elevator or by the coffee maker. Keep it light. Talk about a movie or TV show, sports or recreation.

Script

Hi, my name is Cass Worth. I'm in personnel. In what department do you work? (Assume others want to talk to you because you're smiling, friendly and expressing interest in them, but if you sense bad vibes, leave immediately.)

(Observations provide openers.) *I noticed the book you're carrying is a Lincoln biography. Are you a civil war buff like me?*

I was intrigued with the sticker on your car. You appear to be someone who enjoys the outdoors, am I right?

(Open-ended questions invite discussion.) *What do you think we can do about this cafeteria food? Did you catch National Geographic's show on African art last night? What did you think about the scene with . . .*

Summary

With a few openers in mind, you'll gradually improve your skill at making small talk. The new confidence will make it easier for you to make important contacts at meetings, business gatherings, and social events.

4.6 WORKING THE ROOM
Approaching Work-Related Strangers

Working the room is a politician's term for creating a good impression, making friends, and gaining support from every person present. You may not be running for office, but it'll help you to be perceived as a good representative of your unit or your company. You can't predict the potential payoff from making new contacts. For instance, it's not unusual that meeting a top executive at an office gathering can result in a promotion later on.

People display individual styles working the room, but there's only one criterion. You have to be sincere. Genuinely believe in what you're saying, appear truly interested in the people you talk to. If not, you may as well have PHONY tattooed on your forehead. You may be called worse, and you will have destroyed the objectives you wanted to accomplish.

The reluctance to approach work-related strangers usually stems from an uncomfortable feeling. You can't think of an appropriate thing to say. You conclude you're better off sticking close to people you know than venturing out and making a fool of yourself. All you need is a little forethought to stop passing up great opportunities for future rewards.

Strategy

Prepare emotionally and verbally to plunge. The water's only cold for a few minutes until you start swimming. Decide in advance what you want to accomplish at the event, then figure out a few openers. When no one's there to introduce you, introduce yourself.

Steps

1. Keep current. Read whatever you can about your company to learn who's on what base. After the introduction, when recognition of the name clicks in, compliment people subtly. If you read about their accomplishments, follow with a question about that activity. Listen to newscasts, read books, magazines, and journals and make note of items you can use in conversation. Think up several one-liners to say when making the rounds of an office gathering, workshop, or conference.

2. Show animation and enthusiasm. Walk over briskly. Keep it light and, when possible, amusing. Smile and maintain eye contact as you firmly shake hands. Some people, feeling as uncomfortable as you once were, really welcome a friendly comment. You sell yourself before you sell your ideas.

3. Have a system for remembering names and exchanging information. Always carry your business or personal cards and a pen. Exchange cards, and on the back of cards you receive jot brief notes to yourself. If the other person has no card, jot a note to yourself on one of yours. At workshops and conferences, offer to swap materials.

4. Piggyback on present contacts. Spot someone you know at a table, go over to say hello, and that person will introduce you to all the others seated there. When talking to a stranger, mention names of contacts you may have in common.

5. Follow up on new contacts. A brief note is good, and even better if you can enclose some item of interest.

Script

(Extend recognition.) *I'm glad to meet you, Stuart. I read in the newsletter about the good work you're doing. I'm curious to learn what percentage . . . ?*

Oh, you're on the reorganization committee, aren't you, Pat? Isn't it great news that we're finally . . .

(Give the new contact your references.) *I believe we have a mutual friend, Vicky Black. She contacted me just last week about producing a piece for . . .*

(Follow-up note) *It was so nice meeting you yesterday. I, too, am very interested in modifying . . . If I can be of any help to you or your committee, please call me.* (Or forward an article with a one-line note.) *After our talk at the conference, I came across this booklet on my shelf that I thought you might find helpful.*

Summary

By turning the conversation away from yourself and shining the light on others, you reduce your anxiety and increase your sense of control over the situation. You stop worrying over minute details (Is my hair messed up? Is my tie straight?) and concentrate on making friends. The contacts you make by working the room will bring their own rewards.

4.7 TOOTING YOUR HORN
Bragging Needs the Art of Fine Tuning

Reluctance to toot can mean being skipped over. Your silence can be misinterpreted. If you're too low-key, you may find yourself considered snobbish. In our highly competitive society, you can't rely on a hit or miss system, if you have a system at all. You have to learn how to brag or fall behind.

Bragging with finesse is a communications/human relations skill you can polish. When you become adept, you capture attention as your audience hears and heeds your clever ideas and valuable opinions and suggestions. Effectively executed, you come across with modesty and humility.

Just because you're not a celebrity basking in the limelight every day, that's no excuse to conceal your competence. You also have "publics" you want to reach: office decision-makers, colleagues, members of your professional associations, and civic groups.

You can promote yourself and get appreciation for your achievements without resorting to false images—a true picture of yourself, but making sure your best side is photographed. Create an awareness that you are important to others and to the company.

Strategy

Stop being mute when you should toot. Plan and implement a self-promotion process so that you'll be perceived more advantageously. Work toward communicating mutual interest rather than designing yourself as a slick package.

Steps

1. Learn the difference between tooting and blowing your horn. Tooting is short and inoffensive; blowing is exaggerated crowing. Tooting subtly, quietly promotes goals, values, and respect; blowing is noisy self-promotion without relating the boast to another's interests. Tooting takes in the whole picture, helping others as well as helping oneself. It is honest; blowing is phony. Tooting informs others of your accomplishments while expressing pleasure in your work; blowing tells an excessively high opinion of yourself and reveals only conceit and arrogance.

2. Shed baggage stemming from childhood admonitions. You were brought up being told it's not nice to brag. Today you're uncomfortable when anyone tries to impress others with self-praise. So you hold back, reluctant to let others know your capabilities. Legitimate tooting means you've found a tactful, effective way to inform others of your talented achievements and valuable characteristics. Give yourself permission to toot. Mom would approve.

3. Turn bragging into sharing. Tie your tooting to something another person would need or want to know. Practice linking what you're doing with current concerns. Observe, tap the grapevine, read what your boss and colleagues have written. Find a way to relate what your antennae are picking up to your activities, and you'll turn people on instead of turning them off. You get over the embarrassment of telling others how good you really are by feeling you are contributing to their doing a better job.

4. *Exhibit your work and share the credit.* Mount a bulletin board by your desk and update it with congratulatory notes, photos of a successful project, certificates of awards, newsletter articles about you or your team-mates, newspaper or journal articles of interest to colleagues. Talk about the contributions of others to the success of your venture.

Script

I'm feeling really proud of the progress we've made. As you know, we completed ahead of schedule and I think we've hit upon a shortcut, one you could adapt on a larger scale. (Helping is reason to brag.)

One of the most important results I can report is being able to do this not only well, but also well below the amount we had budgeted. Thanks to careful research, the costs . . . (just the facts, no editorial-izing necessary).

Iris and I made a good team. With the solid background information supplied by Amy and Joe, we were able to convince the group that . . . (One of the best ways to toot is to brag about others.)

Summary

When you concentrate your bragging on yourself, it comes out con-ceit. When you focus your bragging on effective results, others join you in feeling pride. They may not know about your talents or achievements unless you speak up, but be sure you toot your horn—not blow your horn—if you want the boast to boost your career.

4.8 TURNING POINT
Forgetting Your Fear in a Crisis

If you tend toward middle-of-the-road, play-it-safe thinking, you can end up sounding foolish and evasive during an emergency. You pay the price for avoiding conflict at any cost. When you never question ways to improve procedures or policies, you are probably guilty of burying problems that can build up and burst.

Sometimes the crisis is imposed on you as, for instance, rumors of a takeover causing panic and slowdown of production. To help manage a crisis, you have to plan. But under pressure, it's extremely difficult to avoid an emotional, not-well-thought-out decision. You might direct everyone's attention to something negative they probably wouldn't have otherwise noticed. Or deny necessary information because you've dismissed it from your mind to avoid additional tension.

A crisis is not a good time to solo. You can take the initiative and still involve others you trust to supply pieces of news and to bounce ideas off them.

Strategy

Seize the opportunity to demonstrate your leadership potential. Manifest initiative and responsibility in interpreting company policy and in organizing an effective response to the emergency situation.

Steps

1. Gather your tribe of peers who are also affected. Arrange informal pow-wows. Be sure of your information. Verify facts and assess the damage.

2. Inaugurate an instant communications system. Clear up the confusion by telling all employees the straight facts. As soon as you know more, inform them. Even if the news you expect to hear isn't good, you can build confidence only by telling the truth.

3. Propose a backup system. Suggest to your boss steps that could be taken in the future when you find yourselves in a crisis so that everyone's ready instantly to swing into action.

Script

(To your group) *Are we agreed then that changing the policy would help clear up this situation? If our workers regard us as inflexible, then we can take the following steps . . .* (Pull them out of the panic, then talk logically.)

(To your workers) *We are aware of the stories that have been going around all morning. These are the facts now, and we'll continue to keep you informed as any new developments occur.*

(To your boss) *We know you don't want to see a repetition of the little emergency we experienced yesterday. I'd suggest that (1) all man*agers receive crisis training and (2) certain rigid rules be relaxed *so that . . .*

Summary

Begin now to think about how you'd handle a future crisis. If managed well, everyone pulls together. Seize the moment and act like a leader. Deal quickly with your own panic and anger, then begin to think logically how to bring the situation under control. Plan with peers who are also affected, and once decisions are made, confidently voice ways to carry them out. You'll earn their respect and that of top management. The word gets out quickly if you've come through with a cool head while under fire.

PART II

RECOGNITION

BEING PERCEIVED AS SKILLFUL AND INNOVATIVE

You really could do much more but no one's interested. You feel underutilized, untapped, untried, you resent being powerless because somebody else is short-sighted.

No wonder. You're sitting around waiting for opportunity to tap you on the shoulder. In the real world you create your own circumstances. And you *do* have the ability to make something happen.

Everyone can be innovative when it comes to demonstrating potential, getting noticed, garnering support, and manifesting influence. It doesn't require genius or even much talent. Just assign creativity a place in your life.

Try devoting a few minutes daily to a quiet time to relax. Allow innovative ideas and practical proposals to pop into your head—nebulous, farfetched gists at first. Let them lie there, give them time to incubate while you talk to people who've had experience in that area. Gradually the thought will take shape. You'll be able to bring together incompatible elements. You'll hatch the idea that brings you the recognition you crave.

5

DEMONSTRATING YOUR POTENTIAL

The big secret to getting recognized is to give creative thinking a priority. Ten minutes a day will produce possibilities. Concentrate on what's best for the whole organization, not just for your unit or department. The *company* is the message. With your antennae hoisted and with a receptive attitude, you'll discover various outlets for displaying your potential.

Instead of "We've always done it this way," resolve that the status quo must go unless it earns the right to stay. Being innovative is simply seeing something in a different way—reviewing anything for improvement—and presenting your idea without fear of sounding foolish.

It's not so much what you know but the way you show it. Focus on *displaying* your capabilities. Your background, studies, skills, and experiences blend to make you unique. Your objective is to reveal your talent so that you arouse interest in your work. This allows you to rearrange your current job more to your liking, go after a position that's just opened, and volunteer your plans and services when they count.

5.1 LOOK FOR THE HOOK ─────────────────
Dovetailing Talent to Company Needs

Keep asking yourself how the company can benefit from your talent. What can you offer better than anyone else can?

Maybe you have a pioneering spirit. You keep testing ideas within your own unit, always trying out a new approach, a new procedure, a new system. Or you have a high linguistics aptitude. Since most administrators won't admit they can't comprehend technical or governmental gobbledygook, they'll bless you if you blaze through the etymological jungle and translate the wordsmanship. Or perhaps you're a born peacemaker. In the middle of a morale problem, you instinctively inspire staff and peers, enforce policy, and get everyone working together again.

Every company has a rhythm of its own, a way of doing business. Get in synch with the style and be clear on the goals. Begin to develop a *practical* vision for your company that you can help produce.

Strategy

Develop linkage. Search for ideas that tie your talent to your company's need. Very few ideas are brand new. Most are recycled variations. Make note of successful ideas and adapt them to your situation.

Steps

1. Keep an idea file. Clip articles from newspapers, journals, and the company newsletter. Write yourself brief notes after you hear a novel idea at a meeting or lecture. Outline major points you glean from books. All this will trigger thoughts for your own made-to-order assignment.

2. Identify your talent. Whether your capability is natural or acquired, spell out the skill or type of knowledge in which you excel. Something has captured your interest enough to enable you to do this act or acquire this information better than most people can.

3. Research the company's real problems. Tune in to what's happening. Pick up on causes, consequences, and trends. Ask people you want to influence how needs could be met. Press for clarification. Read all you can. Remain alert to pinpoint situations or conditions begging for your expertise.

4. Piggyback on existing ideas. Rework them, change them until they fit both your skill and your company need. Then present the potential benefits from your suggestion.

Script

(You've identified your coordinating talent.) *We've been talking about conflicting policies. I'd be glad to review the manual and list the ones that need clarification.*

(You're especially good at motivating.) *To the average employee, the goals and objectives we've stated will sound highfalutin' and meaningless. We have to translate them into English, something our people can take pride in trying to achieve, by . . .*

(Your gift is the ability to anticipate.) *From everything I've read, this new market has substantial potential, and our diversification would be based on company strength.* (You're no mind reader, but extremely alert.) *Boss, you may need this breakdown when you go into that meeting.* (Supply a need before the boss is aware of it.)

Summary

It's like working a puzzle. After defining your talent and company need, examine every conceivable way to link the two pieces. Think through your selected course of action to note probable consequences, preparing to overcome likely obstacles. You may need more specifics before presenting your plan, or you may have to adjust the methods and materials required. But if you can bring in more customers or increase profit or improve productivity, you're going to be noticed.

5.2 UNINVITED OFFERS
Presenting Your Unsolicited Proposals

At the rate you're going, it'll take another decade for you to get recognition. You cool your heels like a wallflower on the sidelines, hoping your boss will hand you a plum assignment. Stop waiting for the invitation. Develop your own specific proposal. Then sashay on up to your boss with an idea you feel stands a good chance of being accepted.

The boss already knows you possess management skills. Now demonstrate your vision and creativity as well. Show your understanding of what the company should be accomplishing. All organizations need innovative thinking to survive and prosper.

Don't take it as a personal affront if one suggestion isn't accepted. You don't have access to all the information your boss has, and maybe your timing is off. Continue offering carefully crafted, specific proposals. You'll soon gain the reputation as one who can transform a visionary concept into a workable reality.

Strategy

Risk being refused. Keep submitting unrequested proposals. By itself, the offering of good proposals gives you the esteemed reputation as an innovator.

Steps

1. Learn the history before suggesting change. Before challenging a policy, learn who started it and why. It takes tremendous tact to alter a sacred cow.

2. Develop your plan. If you see the need to form new alliances, outline the way to reach target groups. If the boss says costs must be cut, show various places left to snip. If sales have been dropping off, propose actions based on results of your client survey. To retain customers, offer an outline for personalized monthly communication. Answer the problem of 24-hour staffing for your center with a plan combining subsidized child care and flexible shifts.

3. Be specific. Do your homework. Go beyond the concept to realistic estimates: how much it will cost in money, time, personnel; expected percentage increase in quality or quantity or decrease in turnover.

4. Establish a market. Give your proposal a catchy title or slogan that conveys your company's concerns. Decide who could help you polish this proposal or put more meat on the bones. Who else might benefit and lend support? Could you offer potential users a sample, get their reactions, make the refinements, then ask them to answer a brief questionnaire to "document" demand you can take back to the boss?

Script

Boss, would I be correct in assuming when you started this procedure a few years ago, conditions were more stable and . . . (Your actions were right at that time.) *Do you think this is the proper time to make adjustments?*

Boss, you're going to be pleased to learn how much we can cut by having all internal communication done electronically on a computer network (based on experiences of other companies). *This means we go paperless—no more interoffice memos for schedules and messages . . .*

The way to cut costs is to uplift morale. If we were to switch people who are underutilized, put a premium on creativity and excellence, and start an incentive program, we could save the fortune that absenteeism, tardiness, and indifference are costing us. Specifically . . . (Give estimates to back up your position.)

This survey gives us the main reason customers prefer our service, we show genuine concern for them. That's where we have to concentrate. (You moved on your own, gathering information to propose a solution.) *The tone of the monthly would be reporting to them as the higher authority—which, in fact, they are.*

Summary

Get your priorities straight. As long as what you suggest is realistic, getting a proposal accepted is not as important as proposing one. The object is to demonstrate your potential as both a creative, innovative thinker and a practical planner. This is an especially good tack when you feel your talent and experience are being underutilized and you see a way to head a proposed project or new unit. (For hints on writing your proposal, see Chapter 10.)

5.3 REPORTER'S HAT
Relating Results of Your Experiments

A crisply outlined plan inspires confidence. Your enthusiastic presentation of objectives, benefits, costs and other required resources, time frames, and steps to overcome obstacles increases your credibility. And when you add tested results to the mix, you've got a bellringer on the recognition scale. So when you think about testing some new procedure or project in your own unit, plan ahead for sharing the outcome to help your colleagues.

Consider in advance how to quantify as well as qualify outcomes in your report. But don't fall into the trap of setting a number over which you have no control. You can, for example, regulate the number of targeted groups you contact; you can't control the number of sales. You can demonstrate changes, giving a pretest and a post-test, or setting up Control Group A that gets training and Group B that doesn't, but you can't control results.

Although tangible evidence carries the unstated message "I can do," that alone won't sustain your colleagues' interest. Continue relating how this plan may help them and how they can apply or adapt it.

Strategy

Try out your new idea first in your own unit. Then report test results to your boss and peers.

Steps

1. Conduct your own informal research. During casual get-togethers with your peers, extract their thinking. Or do a random sampling among your customers to learn their views and how these views affect your company. Or study your product or service, read your company literature and association journals, and come up with a specific approach: a plan, a method, a procedure that may be a timesaver, a money saver, an efficiency booster, or a sales promotion.

2. Put an idea you've investigated to the test. An ounce of accomplished action is worth a ton of analytical discussion. Some excellent companies have a show-me mentality. Their executives want to see the idea in action before they judge it. In any case, as long as you're not breaking company rules, don't wait for permission to experiment.

3. Furnish believable evidence. Get your sample working smoothly before you talk permanent changes. Be able to show benefits, realistically project costs, discuss roadblocks, and be ready with your own replacement. You tried the idea yourself; it works. Your excitement and conviction will win over your colleagues if you also stress what's in it for them.

Script

I know you'll be interested in hearing about a new procedure we started that's turning our discarded printouts into a profit by reprocessing them . . . (sharing a successful attempt).

If you want to cut staff meeting time in half, let me tell you about this software I've been using. (You have the figures to back up your claim.) *Like the running meter in a taxi, it figures out and prints out how much the meeting is costing us as we proceed* . . .

Now we know a little more about what our customers expect in quality and service. These results of a survey (sure, it's unscientific, but it was quick, cheap, and useful) *among users of both our product and the competitors' products reveal* . . .

Summary

Enjoy friendly competition. Serve up your idea and allow it to be compared. Your plan doesn't have to be universally accepted each time. You'll be applauded as a team player and recognized as one who sees beyond his or her job. Showing your desire and commitment to improve the company earns you another gold star.

5.4 CREATE A JOB
Designing Your Nonexistent Niche

You get what you expect. Maybe life isn't fair, but if you believe you deserve to move up, then be willing to accept the responsibility to go after what you deserve. You can't delegate this responsibility to any other person.

If you're ready to advance and no job is available, invent one. Decision makers are always looking for people who can solve problems and increase profits. If the job you suggest can do that, they're interested.

When companies reorganize, downsize, or consolidate, many positions are eliminated—tough on those being squeezed out, but an opportunity to those remaining. A new structure produces new needs. With reduced personnel, certain vital functions are left in limbo. Leap in.

After spotting a need, decide what you would change to improve the situation. Concentrate on that one problem until you're ready to carry out a solution and you've carved yourself a niche.

Strategy

Search for and defuse a time bomb. Look for trouble spots that appear to be festering. One of the best ways to create a job is to present yourself as an answer to a problem.

Steps

1. Pinpoint the problem. Increased absenteeism related to low morale and lack of worker input? Decreased sales since the last layoff left no one in charge of developing new contacts? Paperwork pileup because managers are forced to fill out streams of meaningless antiquated forms? How much better would the product/service's effectiveness become if you were to . . . ?

2. Carefully construct your presentation. Be careful not to sound as though the problem is due to the boss's neglect. Rather, talk about you and the boss working together as a team. Explain how your knowledge and experience uniquely qualifies you to help handle the current condition. Suggest, if appropriate, a limited test period, a way to measure success, and how you'll be rewarded once the idea is proven.

3. Add the human line to the bottom line. To breathe life into your talk, relate the numbers and percentages to the way people will be affected. When you humanize a subject, you become animated. This, in turn, gets others excited about what you're saying.

Script

Boss, I know that working together we can overcome the demoralization problem. Our communication system is clogged. (Blame the system, not your boss.) *I have an idea for two-way feedback we could implement throughout the department. On my previous job, we found substantial improvement . . .*

According to my estimates, we could have similar small groups throughout the entire department set up and operating in one month. As you can imagine, this will take considerable coordination, but you

can implement my plan without hiring extra staff. (Anticipate and
answer objections before they're raised.) *I would become the coordinator for a test period of six weeks, and . . .*

*Boss, you've been pushing for reports and as you know we're all
having a hard time just keeping up with the work. Please look over
these forms. If you like the way I've streamlined them, limiting data
to the precise information you need, I'd be interested in reviewing all
our forms. I'm sure all the managers would be grateful to you for
speeding up the reporting process* (positioning yourself to be in
charge of data collection).

Summary

The formula for creating a job is as simple as A, B, C. A(company
need) + B(your plan) = C(new job). Keep investigating needs. Continue
coming up with ideas until you hit paydirt. Then you can be sure the
company executives will remember your name.

5.5 COORDINATOR'S CAP
Volunteering to Organize Activities

There's never a shortage of problems, needs, and wants. Constantly
be on the lookout for something vital that requires the immediate attention
of the group because it has a far-reaching effect. For a pressing issue,
suggest that a task force meet for a couple of days and come back with
recommendations. Volunteer for the task force and once the work is
approved, volunteer to implement the action.

Or you may point out the need for a longer-term ad hoc committee
and volunteer to put it together. Aim to chair the group, but at least get on
the committee. Before any deliberation, determine the authority of the
group. Will its decisions be binding or in the form of recommendations? Be
clear on the type and timing of reports.

Watch for opportunities to enlarge your working relationships. At
appropriate times, suggest the advantages of sponsoring a workshop, conference, seminar, public hearing, or sports event. Seek to meet people on
different levels of your company as well as outsiders representing various
organizations.

Strategy

Volunteer to coordinate problem-solving efforts and intergroup activities. Recognize a need as an opportunity for you to be in the forefront and you, in turn, will get recognition.

Steps

1. Volunteer to represent your department. If the activity is one the boss considers important, you could meet many new people, for instance, if you represent your department in coordinating United Way collections or contributions to the Blood Bank. Limit your volunteering at meetings to tasks dear to the boss and that promise high visibility, important new contacts, or a chance to learn a vital skill.

2. Move an ad hoc group quickly and deliberately. Be sure your group is clear on purpose, required resources, and when and how to report. Break down assignments, with each member responsible for securing or studying data in advance of the next meeting. Encourage competing ideas, but don't allow tangential discussions.

3. Prepare concise summaries of each meeting. Ask for group input and modification. Give everyone a sense of having contributed to the end product. Submit the final report, signed by all members, to the boss or other appointing authority.

4. Set up your group for commendation. Arrange for an article on the work of your group or a captioned picture in your company newsletter. If you are giving the report for the group, personally thank each member, acknowledging the parts they played.

Script

Boss, I agree that CPR training is something we should all have. I'd like to coordinate the project for our department (supporting the boss's idea).

Boss, most of our managers appear uncomfortable when approached by the media for comments. What would you think about my setting up a one-day video training workshop to . . . (All you do is *find* the experts.)

Okay, gang, we agreed that for next Tuesday we will have read the literature and be ready to decide on issues a, b, and c. (Keep it moving—don't let committee work get bogged down.)

Each of us has a copy of the draft I prepared summarizing our recommendations. Let's go over this, one point at a time, so that all of you can add to or eliminate parts of this report. (Make this a group product.)

Summary

When an activity is important to the boss and you volunteer to coordinate it for your division or company, the prize is twofold. You've endeared yourself to your boss, while your new and important contacts have witnessed how well you perform. Whether this is a study group or a task force to break up a large problem or an organizational committee for your company to sponsor an activity, as the volunteer coordinator you get the chance to gain recognition by demonstrating your leadership potential.

5.6 DEAD-ENDED
When Your Job and Your Goals Are Mismatched

No matter your rank, you can feel trapped at work, with nowhere else to go. Maybe you've grown beyond your current job and need more challenge but can't afford to quit while seeking something more suitable. Perhaps you've reached a middle-management plateau. Although you've had periodic raises and promotions, you're at the top of your level in the company and you're stuck.

Or it may be that you don't do more because no one's asked and no one cares. Your job is regarded as unimportant when it could be significant if only they'd let you loose to develop it. Well, nobody's stopping you but yourself. Are you so centered on protecting yourself with written explanations and approvals for every step that you won't risk moving out of your rut?

Often you can reshape your job by merely spotting a need and filling it—no questions asked, just step in and do what has to be done, because it benefits the company in some way. After awhile, you're recognized as an essential cog in the wheel. Rewards and recognition come to those who are willing to take the initiative.

Strategy

Show your flexibility. Get unstuck by changing your image from passive to active. Go after whatever you need such as more challenge, training, or staff. Use resources available to you. Observe what is happening in your office to determine where you can add and substract or multiply and divide.

Steps

1. Combine your current job. Take advantage of a layoff or vacancy. Select the important aspects you'd enjoy that are being left undone. Add these tasks to the best parts of your job. Now figure salaries. If the remaining lower-level routine activities from both positions were to be done by a worker earning considerably less than you, even with your salary increase for doing two jobs, that's money in the bank for the company. You've got a saleable plan to take to your boss.

2. Rearrange your current job. You no longer use skills you honed and enjoyed on previous jobs. What tasks could you trade off with your peers? Maybe you noticed the boss doing an activity you like but the boss obviously doesn't. Offer to do that job in exchange for his getting someone else to relieve you of some mundane tasks.

3. Make your work more challenging. When the thrill is gone, request additional training. Take courses. Attend lectures and seminars that will give you material to contribute at group meetings. Consider teaching others your special skill. Offer to represent your organization at meetings. Devise a stimulating project. Start a part-time venture after hours.

Script

Boss, since Ralph left, the purchase orders were piling up and needed to be filled. Here's a report specifying how I've been handling those requests . . . (no explaining why you took it upon yourself to handle the problem—just a report). *If you'd like me to continue doing this, I'd like to suggest . . .*

Boss, I believe I could be of more help to you in the future. You may not know that in my last job I had considerable success as a trainer. Since the orientation sessions always seem to conflict with your other work, I could take over this task if . . . (Get rid of some tasks you find annoying.)

That reminds me of a point the professor emphasized at a program I attended last night on fiscal management. She said that if we want to ... (To be recognized, appear to be more informed and assertive.)

Summary

When you have little faith that you can improve your condition, it's a temptation to hide your frustration beneath a crust of indifference. That only pulls you further down. Look around and you'll discover something you can *do* to alter the flow of events and relieve a stuffy emotional climate. Change your activities and maybe your job itself.

5.7 NOTHING ASSIGNMENT
Making Your Job More Important

You consider your assignment insignificant. You feel locked in to a job that shows no promise of getting you the recognition you seek. You'd like to elevate your status, but you feel trapped.

Then do what every mover and shaker does. Redesign your job description to give yourself room to grow. On your own, align your tasks more closely to your needs and chosen career path. Take it upon yourself to milk all possible benefits from your current position. Use this job as a stepping stone to enlarging your knowledge and contacts.

Look outward. First, comprehend the relevance of your assignment to the total operation. Talk to people who utilize your service or product in any way. Ask how you can transform whatever you produce to be more useful to them. You'll gain a deeper understanding about your business, and you'll spot ways to break out of the shell that's restricting you to a standardized procedure.

Strategy

Personalize your product or service. Whatever kind of work you do, tailor it to fit the needs of the recipients. Build on the base of knowledge you've already established.

Steps

1. Volunteer for additional responsibilities. Forget your job description and position yourself. If your job is administrative, find new ways to support your boss. Asking questions about your job is a good tactic to help reshape it. For example, if you're aiming to become training director some day, volunteer to update the manual. Offering your presently untapped knowledge, skill, or talent sends a tactful message about your accomplishments.

2. Keep reporting subtly. You want your boss to associate your name with accomplishments. Send gentle reminders that you exist and do good work. Give quick, concise, meaty, one-minute verbal updates about a couple of projects you're experimenting with. Submit progress reports even when they're not required. Top your reports with a brief handwritten phrase. Circle an important paragraph with a colored marker. Analyze evaluation forms you had participants fill out after an event you chaired and report on comments. Send copies of your reports to others affected.

3. Contact all who use your work product. Aim to improve your service. Suggest new usages and request reaction. For example, you supply data, and learn some people need headings, subheadings, and indented key paragraphs to more easily extract the information they need. Others suggest you individualize the sequence for different people with different purposes.

Script

(Expand your role.) *Boss, is there any reason why we stopped recording the figures at this point? Would you find it useful if I were to include these response stats on . . . ?*

After the demonstration, we received revealing feedback from our evaluation forms. We learned we could be more effective if we emphasized (1) . . . (2) . . . (3) . . . (You become more important when you can report information accurately and concisely.)

Today's paper has been running stories about the need for students to get practical exposure before entering the working world. Would you be interested in hearing why the student intern program we sponsor is highly successful? (Grab interest by arousing curiosity.)

Summary

If your current job description is too restrictive, move to widen the boundaries. Use the time you're left with nothing to do. Conscientiously offer to do additional work, contact users to make your work product more helpful, experiment with shortcuts that produce better work at less cost. New assignments mean new opportunities, but you have to look for them yourself.

5.8 THE CAMPAIGN
Going After an Open Slot

You hear through the grapevine that your colleague Anne, who holds a higher position than you, is leaving. The rumor mill says Warren is being promoted. Richard, fired two months ago, was never replaced, and the resulting backlog is a major pain for the whole office.

You're watching for one of these job openings to be announced so that you can apply. Don't let such opportunities sail away. If you don't want to be beached, beseech. Ask for information, ask for advice, ask for the job.

Place yourself where you'll hear the latest news. Stop eating at your desk. At least twice a week, lunch with people in your field, inside and outside your company, to help you keep alert to what's going on. When you find a suitable opening, be quick to apply. You can't afford to be shy.

Strategy

Spread the word that you're a candidate. Ask everyone, individually, for support.

Steps

1. Establish squatter's rights. Move into a vacancy and, without legal claim or invitation, take over work that's piling up. Most likely your busy boss will be happy that somehow the job is getting done and won't question how. You reduce the risk of refusal if you work now and apply later to formally acquire the title.

2. Track a rumor to the source. Go to the "departing" person to ask if it's true and to get a better handle on the position. Rework your resumé to reflect how well your qualifications match the *real* criteria. If a selection committee is announced, you're ready to move instantly. Write each member, enclose your tailormade resumé, ask to be considered an applicant, and request an interview appointment.

3. Ask your boss for a frank appraisal. Let the boss know you're interested. Inquire how to enhance your chance to fill the open slot. Relieve the boss's concern over who would do your work if you get the promotion. Beware of booby traps. If you're perceived as too strong, you're a threat. Boast tactfully, not to appear you'll be going after the boss's job next. If your peers believe you're trying to promote yourself by making them look bad, watch your back for false innuendoes ("Bill would be great for the job if he learns to keep his hands to himself.") Learn to spread credit.

4. Advertise your candidacy. Share your ambition to win the appointment with your colleagues. If you're competing with a peer, be open about it—you'll still have to work together. Ask your mentors for advice. People can't help you if you don't ask. Feed the grapevine to plant a tip-off that you're aiming for a higher spot. If you're seen as a strong contender, you'll scare others out of the race.

Script

Anne, I heard you landed a better position. Congratulations (confirming the rumor). *I'd like to try for your job. What unique problems do you run into? How do you see your project developing?*

Boss, I heard that Warren is being promoted, and I'd appreciate any advice you can give me because I want to apply for his position. (Find out where you stand.) *What should I emphasize? Do you think taking a mediation course would improve my chances? Frankly, what do you regard as my strengths and weaknesses?*

You'll be glad to hear that I've taught Angie how to program the computer. (You don't want to be passed over again because "you're too important to us where you are.")

Summary

When you go after a job opening, declare your candidacy and advertise yourself. If you get the job, congratulations. If it goes to someone else, find out how you rated in the competition. Was it politics? You'll set out deliberately to make more friends. Were you the victim of backstabbing? Begin winning over your peers by cooperating with them rather than advertising the fact that you outdo them. Were you less qualified? Perhaps taking a course could make you more proficient in a required skill.

Start taking action now to prepare for next time. And begin looking for ways to become more visible.

6

MAGNIFYING YOUR VISIBILITY

Protecting your position and advancing your career often depend on how well you distinguish yourself among your colleagues who are also highly qualified. It takes a plan to respond to what's going on both inside and outside the company. Then, with the same type of campaign you'd apply to any long-range project, you can feel confident, comfortable, and professional.

Gaining recognition means marketing yourself—raising your profile without raising eyebrows and selling yourself without selling your soul or decorum.You can be unpretentious and still get publicized, and you can explore new channels to showcase your talent.

Develop the knack of thinkng of yourself as a valuable, dymanic one-person public relations department for your organization. If you'll focus on results rather than your activities (not what you did but the effects of what you achieved), an infinite number of options will open up for you. (See 6.1 Mix and Match Visibility Options Chart.) Now pinpoint the reasons others would be interested in hearing about your accomplishments. Press that button and you'll find them receptive to your self-promotion as you proceed to market.

6.1 MIX AND MATCH VISIBILITY OPTIONS CHART ——

TARGET GROUPS	
boss/executives	neighborhood groups
civic groups	professional, trade groups
clients/customers	schools, colleges
colleagues	social groups
general public	subordinates
grapevine	

CHANNELS THROUGH WHICH TO FEED YOUR INFORMATION	
Audio, video tapes	reinforce print and spoken messages with sight and sound
Committees, task forces	show leadership, air views in studying pressing problems
Contests, internal and external	stimulate your workers; win awards in your field
Courses	offer to teach or train
Discussion, face to face, small groups, meetings	show insight, preparation; inject ideas, offer solutions
Displays: bulletin boards, posters, fact sheets, articles, clippings, cartoons, pictures	send visual messages
Grapevine	control flow of information
Mailings: memos, notes, letters and enclosures	send focused message, inform, motivate or get action
Meetings	sway decisions, pose pointed questions, show creativity, offer solutions, share experiences
Newsletters for employees, clients: articles, letters to editor, photo suggestions	report accomplishments; air views, offer solutions

Newspapers: press releases, news or feature interviews, letter to the editor, op-ed article	report aspects, results and coming events of interest to the public
Periodicals, trade or professional journals	submit articles or topics that create interest, support
Printed information: fact sheets, brochures, booklets, manuals, fliers, directories, article reprints	increase flow of precise or special information
Professional/trade associations	gather information; make contacts for yourself and company; gain support, show leadership
Radio and TV: news, talk shows; public service announcements	publicize events and results
Reports, oral, written: progress, meeting, committee; task force recommendations	keep boss informed, get results acknowledged, show leadership
Representative, unit or company, at upper-level meetings; civic groups, association meetings	make friends for yourself and company; publicize activities
Sample product or service	test, use consumer response
Speakers' bureau	win support for company aims; improve your speaking ability
Surveys, studies, questionnaires	put finger on pulse to focus on causes, trends, attitudes, concerns; document demand
Telephone	quickly disburse or confirm information, or take survey
Tested plans	offer result analysis of your time and money savers, efficiency boosters, sales promotion ideas

| Unsolicited proposals | offer solutions, change policies, form new alliances, suggest incentive programs |
| Workshops, seminars, conferences, public hearings | provide training; exchange information; build goodwill for the company and yourself |

6.2 MODEST PUBLICITY
Getting Your Accomplishments Noticed

You've played word association games. You know the kind where I say "white," you say "black," or I say "king," you say "queen." There are two words you want automatically linked together in the minds of others: your name + results. You accomplish what you set out to do.

So if your boss doesn't recognize your successes or never expresses appreciation for your skill and dedication, assert yourself. Even those at the top of their professions want recognition and resent an apparent lack of concern for their feelings. Perhaps you've been in your company so long, always doing good work, that the boss forgets to give you feedback. Ask for it. And find new ways to let the boss know what you've been up to.

It's also essential for your self esteem and reputation that your peers acknowledge your good work. Some jealous types pretend not to have heard about the prestigious award you won, and you feel undervalued. Or they needle you ("That's John, our resident expert in demographics, ha ha.")—a masked dig, unappreciative of the effort involved. Let them know what others think.

Strategy

Make use of new channels to build your reputation as a doer. Tactfully and with restraint, publicize results of your efforts and rewards.

Steps

1. Talk about your success. Generously share credit and acknowledge team support. Disguise your justified bragging by passing the praise around. Use the passive voice to soften self praise. The commendation was thrust upon you, rather than something you instigated. However, be gracious in accepting earned compliments ("Thanks, I really appreciate that.") Don't throw them away by downplaying your achievements.

2. *Report your accomplishments.* Top your final report with a note to your boss. Forward clippings and testimonials when appropriate. Notify the editor of your company newsletter, trying for a photo along with the article. With your boss's okay, submit press releases to the media, interpreting your findings and praising the work of your company. Help a cause and help yourself by chairing a project for your community group, publicizing your company affiliation. As head of your local professional association, express the group's view in a letter to the editor.

3. *Stage contests and advertise awards.* Create excitement for your project by giving it a name that catches on. Hold an amateur photo contest. Or a sales promotion contest with prizes for every idea entry and a bonus for the winner. Friendly rivalry is a great motivator to speed up progress and stimulate interest. Visual and colorful contests may net TV publicity. Award ceremonies are good to show appreciation. Seek joint recognition by suggesting that your company enter local and national award contests in your field and offering to write the entry. Have a friend enter your contribution for an individual award.

Script

Thank you again for your help, Boss. I really couldn't have nailed that contract without your advice and support. (You can boast if you share.)

As you may know, I was asked (passive voice) *to work on solutions for the overcrowding problem. We found that . . .* (You were "forced" to do good.)

(To your newsletter editor) *Yes, we're very proud of the results. May I suggest two others join me in the photo . . .*

(To the company communications/public relations department or local newspaper) *The company takes pride in this award because it shows we are not only concerned with the environment, we actually improved . . .*

Summary

You can remain modest and still take bold steps to get your accomplishments recognized. Occasionally, other people will promote you, but you usually have to take the action yourself. Look over the list of options and select the channels that will work best for you. Then talk and act with pride to get your achievements known.

6.3 WRITTEN VIEWS
Getting Your Thoughts Printed

Companies want people who show they can think for themselves. And one of the best ways to demonstrate this is to reveal your opinions in writing. Search for appropriate avenues when you have something important to say. Look for opportunities both within and beyond your organization.

With foggy reasoning, people seem to feel that whatever is in print must be so. It's tangible. They can refer to it. They believe whatever they read. So it's good to write, or to be talked about and especially to be quoted in an article. Getting your name and activity into a news or feature story enchances your position and credibility. Mixing useful information for the reader along with accounts of your activity enables you to move beyond self-aggrandizement to the service level.

Review the activities you perform for your company, business or professional association, and civic and community groups. If you have an opinion or can report on a better way to do anything, start by writing your thoughts and then polishing what you've written.

Strategy

Get in print. Decide the options you'll try to get your views publicized.

Steps

1. Contact your company newsletter. In a letter to the editor, give your viewpoint about a situation *commonly shared.* Suggest an article if you can connect the activity you're heading to a topic of current interest among employees, or submit a short, factual account focused on one main point. If you won a prestigious award, the editor wants to know this because that type of news indirectly promotes the company as well.

2. Submit articles to your association journal. You discovered a better method and you're willing to explain to your colleagues, for instance, why you think your department is unusually creative. Given enough advance notice, trade or professional journals generally welcome a timely, well-written piece. This will highlight your expertise and increase your credibility.

3. Contact your local newspaper. Check with your boss because this may have to be coordinated with your company's communications or public relations department. Since it helps the company, they may make the contacts for you. If you're on your own, call for an interview or submit a news release. What you suggest must be of communitywide interest, such as a service you're offering to citizens or one that indirectly affects citizens. If you can tie your activity to a current topic of public concern (for example, crime prevention), or if you're the head of a local group, with a strong opinion about what the public should consider, submit an article to the op-ed page or send a letter to the editor.

4. Distribute reprints of any article about your work. Circulate these around the office. Tack them up on bulletin boards. Enclose reprints in appropriate interoffice and outside mailings.

Script

(Submit to the company newsletter.) *To the editor: If we really want a way to reduce absenteeism, it's time we considered flex time . . .*

(Call the newsletter editor.) *You may be interested in hearing about how well we did at the awards banquet . . .*

(Praising your company to a local paper.) *The team of professionals our company has sent to teach this method to students in the public schools means . . .*

(Very brief note with a reprint) *From our last conversation, I thought this might interest you.*

Summary

Articulating your opinions on paper is good practice. Look for opportunities, because it will boost your stock if you're able to get something printed by submitting through the appropriate channel. Read your newsletter, newspaper, and journals more critically. Study the type of stories they run and the kinds of articles they accept. In fact, clip these for a week and you'll have your own textbook. You'll learn very quickly what type and style of story to submit to which channel.

6.4 INFORMAL SURVEYS
Latching on to What's Hot

If you can help your group resolve problems quickly, fairly, and effectively, your value will indeed be appreciated. Informal surveys provide an easy way to keep your finger on the pulse. Interviews, questionnaires, and telephone surveys are among several barometers available to you to gauge attitudes and opinions. Take advantage of them. Sometimes you'll come across the unanticipated.

Taking a random sample is fast and—even though it's not strictly scientific—it's credible for your purposes and will influence decisions. When reporting your survey, boil down your talk to a minute or two, stressing the bottom line. But have all the breakdown figures available for those who want more information.

In addition to researching questions and bringing the data back to your group, try another approach. When participants can't seem to focus on the real issue during the meeting itself, suggest taking different types of quick problem-solving surveys.

Strategy

Poll and analyze needed information. Take any appropriate variation of the survey when you sense a problem exists and present this thinking in its most usable form.

Steps

1. Research attitudes. There were moans and groans a couple of weeks ago when the boss mentioned that everyone would be switching soon to another method. You believed it would be useful to point out, and thus be able to deal with, the real objections. So you circulated a questionnaire. To get frank responses, the instructions were *not* to sign it. For quick compilation, the answers are in numerical ratings.

2. Take a morale survey. There's a lot of tension in the air and you can't quite nail it down. No one you've spoken to is sure why the workers are slowing down, making more mistakes, and generally appearing demotivated. To learn the reasons and how pervasive the discontent may be, prepare a morale survey. List as many reasons as you can imagine with a place to check after each one. Leave room to write in any you've left out ("other _____ "). Add a line to check if satisfied with conditions as they are. Again, ask participants not to sign unless they particularly want to. These answers are easy to compile and will light the way out of the tunnel.

3. Take your own "Gallup poll." Learn how your colleagues or subordinates would choose needs or evaluate effects. This can be executed quickly by phone. Every respondent is asked the same question(s). The results can be useful in reaching or influencing decisions.

4. Suggest a problem census. At your staff meeting, opinions are flying hot and heavy but you're not getting anywhere. No one agrees on what's causing the problem. That's a good time to stop and ask to take a problem census. Without waiting to be recognized, members of the group call out their greatest concerns while one person is assigned to write these spontaneous opinions on the blackboard (or on large newsprint mounted on the wall). Or you can suggest stopping the discussion and brainstorming to define issues and solutions. Or use buzz sessions to break up the large group into small units to secure suggestions for the same question or for different aspects of the same question.

Script

(Questionnaire) *On a scale of 1 to 5, with 1 being weakest and 5 being strongest, in your opinion the proposed change would . . .* (check 1, 2, 3, 4, or 5). *These blank lines are for additional comments you care to make.*

(Problem census) *No judgmental remarks are allowed at this point. just call out your greatest concern. After that, we'll refine the list and decide our priorities. Then we can restate our concerns as positive objectives.*

(Gallup poll) *Are you in favor of . . . ?* (Answers are yes, no, or undecided.) *Would you choose a, b, or c?*

Summary

When you can give your boss essential information you've compiled or you can lead your group in making intelligent decisions, you gain a reputation as a valuable player. When presenting this data in written form, condense results as highlights on one page. To give more detail, separate it from the highlights and attach.

6.5 MEETING PARTICIPATION ————————————
Arranging a Stage to Air Your Views

You feel overlooked. The boss seems disinterested in your excellent performance. She has her favorites who get the best assignments. There doesn't seem to be any opportunity to get recognition. Look again at your staff meetings.

Are they mandatory—drop-everything-to-come-yawn-together-for-two-hours? Or erratically scheduled? Does discussion cover the waterfront without reaching decisions? Suggest to your boss that meetings could save her time (be completed within an hour) and evoke better suggestions if (except for emergencies) all of you were better prepared for issues to be discussed. Offer to prepare and distribute agendas in advance, mentioning the benefits of talking about only one or two issues each time.

Getting your group to meet regularly and informally provides a chance to display your talent and abilities and report on your efforts. You stand out if you take a more active role in the discussion, make intelligent comments, and ask pertinent questions. Doing this well, however, takes preparation.

Strategy

Use your staff meetings to separate yourself from the pack.

Steps

1. Come to meetings prepared. Create interest and prevent yourself from boring everybody when you're scheduled to report. Start with a novel opener such as a one-minute taped interview. Rehearse from key-word reminder notes. This allows you to get right to the point without rambling and deliver the report with confidence. Above all, keep eye contact and don't read. Also, make notes on your agenda of points you want to raise. Cluster your questions to dig deeper and get at the core of a problem. Don't bring up a new explosive issue without giving your boss advance warning.

2. Help guide discussions. You don't have to, and shouldn't, comment on every topic. Save your comments for times when they count. Listen to the views expressed before you jump in. Then you can ask a few questions that open the door for your ideas as you summarize and narrow down the problem for the group.

3. Step forward when the group can't resolve issues. If there's insufficient information, suggest talking about it next time. If there's a heated debate, suggest breaking up for discussion into several small groups. Volunteer to brainstorm with a few others after the meeting or be part of a task force to bring back recommendations. Joining committees that report to the whole group gives you good experience in articulating your thoughts and practicing brief talks.

4. Develop post-meeting summaries and proposals. If your boss doesn't recap meeting results and assignments, volunteer to prepare from your agenda notes a succinct wrap-up, ready for the boss's signature. If an idea struck you that you weren't ready to talk about during the meeting, think it through, briefly outline your plan, and have it on your boss's desk by the next morning. Or, if you expressed an idea at the meeting for which the boss wanted more background, provide a written summary with specific information.

Script

(Clarify an ambiguous opinion.) *Mary, can you give us an example of how that would work? (*Asking clarifying questions when everyone's confused.) *How long would it take? Why isn't that satisfactory?*

(Share credit as you piggyback on another's idea.) *Jane has a terrific idea. Do you think we can expand on that to . . .*

(Improve discussion by stopping the rambler.) *That's a good suggestion, Ted, why don't we schedule it for next time. Our problem now appears to be . . .*

(Summarize discussion, then point the way to go.) *So it really boils down to this. The basic question we have to ask is . . . and it seems to me that we'd be better off . . .*

Summary

Participating in a meeting can put you in the spotlight. You're seen as wanting to be part of a group effort as well as advancing your own career. Use the staff meetings to gain new insights into your organization and its needs and to figure out where you best can shine.

6.6 BROKERED INFORMATION
Milking Your Significant Data

Don't let the data you've been collecting collect dust. You've gathered a great deal of knowledge from reading newletters, newspapers, journals, periodicals, and books; from attending courses, seminars, workshops, and conferences; and from talking with people in your field, inside and outside your company, and to your customers. How can you use this knowledge to make yourself more visible?

As you read, listen and observe, determine the direction in which your organization is moving and how that fits in with current trends. That can help you figure out the kinds of data or information significant to others. Maybe from amassing and analyzing statistics, you can suggest an adjustment in current operations. Or by recognizing patterns, you can show that your company should be targeting another market. Or, after learning a new method at a conference, you share this know-how with your colleagues.

Just as a broker collects a commission for an exchange, you rake in recognition if you supply needed information in a proper, effective form.

Strategy

Make your data matter. Plan ahead how you can use your information to help your organization and yourself.

Steps

1. Find a handier format. If your job includes preparing reports of any kind, consider what you know about those who use your reports. They're probably in a hurry for specific bits of information, yet have to plow through a lot of reading. How can you personalize your data when everybody gets the same general content? You can top each report with a tailormade, concise, one-page memo for instant reference. Try a fact sheet format with a snappy, staccato style. Substitute phrases for complete sentences. Capitalize each one- or two-word topic, follow with several dots, then a paragraph of boiled-down extract.

2. Initiate requests for the data you have. If you hear a lot of rumbling that company directives are confusing, conflicting, or verbose, prepare a useful checklist and offer copies. When you send concise memos to your boss or colleagues, end with a request for specific action and offer them more detailed information. Study national and local journals and magazines searching for a peg—some issue of great interest to which you can relate what you're working on. If you find the link, submit an article for consideration.

3. Translate complex issues. Comprehension often requires more persistance than genius. Most people aren't willing to take the time to study; they skim the headline without reading the article. Make yourself visible by volunteering your knowledge. Interpret and present research reports in simplified terms. Extract the essence of articles and talk in terms managers understand and can act upon.

Script

(Personalizing reports) *Josie, from the report I send you each month, tell me what's the exact type of information you need to know for your work? I can pull that out for you so that you don't have to wade through the whole thing.*

I found I needed a quick reference to look up directives. If you'd like a copy of the summary I prepared, call me. (Get others coming to you.)

(Query letter) *Since the journal leans heavily on reports of successful consolidation efforts, would you be interested in an article describing how we . . .*

(Interpreting data) *The bottom line of these reports shows we can't compete with big discount suppliers, but surveys indicate their customers do have a need not being filled. We have to target another market, offering a delivery service . . .*

Summary

For an additional way to raise your profile and be applauded, consider interpreting and distributing useful information you've gathered. With a little extra effort, you reshape and expand your job. Or you can reduce to writing quick reference material. Or submit articles. Or put technical talk into everyday language. The key to getting more mileage from your data is to personalize the presentation to meet the needs of the recipients.

6.7 THOUGHTFUL GESTURES
Little Things Bring Big Dividends

In this age of instant everything, for most of us five minutes is too long to spend showing consideration. So if you want to be different from the majority of your colleagues and become more visible around the office, take the time for a little thoughtfulness. Show others, without the thought of a payback, that they matter to you.

Be generous in your appreciation. Make quick phone calls or send brief thank you notes. So few people do this today that your action is much appreciated and long remembered. It's especially helpful to send a note to the supervisor of the one who helped you, with a blind copy to the subordinate.

Supply your boss, colleagues, and subordinates with bits of information they may find useful—an easy reminder that you exist and are thinking about them. Be kind and professional when you disagree by taking another minute to soften the sting with a polite phrase.

Strategy

Show sincere concern, but aim for mutual support. Being thoughtful of the feelings of others earns you grateful recognition as well as eternal loyalty.

Steps

1. Use gratitude to build bridges. Thank a few of your peers who helped on your project by inviting them to a surprise lunch and centering the talk about their roles in making it a success. Post items on the bulletin board that cite the part others played. Feed your gratitude into the grapevine, mentioning how well someone is performing. And don't forget to call or send brief notes of acknowledgment.

2. Get your name remembered. Use the Madison Avenue repetition approach. When you distribute "This may interest you" material, circle paragraphs or reprint important data, jot a note and sign your name. When you prepare any special information, take credit for authorship. Look for good cartoons you can mount, pen a one-liner and sign your name before posting it. Don't wait for people to struggle trying to remember your name—go up and immediately identify yourself. Request that satisfied customers convert their spoken compliments into quick notes to your boss.

3. *Invite your boss to lunch.* Make it a business lunch, not to cultivate a close relationship or ask for special privileges, but as a nice gesture to create an opportunity to express opinions and learn how well you're doing. You have some ideas you want to discuss without interruption and have figured out how the boss would benefit. Or you think you know how to meet a particularly troublesome situation. You're acquainted with a whiz in that perplexing area, whom the boss may want you to invite to the next staff meeting.

4. *Correct others graciously.* Smile as you set someone right who has your name wrong, or mispronounces it, or calls you by a nickname you detest. Disagree inoffensively about issues. Rather than tell others they're wrong, show good manners by stating your concern or confusion or asking for an explanation or politely showing contradictory evidence.

Script

(To the office gossip) *Well, you know, Jim, I really couldn't have pulled that off without Linda's research. Her work is terrific.*

(Assume others can't remember your name.) *Hi Joe, I'm John Stoneface, good to see you again.*

Boss, I'd like to talk you at length about a matter I believe could help you. Are you free to have lunch with me on Thursday?

(Correcting without offending) *I believe the figures have been misstated* or *I'm afraid my colleague was given some misinformation.*

Summary

If you want to be praised and raised, you need every friend you can get. Make it a habit to devote five minutes a day to increasing your recognition and visibility via thoughtful gestures. Think: Whom can I thank today? Who could use this information? How can I help others while getting my name in front of more people? Just as tossing off an insensitive remark can cause someone to carry a grudge for a decade, being considerate can make a friend for a lifetime.

6.8 TEACHER/TRAINER

Offering to Share Your Expertise

You've trained yourself to excel in your area, and this unique talent helps you to stand out from your colleagues. Whether your skill is interpreting laws that affect your company, writing contracts, or programming computers, whatever you do is of special use to the company. Tap into that and expand your usefulness.

Offer to share your expertise by talking to, teaching or training company classes. Or you might offer to put together a panel and volunteer to serve as the moderator. Doing so not only reminds the boss of your expertise, but also demonstrates your genuine concern for the company. In addition, use your contacts outside the company to volunteer your knowledge to produce, for example, a workshop for your association.

Gradually you'll become recognized as the expert in your subject. You'll become sought after for your opinions. With increased visibility, you'll feel renewed energy and zest for your job.

Strategy

Become an authority on one aspect of your field. When you are a recognized authority, you are asked for your opinion, invited to speak before groups, and you're quoted by people in your company as well as the media. That's visibility.

Steps

1. Volunteer to teach a course to colleagues or subordinates. N o t only are you seen as the expert, but you also protect future promotions. Some qualified workers have been stuck in one position because no one else knew how to do their work.

2. Offer to lead problem-solving groups. Become the recognized expert in resolving difficult issues. For example, at meetings you can take a problem census, organize buzz groups, role play a technique, or discuss forming quality circles. Or volunteer to coordinate a workshop centered around a problem area.

3. Solicit and give talks. Use your network to build contacts and keep updating your contact file. Where relevant, talk to students during their job-study programs. Talk to groups that your friends and colleagues belong to. Tell them you're available if they need a speaker or panelist. Mention your subject and availability to the program chairperson of your professional association.

Script

Boss, I've been talking to Rob, Bea and Benny. They've expressed an interest in learning to write contracts. If you have no objection to my teaching them, I'd like to give us a backup . . . (good for you and the company).

One way we could improve this situation is with employee participation through quality circles. I'd be glad to train the workers in the various techniques they'd need to study the issues and present recommendations. (advertising your expertise).

(Approach the chairperson to be invited to speak.) *As you may know, my specialty is producing motivational tapes. If you'd like to have a program with visuals on that subject, I'm available on* . . .

Summary

One of the best ways to become more visible is to teach or train others. Look for opportunities in your company and in the organizations you and your friends belong to. Your recognition grows along with your reputation. Becoming more visible requires good planning. Decide:

- What is your message? Your goal, aim, how you want others to see you.
- Whom do you want to reach? The target audience that can help you reach your objective.
- Through which channels? The most effective ways to reach them.
- What are the best tactics and techniques to use?

And now that people know who you are, consider how to build up and display your base of support.

7

SHOWING A BASE OF SUPPORT

Everybody's scrambling to get heard, but very few *take the time* to figure out specific opportunities that are open through an internal support network. To gain a reputation for skillful, innovative leadership, you need a base of backers. This intangible hookup allows you, your boss, peers, and subordinates to collaborate in producing the best product or service you can. Each one, at every level, is your potential assistant, even your competitor colleague.

All of them are available to help you move more quickly and accurately. So it's important to define the ways they can help you as well as to know how you can help them. You build your support by synchronizing mutual interests.

Admittedly, it's a bit nervy to position yourself as a leader without title. But nobody's knocking down your door. You have to create your own circumstances to win trust, make friends, get your thoughts across, and motivate everyone around you. You don't need to know all the answers; you just have to know where to find them.

7.1 RELIABLE ─────────────────────────────
Winning Trust from a Skeptical Boss

The boss, of course, is the key player in your support system. If your boss is skeptical, consider the reasons. You may be perceived as a threat. Or you may have ticked off people friendly with the boss. Anyone you offended could be spreading stories about you, and a negative reputation takes a long time to shed. So one of your first objectives is to make friends throughout the office. Work on becoming more pleasant, cooperative, and tactful.

Keep unrelated personal problems out of the office. If you can't keep them secret, the assumption is you can't be trusted in the office with confidential matters.

Earn confidence by being consistent in the quality of your work and by keeping your promise. Become known as quick and dependable. If you've turned in inaccurate information, from now on, double check to rebuild credibility. If a warning bell goes off in your head, review again. Before you offer a new idea, check if it was tried before. Don't hide negative aspects of a proposal, but be prepared to discuss them. Anticipate and think through the entire sequence before you take action.

Strategy

Augment your reputation to convert skepticism to trust. Become known throughout the office as one others want to work with because you get things done.

Steps

1. Keep your boss informed. Even when not required, send periodic progress reports so that the boss knows he can trust you to come through. Don't bypass your boss and avoid surprises, good or bad. They can embarrass your boss, who always has to be ready to respond to his boss.

2. Observe deadlines. Meet yours and help others meet theirs. Your cooperative, dependable attitude gets back to your boss. Before promising, think through the required steps. Give yourself a little leeway so that you always deliver on or before deadline. A tickler file will help you to follow through and remind others whose work you need so as to finish yours on time.

3. Seek a chain of quick, small victories. Establish a decisive work style. Work first where there's the highest interest and chance for fastest results to develop the boss's confidence and restore your own self-confidence. In advance, consider how you'll measure results to demonstrate improvement. And then interpret the results. What's obvious to you may not be obvious to your boss. Go ahead and spell it out.

Script

> *Boss, I think you'd want to know that we're having a little difficulty with the Warren contract. It seems Mr. Warren has added a few new conditions, and I think we might handle it by . . .* (To inspire trust, it's better that the boss hear the trouble from you.)

> *We're showing demonstrable results with our contest to increase sensitivity. The panel of judges rated the last session . . .* (Tangible evidence increases trust.)

Summary

In building an internal support system, your first concern is having a boss who trusts you. After exhibiting your loyalty, if you can't figure out why your boss seems skeptical, have a heart-to-heart conversation. Remember people talk, and what the boss hears influences the amount of trust in your ability. So be straightforward, considerate, and dependable.

7.2 NO YES-MAN
Telling Bosses What They Need to Know

Think it's dangerous to be right when the boss is wrong? Not really. In fact, handled correctly, your reasoning can boost you up, while being a bootlicker can boot you out. For your opinions and reports to be of value, you have to show the courage of your convictions. At times that means disagreeing with and actually bossing the boss.

You can't afford to be intimidated by authority. You just have to be tactful and polite while standing your ground. The temptation is to report only good news, but what the boss needs to know is not necessarily what the boss wants to hear. Know his or her objectives and guidelines. Quote from the credo. Using the boss's own words in your message makes it palatable.

Be aware of how your boss comes across. If you spot something that's creating a poor impression, plant the idea for improvement and then cultivate your plant. Rather than telling the boss what to do, use questions to focus on alternatives and to inquire about progress being made. Go the extra mile to make your boss look good.

Strategy

Pretend you bought the company. You have a vested interest in its success. Now get up the nerve to state what you believe to be best for the boss and the company. Assume a leadership role with the message, "I can help you meet your goals."

Steps

1. Save the boss's time. Be selective and concise in your oral and written reports. Organize your thinking to eliminate extraneous time-wasting, tangential information. But when you hear pervasive grumbling from workers, talk up while there's still time for the boss to correct the problem.

2. Start a disagreement with points on which you agree. You'll both be more comfortable. You want the boss to feel that you're pleasant to be with. If you're on friendly terms, very mild teasing shows you're not intimidated, but never question the boss's authority.

3. State the expected consequences. Offer the long view, the anticipated outcome of the decision being discussed. Give it your best shot, and if the boss still disagrees with you, smile and let it go. Sometimes a bad decision has to be implemented before the boss can see it was flawed; sometimes the boss was right all along.

4. Go out on a limb and offer creative suggestions. Take the risk because that's the only way your efforts will bear fruit. Research the issues or equipment the boss has expressed an interest in. Then, without being asked, you can offer an educated opinion.

Script

(Quoting the boss is your strongest argument.) *You've often said our priority should be . . . It seems to me this would shift our direction in two ways . . .* (factual, unemotional, avoiding hostility).

Boss, while I agree with your reasons for the delay, I think we should review point number 3 again. That might be a reason to expedite . . .

Perhaps, instead, we could . . . (Start by agreeing, then offer your alternative.)

(Tactfully offering your idea) *You've probably already considered the need to do something about* . . . *I have an idea, but I need your advice on how to approach* . . . (acknowledging the boss's skill).

(Moving gently on a procedure the boss initiated) *As you know, because of today's changing market, we've been having some distribution problems. We can expect the delays to increase until we find* . . . *In light of these conditions, we should* . . . *Well, maybe you're right.* (Give your view, then back off if the boss is intractable.)

Summary

In telling the boss what the boss needs to know, there's always a risk that the messenger gets shot. Even a secure boss can feel "This is something I should have thought about and didn't" and then feel resentful toward you. But if you learn how to disagree, and even boss the boss, you'll be recognized as a valuable advisor. The skill requires tact, knowledge, and a clear understanding of mutual goals.

7.3 IMAGE MAKER
Helping Others Look Good

Not only do you want to make your boss look good, it's also in your interest to help everybody else look good. Colleagues and subordinates whom you've helped develop potential will become your staunchest supporters.

Most of us are egocentric, focused primarily on what we want. We think we earn points by carefully staying within the lines, tending our own business. Helping others is often a tit-for-tat situation. Some don't even think about aiding. Some are afraid of competition.

Therefore, when you help others grow, you stand apart from the rest. What's more, you get an extraordinary return on your investment. As individuals improve, the unit improves. News of your efforts filters back to the boss, whose main concern is the unit's output. The boss is impressed. You feel good about yourself. And you keep filling the stands with your enthusiastic cheerleaders.

Strategy

Make each person you work with feel happy to have had the chance to do so. Go out of your way to be helpful.

Steps

1. Bolster confidence. We all need reassurance that we're moving in a good direction. Be generous with sincere, deserved compliments. Don't worry about coming up with the right words. An honest expression of your feelings makes the words "right." Ask questions at your staff meeting that you know certain people have specific information about and are dying to answer. Give them the stage.

2. Be a coach, not a crutch. If you play mother hen or complete a difficult assignment for a colleague, you're hurting, not helping. For people to grow in their jobs, they must assume responsibility for their own actions. You can offer good routes, but leave the driving to them.

3. Help others articulate their ideas. Everybody has thoughts and opinions. Pull them out. Offer suggestions on how to refine their ideas to meet what the company is looking for.

4. Define ways others can help you. People are uncomfortable always being on the receiving end, so it's important to let them do something for you in return. Make tactful suggestions.

Script

(Honest compliments) *I like what you did. That was a truly inspiring story. Really good work, congratulations.*

June, you know you're very capable of pulling this together by yourself. I might suggest that you emphasize these three points. Show me your draft and I'll be glad to critique it. (Don't let flattery ensnare you into doing someone else's work.)

Are you saying that we'd be better off by changing to this system? In that case, why don't you outline the steps and ask the boss to . . . (Some need help in extracting and presenting ideas.)

Michael, you have such unusual ideas, I'd consider it a great favor if you'd think up some titles for this project (suggesting how he can pay you back).

Summary

Helping your colleagues and subordinates polish their potential is good for everyone. You're not trying to create a phony image but to assist them to use their talents and creativity to help themselves and help the company. You might establish a model they can copy, changing your own little corner of the world and sharing methods you found practical. You might convey information you picked up that they could use. You might alert them to some program of interest. However you coach or encourage, helping each one feel important is a kind deed for which you'll be repaid over and over.

7.4 TEAM PLAYER
Pitching In and Helping Out

The significance here is not so much that being a team player helps you, but that being perceived as *not being a team player* can seriously impede your climb or send you tumbling down.

When colleagues act hostile toward you, there's often a feeling (deserved or not) that you do certain things just to make them feel inferior. The other person may have a self-esteem problem, but you get the brunt of the attack when he or she doesn't feel respected.

Therefore, it's important for you to examine if the perception you've created is netting you enemies. Is your idea of success making everyone else look bad? Are you flaunting the fact that you do everything better than they do? Do you walk around with a chip on your shoulder? Are you intent on exposing what you consider to be another's petty politics?

Pitching in and helping out is a lot more than working an extra hour during an emergency.

Strategy

Create synergy. Develop cooperative action among all who work together. You really can't do it all alone, ignoring contributions others make. When everybody pulls together toward common goals, you accomplish more than if each of you were working in a vacuum.

Steps

1. Become a better listener. Listen to what others are saying and especially for between-the-lines meanings. Accept their disagreement with you as a chance to reexamine and perhaps improve your statements. You can benefit greatly from your colleagues' assessments.

2. Support decisions. You took part in the discussion and the matter was resolved. Now go along with the group without pouting that you didn't get your way. Bend a little.

3. Be quick to do favors. Create opportunities to contribute your experience and share new information to help others. When you see someone overburdened, even though "it's not my job," think of yourself as working for the whole company. Offer to switch shifts when your cohort needs time off. Do more than necessary and do it graciously. More than looking out for yourself and your boss, start looking out for your team.

Script

What, specifically, don't you like about the idea? (a valid argument). *I see, well, maybe it could be produced faster. I'll have to give that more thought.* (Be willing to reconsider.)

My appraisal proved to be right on the mark. How did you do with yours? (Stop trying to show up your peers, and offer genuine help.) *I found a little trick that's helped me make better appraisals. Maybe you could use it too?*

Summary

Being a team player is doing whatever you can to be part of, and improve, what's going on. Stay alert, looking for ways to relate to any issue, problem, or objectives you hear about. Give support to get support. Think more globally, not just about your job, but also about your department, division, and the company. Help to resolve little problems before they magnify.

7.5 PROTECTIVE ARMOR
Lining up Your Allies in Advance

You never seem to muster enough support for your suggestions on important issues. Your ideas don't get explored, or they die in committee. You're left holding the bag on a proposal you'd mentioned to a couple of colleagues who seemed to go along and then spoke in opposition when you presented it.

What's really upsetting is when peers you had assumed had the same goals as you openly oppose your position. Or you find yourself under attack by the "oh, it could never work" doom-and-gloom crowd.

Your best bet may be to find a sounding board—a few people you admire for clear, logical thinking and whose reactions you trust as to the effectiveness or acceptability of your idea. Perhaps you're friendly with an astute executive who likes you and is willing to guide you simply out of a desire to see you succeed. This mentor can be of tremendous help not only in paving the way with new contacts, but also in sharpening your preparation and presentation skills.

Strategy

Garner support before you're attacked. Either take people into your confidence in the planning stages and have them co-sponsor your proposals and/or be better prepared to answer anticipated objections.

Steps

1. Listen, modify, and join forces. While the idea is still nebulous and hasn't yet jelled in your mind, ask questions that will evoke the opinions or suggestions of others. If you can modify your plan to accommodate their viewpoints, try for a joint presentation. Or if you can compromise a little, you may not get outright support, but you've probably stopped them from speaking out against you. And even if they do speak out, you'll know what to expect and can be prepared with a counterpunch.

2. Move before your opponents can mount a defense. When you know you have something controversial, don't talk about it until you're sure you have all the information and your facts are solid. Otherwise, your idea will get picked apart as you go from person to person in advance of group discussion. Instead, present your idea confidently, knowing the benefits and anticipating and answering every objection with extreme tact.

3. Be prepared for wet blankets. Almost every group has certain people who insist something can't work before letting you state your case. Their premature pessimism destroys your enthusiasm and turns off everyone else. You have to stop the unwarranted attack. Begin your talk by briefly summarizing the problem, alternatives, and your proposal. As the chorus of nay-sayers start, interrupt the interruption. Keep talking, presenting your evidence (studies, articles, testimonials, whatever can back you up). Keep it light and control your annoyance. But if they persist, pressing them for specific objections will stop them cold.

Script

Frank, do you think our workers are feeling the stress today as much as we managers are? . . . Under what conditions do you see extending the stress management programs to include . . . ? (getting a feel for opinions of others).

(Countering objections) *Yes, Amanda, you're right, we do have to use utmost caution not to build false hopes. That's why I propose mixing both groups to develop the plan and work out . . .*

(Interrupting and refusing to surrender to the wet blanket) *Excuse me, Andy, I have two more points to make and then we can discuss your objections . . .* (and when you've finished) *Now, Andy, please tell us specifically what it is that makes you feel this is impractical.* (You sound fair and friendly.)

Summary

While you know you can't win every time and people have a right to disagree with you, you want to put up a good fight. To line up support in advance, get a better reading of the pulse of the group. And then do a better job of selling yourself while selling your message.

7.6 AMALGAMATOR
Molding Individuals into a Team

When workers feel pride in the company and pride in their unit, their own self-esteem swells. They want to belong. They want to accomplish. So if you wish to be recognized as a manager who gets great results, start reshaping the various segments you supervise into a more cohesive whole. Instill a strong common purpose. Link the parts by interpreting company goals into unit goals and unit goals into results you expect from individuals.

Then free your subordinates from your need to regulate their thoughts and styles. With simplified structure and a flexible motivational style, allow people to feel they have some measure of control over their own jobs. Overall policy, final decisions, appropriate technical assistance, and communication strategies can still come from the top. But make each segment feel responsible for improving its own operation.

Level with your people, giving honest information instead of playing games. Explain changing circumstances and explore ways to adapt. Let all of them know you need their creativity and you value their knowledge and insight. Reward innovation. Before long, you'll have molded all the diverse parts into a dedicated entity.

Strategy

Balance company and unit goals with individual freedom. After you've defined the objectives, duties, and restraints, give your workers the flexibility, latitude, and authority they need to get the job done.

Steps

1. March to the same drummer. Send the same message to all segments. Make it crystal clear that the beliefs, principles, and goals you enunciate are the guidelines for operations. Say what you want achieved, give them what they need to achieve it, and watch their imaginative ideas burst forth.

2. Decentralize. Think less control, allowing components maximum autonomy and supervisors individual managing styles. Eliminate unnecessary layers of people approval, but don't let subordinates pass the buck by making their problems your problems.

3. Encourage self-correction . Devise a system that allows each segment to correct itself before higher-ups clamp down. Encourage them to ask for technical assistance, to learn what they're doing well and what deviates from accepted standards, to work with the experts to improve themselves.

4. Be flexible. Regroup, expand, or contract as you increase and decrease projects, alter directions, or find cost savers and product improvements. When your unit is well molded, you have the ability to adjust quickly to changing conditions. Facilitating work teams and problem-solving task forces can be pulled together instantly, as needed.

Script

Keep in mind the company creed and these objectives which form the basis for your decision making. They are also the standard by which your results will be measured. (telling what you expect and why).

I'm visiting your site to bring you the latest update and answer your questions about the new acquisition. (You're accessible and communicating.)

That's a good question, one you'll want to discuss in your own group. I know you're smart enough to come up with a workable answer. (Don't tell them answers they should figure out for themselves.)

Summary

Charisma alone is not strong enough glue to hold together your entire operation. Build from a solid base, explaining company and unit purpose and instilling pride in that purpose. Then allow your subordinates to be responsible for part of the planning and they'll be there for the problems. Autonomy, responsibility, and creativity are powerful motivators.

7.7 PERSUADER
Getting People to Buy Into Your Plan

You're not trying to manipulate your workers, and there's really no need for high anxiety. But you do want to make changes, avoiding the resistance you usually run up against. This time you're hoping that if you provide information early, you can get your workers to help you with the planning and implementing and in the process go along with your ideas.

You've learned that people feel anxious and insecure when they don't know what to expect. They worry about being transferred or replaced during a reorganization. They fret about having to learn new procedures or techniques.

So one of your first concerns is spotting and dealing with unwarranted assumptions. When people don't know the answers, they tend to make them up. Be straightforward in relating your information, telling them what they most want to know: how they'll be affected, the good and the bad. To get their help and cooperation, you'll have to have them understand the need for the change. Then listen receptively, encouraging a free-flowing discussion. You may hear some useful new ideas, as you start building toward a consensus.

Strategy

Reinforce your workers' sense of belonging. Concentrate on a comfortable climate in which there's a clear sense of direction, accurate information, and uninhibited discussion.

Steps

1. Strengthen your subordinates' confidence in you. They can't latch onto Milquetoast comments, but say you have a plan, and their ears will perk up. Your self-confidence inspires their trust. Now that you've got their attention, get support by showing you've done your homework. Start with your conclusion to the existing problem. Then give the reasons, followed by the advantages and drawbacks they can expect. Don't build up to and drag out stating your decision because the anticipation creates too much anxiety. Some would stop listening and start misinterpreting your remarks.

2. Correct misconceptions. By asking how others feel about an issue, you learn who is misinformed or uninformed. Counter with as much specific information as you can provide. Be accurate, telling exactly what you believe to be involved. Give estimated numbers, such as expected time and costs, or how many involved. Be sure your body language matches your spoken words. Don't, for example, nod yes as you're listening when you really disagree.

3. Listen with an open mind. Encourage your workers to make suggestions. They might have some special insight. Maybe your way is good, but you could hear a better way, or perhaps by combining, you can get an even more effective solution. Don't, however, ask employees for their opinions if a decision is carved in stone and can't be changed.

Script

(Candidly share updated information.) *We expect the changeover to take two months.* (Don't hedge with "it may take quite a while.")

Yes, Carly, I'm aware of some of the reaction, but it would help me to understand if you'd tell me what you're thinking. (Encourage open discussion.)

But if that were the case, David, wouldn't it be logical to expect an increase rather than a decrease? (Get them to examine their thinking.)

Okay, then, are we in general agreement about the best way to proceed? Good, we'll meet again next week to review our efforts. (Although you have authority to move without them, aim for consensus.)

Summary

To avoid resistance and gain cooperation when you want to make changes, have an open and frank discussion with everybody involved. Frequently updating accurate information, letting others know where they stand, and giving them the opportunity to improve upon your plan leads toward acceptance and support. Also, to generate additional interest, take a little extra time to create a memorable title or a descriptive slogan for your proposal.

7.8 CONCILIATOR
Resolving Issues That Cause Tension

You're not likely to win any special recognition if your workplace isn't a good place to work. Tension and stress among your workers lead to skirmishes, backstabbing, absenteeism, production loss, and even sabotage. That hardly makes you eligible for Manager of the Year.

Since your success depends on the continuous good work of your subordinates, you have to take steps to prevent interruptions. When you find your workers are at each other's throats, look for underlying causes.

Examine first the emotional climate and how it can be improved, then ways to release tension and resolve issues. After that, you can get back to coaching, motivating, and rewarding. Good results from your team mean plaudits for you.

Strategy

Concentrate on improving your policies. Examine them for perceived unfairness, clogged communications, issues never resolved, opinions never sought, and appreciation never expressed.

Steps

1. Establish a policy of fairness. Stop rewarding nonperformers for *not* doing what they were assigned to do. When poor workers and goof-offs get all your time, you tend to ignore your good workers. They feel hurt, resentful, and revengeful. Cease and desist from psychoanalyzing poor performers and deal with the poor performance.

2. Give good feedback. Provide frequent, specific, constructive comments focused on bringing performance up to your expectations. Be extremely clear about consequences. Instead of imputing motives, coach by giving examples, or role playing scenarios, to show better ways to have handled difficult situations. Present simulated conditions and ask workers to identify potential alternatives. When appropriate, suggest additional training.

3. Institute a form of employee participation. Put into place a system that lets ideas float up from the bottom to the top. You're not surrendering power, you're just improving the climate by acknowledging employee intelligence and extracting their valuable insight. The mechanism can range from simple, regularly scheduled, informal get-togethers, such as rotating small groups for monthly breakfasts, to more complex study groups or quality circles. To encourage input, assist those who have difficulty articulating a point of view. Allow impersonal criticism but insist on respect for everybody, giving all ideas a fair hearing.

4. Establish a reward system tied to performance. An accomplishment provides positive reinforcement for your workers, but this needs to be followed by praise and/or reward or else your workers may cease trying. Think this through carefully before you start so that you don't find yourself rewarding quantity at the price of quality. Your measure of success should match your desired outcome.

5. Create a little fun and excitement. Release tension with friendly competitive teams. Show workers you rely on them by rewarding innovations. Use contests and prizes to generate imaginative solutions and lessen stress. Lighten the atmosphere with humor, anecdotes, an easy smile and laughter, as well as organized leisure activities such as bowling leagues.

Script

Pat, you seem (worried) (angry) (upset). What specifically is troubling you? (letting employee express feelings before dealing with the problem) . . . *I know you're smart enough to understand the consequences we've discussed. So what do you think you can do to make sure you arrive on time every morning?* (You've been spending too much time with Pat, making excuses for poor performance.)

(Pleasant remark before criticism) *I'm sure you gave the problem consideration before you acted. However, let's examine . . .*

(Helping the inarticulate) *Cindy, I'm not quite sure what you mean by that. Are you saying that we could reduce costs by . . . ?*

(Resolving touchy subjects) *Okay, obviously we can't have people adjusting the thermostat every few minutes. Instead of reviewing behavior, let's admit that some individuals are more comfortable . . . What suggestions might we consider?*

Thank you, Tim, that was good work. In appreciation of your improvement, you have earned this week's award for . . .

Summary

Once you can reduce the bickering and give everyone a sense of belonging, you'll see an increase in pride, morale, and the quality of the work. Respect the ability of your workers to meet challenges and come up with answers you never would have thought of by yourself. Your employees need the satisfaction they receive from expressing their ideas. Don't deny them this opportunity.

In addition to the internal-support network you've constructed among your superiors, peers, and subordinates, start using other power you may not realize you have.

8

MANIFESTING YOUR SOURCES OF POWER

Okay, you're not the CEO, but you still have more power than you think. And it's up to you to tap the potential that's out there. You'll be perceived as having clout to get things done and ability to influence outcomes. Influence gives you power and power gives you recognition. Some power is given you with your title. Some you take because others think you have it.

Power is derived mainly from four sources. *Position power* comes with the job or is delegated. *Knowledge power* comes from information or expertise others need and from observations that let you plan strategically. *Persuasion power* is the ability to influence decisions or motivate others to act in a given way. *Mobilization power* is both a network of people you relate closely to inside and outside your company and contacts you make among the potentially helpful.

If you use power correctly and have realistic expectations, you can achieve goals for yourself, for others, and for the company. The best part about expanding this base of support is that you don't have to be handed power. It's there for the taking.

8.1 AUTHORITY _____
Overcoming a Wimpy Image

First, make wiser use of the power you already have. Your official position automatically anoints you with command over subordinates. You control resources allotted your unit, you reward (with pay raises, days off, better assignments), and you punish (demote, transfer, send to Siberia). You can't be afraid to enforce your rules to achieve company goals.

Stop figuring out for your workers what they should figure out for themselves. You can give up this kind of control and still uphold your standards if you give your people what they need. Their performance will make you look good, increasing the perception of your power.

Sure you want to be well liked, but leadership is no popularity contest. To get recognized, you need respect from above as well as from below. No namby pamby checking with your boss on decisions that are yours to make.

Most bosses are happy if you relieve them of a responsibility they're not interested in maintaining. Expand your unofficial authority and you increase your power.

Strategy

Act as if you have power. Without being a tyrant or a timid soul, show that you know the proper use of authority. Display your confidence, concern, and desire to do good.

Steps

1. Accept nothing less than your standard. Stop worrying about appearing pushy and start correcting subordinates tactfully. Critiquing can be motivating as you influence decisions that support company goals. Delegate responsibility to those you trust because sharing power increases your power base and frees you for more important matters. If you hoard power, the work suffers and you risk being sabotaged.

2. Take control of your own little corner. Don't erode your power by constantly suggesting to your boss ways you might carry out your assignments. If the boss reacts with thumbs down, you weaken your position, already weakened by asking permission. Show self-confidence by accepting the power given you. Speak with assurance. If you're doing something wrong, you'll hear soon enough. But most likely, unless you confer, the boss doesn't care how you get the job done.

3. Gain authority by default. Be alert to fill in when your boss repeatedly fails to do something important. You gain power by default because you've just enlarged the area of responsibility for your current job. And the boss is probably glad to be relieved of the headache. Taking over duties the boss doesn't like to do is seizing power, but this is one theft that's usually rewarded.

4. Accept responsibility for boners. So you made a mistake or somebody under you did. Don't be a wimp and don't limp away evasively. Own up to it quickly and apologize. A real apology, not the passive voice "Mistakes were made." That cop-out fools no one, and you rob yourself of the respect and recognition you seek. Stop excuses and correct mistakes made under your watch. That responsibility comes with the territory.

Script

Paul, these contracts aren't prepared correctly. You need to change this section to conform to the new policy we've discussed. Please redo the contracts and get them back to me by early afternoon. (No big deal, but impersonal and firm, with a friendly tone.)

Boss, just a quick update. I contacted three agencies, picked the best deal, and they've already started planning the . . . (Carry out assignments, knowing the boss thinks you're competent. If you ask approval before proceeding, you lose respect.)

Boss, I've reduced this information to one page, so that you can send it to . . . (Increase power and insert your emphasis by taking on an important task the boss keeps putting off.)

(Stop blaming some abstraction for your error.) *My unit was caught in the reorganization confusion which caused the delay.* (Accept your responsibility.) *I apologize for the delay. I've taken steps to assure that the material will arrive . . .*

Summary

Position power requires a telescopic view. See the whole broad picture without getting bogged down in details. Take a more confident stance by carrying out your assignments without asking permission at each step. Extend your power by seizing responsibility your boss obviously doesn't want. Expand your power base by delegating authority to those you trust.

8.2 REPRESENTATION
Using Delegated Authority

When your boss asks you to represent your company, division, or department, your official authority is extended by delegated authority. Your power has expanded, and there's a general perception that your influence has increased. But why wait to be asked? There are plenty of situations for which you can volunteer and receive delegated authority.

Offer to speak for your company to influence outside opinions of groups or agencies. For example, translate government regulations into business terms your audience can comprehend and appreciate. If your boss is reluctant to accept a request to speak to a civic organization, volunteer to go. If your company has a speakers' bureau, sign up.

You can "speak for" your company by writing a trade/professional journal article about a successful company method or project. You can head outside projects that will publicize you and your company along with the event. With permission, you can involve your company in co-sponsoring activities that can win new clients and create good will.

Strategy

Identify opportunities and volunteer to represent your unit within the company, or your company to the outside world.

Steps

1. Volunteer to attend meetings your boss can't attend. A zoning meeting at City Hall, your trade association get-together, the Chamber of Commerce luncheon. Let it be known you're willing to attend night meetings or you're glad to sit in and report back on board meetings of civic organizations, and the boss might suggest you become a permanent replacement.

2. Volunteer as a representative in communitywide drives. Your local school board, for instance, is recruiting business executives to teach one hour a week. Offer to be the recruit coordinator for the company as well as a teacher. You establish rapport not only with professionals in related fields but also meet a lot of people within your own organization.

3. Volunteer as a rainmaker. Look for opportunities and serve enthusiastically as a speaker, panelist, or coordinator for events that can win new clients for the company. You can suggest the company sponsor or participate in seminars, conferences, workshops, public hearings, or sporting events.

4. Enhance your performance as a representative. Position yourself in high-traffic areas near the entrance, buffet, or sign-up tables to make contact with the maximum number of people. Wear something (a pin, tie, cap, name badge with a slogan) that arouses curiosity and attention. It's an ice breaker to lead into talk about your company. Follow up on contacts you make with brief notes or calls or by forwarding reprints of your talks.

Script

Boss, I know you're tied up with the Alson matter. I'd be glad to attend the zoning meeting tonight on the fifth street property . . . (Keep alert to extend your delegated authority.)

We have a great opportunity to help the community and ourselves by joining this effort. As the company coordinator, I'd like to know the best days for you to come . . . (expanding your authority and power).

There appears to be a lot of confusion about how we'll be affected by the new tax regulations. I'd like to put together a panel of experts . . . (You don't have to be an expert, just know where to find them. By talking for the company, you enlarge the perception of your power.)

Summary

Don't just sit there, waiting to be selected to represent your company, department, or unit. There is additional power in delegated authority. Demonstrate your ability to keep your head when handed the unexpected, to speak well before groups, and to mingle easily. Then volunteer to report on meetings or to speak or coordinate activities for the company.

8.3 KNOWLEDGE
Utilizing Your Expertise

You may be the only one in your office who can interpret certain data or program the computer or know how to reach key people the boss wants to meet for a business venture. Whatever your special knowledge or skill, look to fill a void in a significant area unfamiliar to most. You'll become the company's resident expert. You'll be asked your opinion; your remarks will be quoted. Having accurate information at your fingertips or acquiring a unique skill can reduce your dependency on the boss and increase your appearance of power.

If you have no such expertise, prepare yourself to be more adaptable. Reexamine your capabilities to suggest a new direction. Grow to be more valuable by increasing your knowledge of issues, technology, or skills. By becoming an expert in an important area, you also create a safety net for troubled times. Your job security doesn't depend as much on changes within your company as on your having transferable knowledge or know-how. So stop thinking of yourself as committed to one job for the rest of your life. Times change. As you become more valuable to your company, at the same time you become more valuable to the competition.

Strategy

Investigate new avenues to acquire knowledge. Then find better ways to present your expertise.

Steps

1. Pinpoint trends. After a full day's work, most people want to relax. A few will pursue new studies. If you do, you can extend your power base. Take notes when attending lectures, conferences, and work courses. Read books and trade publications to stay on top of trends. Most associations publish career brochures or monthly newsletters or magazines that also zero in on trends. The information you write up as forecast highlights can become invaluable.

2. Preserve your assets. It's important to share, but don't give away your knowledge to others who'll take credit for it. First, date and sign all the material you prepare. Second, be concise. If you fill in every fact, figure, and possible explanation, no one has to come to you for help or more information, or invite you to their meetings. Focus on your conclusions, give basic reasons, but make them come to you for more details.

3. Quantify your information. Report your recommendations after analyzing the evaluations you collected as head of a project or program. Almost every activity can be measured to see if the desired results were achieved. Decide before you start how you can state objectives numerically. Your message carries more weight when you show evidence that the mission was accomplished.

4. Meet regularly with your counterparts. Keep alert to what's going on. If a problem will affect you, you'll be forewarned by the information you pick up. Listen carefully when others talk.

Script

This trend hasn't been highly publicized, but considering all the factors, I think we should move quickly and beat the competition (finding trends others miss).

If you'd like more information, please call me. I have a lot more material on this. (Give people only as much information as they need.)

The effectiveness was rated on a scale of one to five, and we found by measuring before and after that . . . (Point to your accomplishments by quantifying as well as qualifying.)

Summary

Identify an important area where you need additional training. Seek to acquire specialized knowledge or skills. In the event that you want to, or have to, change positions, familiarize yourself with a new interest while still working at the old job. If your company doesn't spend much on retraining, watch for seminars, workshops, or courses you can attend. When you have knowledge you can be enthusiastic, and enthusiasm is persuasive.

8.4 RESEARCH
Presenting Data That Affect Decisions

The ability to collect and process information into an immediately usable form distinguishes you and increases your power. Besides reporting trends, you select emphasis and help plan more realistic goals.

With some initiative, you can obtain much information by studying company records and budgets. Annual and quarterly reports go beyond the money picture and tell who's being hailed, what or who is being blamed for pressing problems, and what's planned down the road. Your financial officer can answer questions about your department. And personnel usually knows what's about to occur and where there'll be transfers, layoffs, hirings, or bonuses.

Next correlate what's happening in your company to what's going on outside. Study business publications and dissect reports by leaders in your field. Monitor the effects of political and economic news upon your industry, ready to sound the alarm to prevent problems. Now report what you've learned, compressing your data into a comprehensive but concise format.

Strategy

Collect and present pertinent data. Insert yourself into the planning process by offering data in a practical form management can use in its decision making.

Steps

1. Follow the money trail. Knowing where the company is allocating its money clues you into future priorities. You can make valid suggestions about what your department should be stressing. Check where marketing dollars will be going, and you'll spot projects to be getting the most attention or departments to be increasing staff. These are places where you may want to team up. Compare current and past budgets, noting items obviously important because they remain despite other budget cuts. This tells you what to emphasize. Your financial officer can explain the fine print and answer questions. Also note who's making decisions and setting goals and the amount of latitude given the various departments.

2. Interpret results for the boss. Reading studies, evaluations, and analyses, the expected impact may seem obvious to you. It probably is not that obvious to someone else who hasn't devoted the time you have to studying. Relate your conclusions to issues of greatest importance to the company. Use terminology you picked up from reading company reports and phrases top brass use to describe their priorities. Look for information that will save the boss's time and remove some load off the boss's back.

3. Talk trends within your industry. Read the business sections of newspapers, business magazines, trade or professional journals. Tune into radio and television economic shows. Monitor patterns and track data, alert for anything unusual. Be able to discuss developments, laws, and regulations. Memorize a few vital statistics to toss into conversations.

4. Prepare data in a usable form. Start by stating your recommendation and the reason. If this is a written piece, don't clog the top page with details. Instead, attach concise background facts and figures. A particularly useful format is the fact sheet or a series of fact sheets or a checklist.

Script

Boss, since our annual report stresses the need for innovative techniques to cope with the shortage, this seems the right time to try out a successful approach reported by . . . (Link potential solutions you come across to company priorities you've read about.)

The impact that the new, faster, and cheaper computers are having on the ability to handle increasingly complex tasks—we're up to 4 million transistors on a typical memory chip—points to a potential solution for us in . . . (Keep statistics to a few more dramatic ones.)

Since we can't match salaries, the only way our nonprofit group can compete with private companies for high-caliber people is by changing our benefit and retirement package. According to a recent article in the Times . . . (Report emerging patterns.)

Summary

Expand your power by playing a growing role in goal setting, decision making, and planning. Read and digest all you can about business news. Study the effects of politics and economics on your company and industry. In clear, concise language, put together factual and analytical data.

8.5 OBSERVATION
Seeing What Goes on Beyond Your Desk

Pick up your head and look around you. What's happening out there? You need to know because what you observe is another source of knowledge power.

What assignments seem to get the most attention? What unit is getting new equipment or office space? Who's getting additional staff support?

Where are the little cliques and alliances in your office that have the potential to influence others? Who's always talking to whom at the water cooler? What people go to lunch together all the time? Who vote in blocks at the meetings?

Watch also for a lack of leadership. You don't need to be appointed a leader to become one. Form your own persuasive group. Identify people who can help you reach other people. Pick out those who appreciate your guidance. See what's in front of you, but also use your peripheral vision to broaden your power base.

Strategy

Link up with people who get results. You've located the action with careful observation. Now figure out a way to utilize the information you've observed.

Steps

1. Work with projects and people who are highly visible. Make the effort to become friends. Propose a joint activity that would be mutually beneficial. If that goes well, you gain more recognition.

2. Identify influential cliques and alliances. Some cliques ban together to support members who'd be weak by themselves. Let them be, for their influence is limited to their group. Other informal alliances are formed expressly to influence goal and policy decisions and to get more control over resources. They can be powerfully good or powerfully destructive. If you can guide the clique leader into doing what's best for the company, showing the mutual advantage to the clique, you'll gain recognition from above.

3. Be alert for a need to form your own coalition. As soon as you observe a leadership vacuum, step to the front of the line and appoint yourself. Arrange frequent, informal get-togethers with your counterparts in other units or departments. Listen carefully for tidbits of news you can later piece together. Be acutely aware of unspoken signals people send one another. Take every opportunity to pursue common objectives. Talk to members at meetings, coffee breaks, waiting for the elevator. During a controversy, automatically and calmly guide your group. They'll turn to you for guidance in a crisis, and this confidence in you will be noticed. More recognition by higher ups is an extension of your power.

Script

(Try a joint activity to tap into the popularity of a counterpart.) *We came out with some really good ideas staging a contest for our department. Could I interest you in a bit of friendly competition between our departments?*

(Interpret an unpopular company decision to a clique leader to win support of the group.) *Yes, Ken, I realize the new schedule imposes a little hardship on some of your friends, but let me list the benefits we all get from the additional revenue.*

(When you observe a leadership vacuum, jump in and fill it.) *I've asked all of you to come here this morning because we have a serious situation that's developing. We ought to put our heads together and decide . . .*

Summary

What you observe around the office can become an important source of knowledge power. Learn all the players and which ones carry weight. Identify clique leaders to move them closer to company goals. Pick out influential people and put together a group that will look to you for leadership.

8.6 INDUCEMENT

Focusing on the Vital and Doable

Think beyond tit-for-tat: If I do them a favor, they'll feel obliged to do one for me. Persuasive power that allows you to influence behavior is legitimate when the potential is there for everyone to benefit. Rather than manipulating others with what they want to hear, *tell them most sincerely how to get what they want.* Focus on that one point. Believability is a vital factor. They must be convinced that what you're suggesting can be attained or accomplished.

The ability to motivate and persuade superiors, peers, and subordinates becomes significant personal power. The key is to tie what you want to the wants of others. Refer to their personal experiences so that you mix what is familiar to them with the unfamiliar you're about to suggest.

Begin by listening to their concerns. Manifest a genuine interest as you encourage others to think along with you. If you can get them to express their thoughts, they'll probably continue going along with you. When their answers go off the track, suggest a slightly different version. Guide and glide rather than force your conclusions.

Strategy

Help others get what they want by doing what you want.

Steps

1. See the situation through another's eyes. Watch for clues that tell you the yearnings. Adjust your plan to fit individual desires (to be noticed, feel appreciated, have a sense of belonging, get more money, time, knowledge, challenge, or culture, to name a few). What people want depends on what they already have. But generally, you can appeal to self-image. Acknowledge their importance and let them shine with you. Be instrumental in awarding pins, scrolls, framed certificates, and coupons redeemable for time off or applied toward an employee trophy.

2. Use involvement techniques. Wait until people get past an emotional state (high, low, excited, angry) and can concentrate before you offer your idea. Be honest in presenting negative as well as positive aspects. Defer to them, asking how they feel about a situation. Challenge them. Explain why you need someone's special ability and why he or she would want to comply. Show your own enthusiastic, confident, positive expectations. Your knowledge gives you the courage to try. They believe because you believe. To lure, act sure.

3. Go for fast results. To hasten acceptance, concentrate on uncomplicated areas that can be completed with quick victories. Look for actions that yield dramatic results. Before you start, spell out specific, measurable objectives so that you have something to point to when you succeed.

Script

You've mentioned a few times that you always feel pressed for time on Tuesdays. I could incorporate your part of the orientation with mine to free up an hour for you . . . And frankly, I need more practice with informal talks. (He wants more time, you want more exposure, a good bargain.) *Do you think that would work out?* (deferring) *Is there anything about that idea that doesn't hit you right?* (No tricks, everything's above board.)

(Allow others to feel important.) *I wonder if you could help me with a little problem I have.*

(Pull out their thinking.) *Perhaps there's some point you'd like me to explain in more detail. Was any part unclear?*

(Offer an alternative when the suggestion gets away from your purpose.) *Your basic idea is sound. However, we could probably get more action if we were to* . . . (Do it my way.)

Summary

Persuasive power is more than piling up chits and calling in your IOUs. It is comprehending what others really want (as distinguished from what they need) and helping them get it. This applies to all levels—boss, peers, and subordinates—and substantially expands your power base.

8.7 NETWORK
Cultivating Closer Relationships

Your personal network is a group of people, inside and outside your organization, who are all tuned into the same channel. The support you give one another can be a tremendous source of power.

It's hoped that you have a mentor among top management to guide you—someone who likes you and derives pleasure out of advising. They aren't too hard to acquire because most people enjoy having their opinions sought after. In addition to mentors, cultivate good working relationships among upper level, colleagues, and subordinates you perceive to be influential. Not only do you have the chance to improve techniques and exchange assistance, but also you'll find such kinships a source of invaluable information. Ask questions and listen carefully.

Establish rapport with professionals in related fields. To learn more about what's happening right now in your area, join associations and attend the monthly meetings. In between, meet for lunch, play tennis, or talk on the phone with those you feel especially simpatico.

Strategy

Increase the number of people in your personal network. Look both inside and outside your company to expand this power base.

Steps

1. Volunteer for assignments. Watch for ones that will put you in close touch with people at all levels of your company. Attend periodic meetings, discuss progress, be in on the planning. Look for projects or task forces that focus on ways to improve your product or service. If you help customers, the ones your company depends on most, you'll earn new respect.

2. Establish a closer bond with supporters. If your job depends on approval from some other unit, agency, or funding source, don't assume required reporting is sufficient or you may find the rug pulled out from under you. You can't take for granted that others are educated in your subject. Go beyond reports and establish rapport. Visit, or at least call. Be sure to talk to these decision makers periodically. By exchanging information, you learn what they are *currently* looking for.

3. Become active in your professional/business group. Local chapters of national associations usually meet monthly. Most people assume that if you do good work here, you must also be effective in your job. This can lead to your getting important recommendations. Also, if your company specializes, and you've made friends with a representative of another specializing company, you may be able to impress your boss by cross-selling.

4. Join community groups. Stop hiding behind your desk and go out and meet executives from your company and other companies, civic leaders, and media people. Civic, social, and neighborhood groups provide excellent opportunities for networking. Volunteer for an important committee or to serve on the board. Be a friend to people who may be able to exert influence where it will count.

Script

Joan, are you free to meet with me on Tuesday at about one? There's something I'd like to discuss with you. (If you're going to meet, limit phone conversations to making the appointment. Aim to keep supporters updated while learning what might be around the corner for you.)

(Don't be shy about approaching the president, who's always looking for good assistance.) *If there's an opening, I'd like to volunteer to chair the program committee next year.* (Choose activities that can help you establish closer ties with influential members.)

Summary

Networking power has two prongs. By expanding your close relationships, you can become more effective in your current job. However, networking is also important in protecting your future. At some point you may want to, or have to, leave your job. You'll want a little help from your friends.

8.8 CONTACTS
Reaching Potentially Helpful People

Besides increasing the number of close relationships you have, you can expand your power source by continually making new contacts with people who have what it takes to help you in some way. Maybe they supply information, give you new insights, or help you gain more recognition.

Contacts are also useful leads to openings when you want to change jobs within and outside your company. Even if you're not actively looking for a new position, it's important for you to keep current on what's out there. If for no other reason, you will act with more confidence when you know other options exist for you. Most jobs aren't filled by advertisements, but by recommendations from company employees. Let your contacts know to keep you in mind so that you can keep your options open.

Contacts grow easily. People introduce you, or you introduce yourself. You go where you can position yourself to make more contacts, and you follow up on the ones you make.

Strategy

Devise a system for expanding your contacts. Plan how you will identify and meet new people in your area of interest, especially ones who can open a door for you to display your talent.

Steps

1. Set goals to make yourself keep trying. Decide on X number of attempts per month; or spending X number of minutes a week on calls. A half hour on Wednesdays is a doable, measurable plan. If you have permission to discuss your project with the media, promise yourself to talk to X number of potential media contacts.

2. Approach people whose support will expand your power base. Move from table to table or row to row introducing yourself and chatting at company functions. Approach people you don't know at meetings, conferences, and workshops. Meet the leaders and follow up with a note. Exchange business cards. Call cold for appointments, using a direct, uncomplicated, friendly approach. You don't need a third party to introduce you. Just call, identify yourself, and in one sentence tell why you'd like to talk.

3. Develop a routine for keeping in touch. Many people refer to an index card contact file, like this:

ANDERSON, ANNE	Phone: _____
Company: _____	Address: _____

6/6   I called. She's out of town for 2 weeks.

8/7   Sent congratulatory note, for Outstanding Employer Award.

9/24 Lunch. Discussed opening in her office.

Start by listing everyone you know who can lead you to other people. Your personal phone listings and Christmas card lists are a good place to begin. Then decide how much time, and at what time, you'll devote regularly for making appointments for lunches or meetings. Set aside a similar time block to make catch-up calls or jot brief notes.

4. Find places to display your knowledge. Market yourself creatively with interesting personal business cards. Talk to the program chairpersons of associations in your field and of other groups seeking guest speakers. After your talk, take the time to converse person to person to make new contacts and exchange cards. Offer to serve as a moderator for panels you put together. Contact editors of business sections and trade magazines. Gradually build credibility as a resource person.

Script

Ms. Mason, I enjoyed the talk you gave at the meeting yesterday. I've been thinking about what you said, and I have an idea or two I'd like to talk to you about. (When you introduce yourself, people are often more accessible than you realize.)

(Hand your card as you introduce yourself.) *My specialty is designing systems for reducing paperwork. If you think the members would enjoy a helpful as well as entertaining program on this topic, I'd be happy for you to call me.* (Be very friendly, but remember, you're also doing them a favor.)

Summary

The most important point about enlarging your contacts is to develop a plan and stick to it. How fast or how slowly you move is up to you, but discipline yourself to follow through with a regularly scheduled time slot. It's not enough to go to functions or meetings. You build on the introduction made by finding a way to follow up.

PART III

ATTENTION

BEING PERCEIVED AS A RISING STAR

To stop feeling you're at the mercy of a pink-slip-doler boss, manage your career as though you held an elective position. If you were elected, you'd continue campaigning from day one in office, always running a little scared, constantly alert to pick up signals others send you.

You'd concentrate on creating more attention during your conversations, group discussions, and presentations. You'd make a deeper impression with your writing and phone calls. You'd improve the way you channel information and insert yourself into the office information loop. And you'd redirect work habits and personality traits responsible for any unfavorable labels you're stuck with.

Such self-improvement efforts not only put you in line for a meteoric rise, but also are insurance premiums against future company shake-ups. Most people want to work with those they sense are on the way up. They'll support you if they believe you deserve it. Yours will be the first name to pop up when someone's needed to shepherd a project through to completion or round up others to get something done.

Rising stars appear more committed to fulfilling a mission than their colleagues are. Nothing is too much trouble. Their work, impressively performed with ease and confidence, shows a sweeping grasp of what has to be accomplished. Bosses, peers, and subordinates all sing their praises.

9

CREATING INTEREST
AND EXCITEMENT WHEN
YOU SPEAK

People you work with just don't hear what you say. Your suggestions fall flat or are unconvincing while you want to be perceived as dynamic and important to listen to. You wish you could evoke more than a one-grunt response and that rude colleagues would stop talking to each other while you have the floor.

In short, you want to be noticed. Getting favorable attention requires combining several skills. The aim is to focus the concentration of others on what you're saying or doing. Begin by realizing people don't deal well with more than one idea at a time. And we don't even try to pay attention unless the effort in some way serves our own interest.

Getting attention is a one-shot attempt. *Sustaining* interest presents another challenge: Set the stage for others to keep discovering something new about your ideas or activities. The key is to link your innovation to something already familiar. You may, for instance, suggest that the same objective could be reached more easily by trying a new method. Sculpt the new into an old familiar shape.

9.1 TUNED IN
Listening While People Talk

Most of us retain only a small segment of what's said to us because we've never been taught how to listen. We usually think listening is trying to figure out what other people mean, or trying to convince them to accept suggestions, opinions, or information we present. But effective listening is much more involved.

Hearing is only the first part. Then we interpret the words correctly or incorrectly. A sifting or screening process takes place because of our preconceptions. Or lack of concentration. Or emotional blocks, for instance, when the speaker espouses a view we're totally opposed to, or puts us to sleep with boring repetition. After we interpret the information, we determine how to use it or react to it.

Listening skills, which can be learned or improved, are the first steps in influencing others. Your company has to listen before it can respond to what your customers are saying. You have to be a better listener to get others to pay attention to what you say.

Strategy

Listen harder to get the most out of what you hear. Listen unemotionally, and clarify any points you're not sure you understand.

Steps

1. Listen with emotions on the backburner. Put your anger, accusations, and disapproval on hold to open your mind to what's being said. Don't allow yourself to be distracted by someone else's emotions, gestures, or delivery. Pick up the significance of the words. Listen to determine what others want to know.

2. Listen to the whole message without interrupting. Show you're paying attention with a nod or an "I see." Before counterpunching or responding to a specific point, hear the entire case. Be alert for hidden meanings. Keep eye contact to show interest and to observe if message and facial expressions match. Listen for key words or central ideas rather than trying to remember a lot of facts.

3. Draw out the other person. Ask the basic who, what, when, where, why, and how questions. Really concentrate on answers to get a better understanding of what other people are thinking and feeling. You don't have to agree, just get a handle. Show you comprehend why each of you reached different conclusions and that what they're saying is important to you.

4. Paraphrase what you think you heard. Recapping the remarks serves a dual purpose. You make sure you understood correctly, and you also get others to reexamine what they said.

Script

(Draw out with questions.) *I'm not sure I understand. How would your suggestion improve the morale of our workers?*

(Show understanding of another's view.) *I can see how you might come to that conclusion, however, did you consider that . . . ?*

(Clarify by rephrasing.) *I think I heard you say . . . Would I be correct in stating your position as . . .*

Let me see if I have this straight. You're saying that . . .

Summary

Sharpen your listening skills with more pointed concentration. As you are better able to read what people are saying to you, directly and indirectly, you know what their interests and opinions are. Listening lets you help people achieve their goals, and that's a sure way to be regarded as a rising star.

9.2 LURES
Getting Others to Listen to You

Some things you say pull people in, like a magnet, while other comments repel your listeners, and they tune you out. Basically, they have to hear, or at least sense, some connection between themselves and what you're saying—either something they want to know, or need to know, or the benefits or detriments that will affect them. A smile also acts like a magnet because it's a way of reaching out and linking up.

If you are painstakingly thorough and conscientious, you may feel the need to give some background before making this connection. But if you're determined to make them sit through the why before you give them the what, they've already stopped listening to whatever you want to communicate. Also skip the apologetic preamble. No one cares.

If you're being falsely modest ("Please excuse my ignorance on this subject, but . . ."), that's a real turn off. Above all, be yourself when you're talking. Instead of trying to imitate others, extract from your own experiences and knowledge. This is what makes you unique and interesting.

Strategy

Concentrate on making a connection between yourself and your listeners. In addition to tailoring pertinent information to fit them, present it in a clear, crisp, tactful way.

Steps

1. Practice summarizing your concepts. Use your daily newspaper as a drill book. Read a short article, summarize the basic idea in one paragraph, then keep editing until you get it down to ten seconds. Notice on radio and TV newscasts how many sound bites are 10 or 15 seconds or less. Being clear, concise, and specific (saying "367 times" instead of "a lot of times") strengthens your credibility and clarifies your meaning. Without going into minute detail, have documentation ready to back up what you say. Avoid cliches, unless you come up with a really good play on words.

2. Get to your point and stick to it. When you start with a long buildup, you're manipulating people to react the way you want. But instead of hearing your meaning, they get impatient or defensive and often jump to the wrong conclusions. Start instead with a confident, strong attention-getter and explain your point without rambling. Keep focused on your main point and resist deviating with unrelated ideas. Articulate a clear vision of where your company, department, or unit should be going and why. Show how you help meet a need. Give the standard by which your idea can be measured and be ready for anticipated criticism.

3. Make sure listeners comprehend your meaning. Restate the same idea in a few different ways. Try the tactic of groping for the right words. This prompts listeners to fill in the blank, letting you know if they understand. If you're not sure they heard you correctly, stop and ask.

4. Encourage listeners to express disagreement. Sometimes people feel intimidated and keep their thoughts and feelings hidden. Let them know you enjoy a debate. Also, watch your timing. Wait until the listener levels off from a high or low emotional plane before feeding information, or nothing you say will sink in.

Script

(Get to the point to avoid uneasiness or wordiness.) *Although the company policy restricts the amount of resources we can allot your project, we will make an exception in your case.* (Restate to show immediately your interest in the listener.) *We know you need more help to meet the deadline. We're prepared to give it to you.*

(Check to see if you were understood.) *In your own words, what do you think I've just said? How would you sum up my position?*

(Encourage free flow of ideas.) *From your expression, I sense you're not in agreement. What points are giving you trouble?*

Summary

Give your proposal a short name listeners can remember, something new and unexplained to intrigue them. Encourage listening workshops in your office. You can do this without a professional trainer. There's abundant material available in books, articles, films, and video tapes, and your group can role play actual situations as an exercise. Above all, get right to the point and stay there. When you become more magnetic, attention is riveted on you.

9.3 SHOWMANSHIP

Humanizing and Dramatizing Your Talks

Help put a little fun back into working. You can take your job seriously without taking yourself so seriously. You aren't breaking any company rules if you uplift spirits around the office.

Showmanship is a style that lets you involve everyone around you, at every level, by getting them caught up in your excitement. It's smiling easily and frequently to help create a pleasant atmosphere. It's letting unimportant negative remarks bounce off you with a simple "You may be right." Or poking a little fun at unquestioned and outdated routines. Or exaggerating to make a point. Or arranging humorous right- and wrong-way demonstrations. In fact, many other programming techniques can be utilized to pep up a performance.

Showmanship is appealing to people because you're talking about people and not speaking in generalized abstractions. Even an inanimate piece of equipment takes on life when you zero in on the time it saves workers or the pride workers take in an improved service.

Strategy

Lighten up. Create interest and improve attention and retention by talking about people. Speak about those who are affected by the subject under discussion, and why that should interest this audience. Find ways to demonstrate the points you make. Stop worrying about advertising yourself and start talking as though you're speaking to friends.

Steps

1. Involve your audience in your talk. Tell them right away why they'll want to hear what you have to say. Stop your talk to ask the audience a question. Act as though you're having a conversation with them. Keep any request you make of the audience simple, but make it sound important.

2. Personalize your remarks. Talk about not just the concept, but the people affected by the concept. Try to tell your listeners a story, an anecdote, make a taped interview part of your report, anything to avoid boring them with the impersonal. Keep current. When you hear or read an interesting story on radio, TV, or in a magazine, jot down a note to help you remember it and put it in your talk file. People remember more about one person having difficulty than about a general discussion of the problem.

3. Dramatize your talk. Add colorful language to help listeners visualize the situation you describe. Give examples and analogies, and choose strong, positive, active words. Plain English without any jargon has an essential believable ring. Visual aids add interest and clarity, but use them in small doses not to drown out you or your message. Try flow charts and stick drawings on the blackboard, mounting exhibits on easels around the room, use photo blow-ups, display before and after pictures, cartoons, and posters on the walls, or play audio and visual tapes, films, and slides.

Script

(Talk to a group as though it's a one to one conversation.) *How often have you been disturbed by that situation? Well, I have a suggestion that will help you . . .*

(Rather than saying *Analysis shows this plan would decrease absenteeism by 21 percent,* personalize.) *Twenty-one percent of our workers who are staying home because of this difficult problem would now be able to report.*

(Substitute more active or descriptive verbs.) *The competition is floundering in that area* (rather than *The competition is in a confused state when it comes to that area.*)

Summary

Showmanship uses your creativity to see and describe situations in a new light. Pointing up the humor in everyday activities won't detract from the quality of performances. On the contrary, it makes you feel energized. Permit yourself and others to enjoy your work by humanizing what you say and talking to people as though they are your friends. Giving them this kind of attention attracts attention.

9.4 CONVERSATIONS AND DISCUSSIONS
Counteracting Indifference

Whether you're in a one-on-one conversation, a group discussion, or a meeting debate, you have to get and keep attention if you're going to be considered a rising star. We know that people are insulated by their own self-importance, and for you to penetrate that wall, they have to hear you say what's in it for them. Or at least understand that what you're about to say is important to them.

At times, the most meaningful part of the conversation or discussion will be the questions you ask. People are impressed when you put forth questions that pinpoint problems, help dig out the real issues, and sort out solutions. Questions are an important means of controlling or directing a discussion as well as drawing out your listeners.

Strategy

Sharpen your conversations and discussions with better timing. For maximum effect, watch the order in which you present ideas, when you come in and stay out of discussions, and when to keep still and utilize silence.

Steps

1. Focus your remarks. People can deal with only one issue at a time. First get their attention by telling them the answer, then why you think that's the way to go and how it could be accomplished. Keep your comments short, limiting your information to what they want to know. Say less and let them question you. Respond with strong, simple language and an unambiguous message. Don't beat around the bush or weaken your remarks with "I think" or "I believe." Sound confident and stop begging for approval.

2. Enjoy the competition of ideas. Pick your topics, deciding when to clam up and when to jump in. By not commenting on everything, you get more attention when you do speak. Jot notes to yourself while others are talking to bolster your confidence and respond effectively. Ask questions that clear up confusion for everybody. Then come in toward the end of the discussion with your arguments, keeping your disagreement pleasant and professional. You can be spirited and not sound opinionated. Start with a point of agreement, then give the action you suggest or perhaps a summary that can move the group forward.

3. Use silence to your advantage. When talking person to person and there's no immediate reply to your comment or question, keep still. Don't rush in to fill the void. Your worker, for instance, may need a little time to consider or may be avoiding a problem that has to be faced. Your waiting patiently forces an eventual response. If colleagues give you the silent treatment, without sounding accusatory, ask what the problem is and if you can help, and explain how the silence makes you feel. Be ready to accept some straight talk in case you've been doing something that embarrasses them.

4. Keep track of conversations on pending matters. After an unexpected but important talk, jot a note to yourself for the appropriate file with date, person, and summary. This will save you time and misunderstanding later. If warranted, dash off a brief memo, saying you're glad to have had the talk and add a synopsis of the discussion.

Script

(Start with the solution.) *The answer to absenteeism is providing incentive bonuses. We have to motivate our people to work a little harder. We could start this kind of program by . . .*

(If you see listeners squirm.) *What's significant to you is . . .*

(Summarize, then point the way at the end of a discussion.) *It seems what everyone's really looking for is a faster way to move the material. This could best be accomplished by . . .*

Summary

Whether made up of one or one thousand, your audience is essential to your getting attention. Study your audience, and if you still don't know their interests, ask. Talk about what you may have in common. Give examples they, too, have probably experienced. In a group discussion, you come on stronger if you wait to be the rebutter or summarizer.

9.5 PRESENTATIONS

Preparing Verbal Reports and Proposals

Whether you're considering a one-minute suggestion for a problem plaguing the staff, or a ten-minute proposal to the board, or a major address to a conference, start by asking yourself the same questions and thinking through these points before deciding anything you'll say:

1. What's the purpose of the talk or report?. Are you trying to inform, motivate, persuade, or teach? What do you want the audience to do: make a decision, rally in support, take some action?

2. What information does the audience want? How much do they already know? Will they need background up to this point? Why do they want to know this information and how will they use what you tell them?

3. What's the main message you want to present? What's the one key thought or solution you'll be talking about.

Prepare. Unless you do, your talk may be one uninspired, tedious yawn.

Strategy

Mull over your report or proposal before you try putting your thoughts together. As you go about routine tasks, jot notes as thoughts pop into your head. You'll use these in the preparation in order to get and keep attention.

Steps

1. Define your message or conclusion. Review your notes until you can detect the essence of your talk. Everything hinges on that. Write out your one main idea. Now take the supporting ideas you've listed, categorize them into three or four points, and shuffle for logical order.

2. Keep your meeting reports to only one or two minutes. It's better to tell the group what you know they can absorb, later answering whatever questions they have, than to try to tell them more than they want to know in one spurt. The short talk can take as much time to prepare as the long one does. You cram so much information into such a short space that every word must count. Here, especially, remain focused on your main point without going off on any tangents.

3. Gather back up material. List the facts the audience needs or wants to know, such as a comparison of past and anticipated costs, the time and labor involved, and expected results. Use statistics selectively, sticking to a few of the most impressive ones. Strengthen or interpret your remarks with appropriate examples or analogies.

4. Work hardest on your opening and closing. Snag their attention right away or forget about getting it later. And bolster your good presentation with a strong dynamic ending. Avoid jokes (even polished comedians can bomb out) as well as apologies and trite expressions. They're deadly. For a longer talk, alert the audience you're finishing. Restate the message you gave at the beginning. That's what you want the audience to come away with.

5. Hone and buff your words. Review your notes for clarity, sharpness, simplicity, and dynamics: language appropriate to the level of the audience; everyday, conversational tone; and strong, colorful, positive, action-oriented words.

Script

(A dramatic statement can open or close.) *In just two months, we turned a plague into a profit.*

(Or a question.) *How many of you have ever been faced with the dilemma of choosing between . . . ?*

(Or your personal experience.) *A customer called me yesterday to complain about the time it took for his order . . .*

(Let the audience know you're about to close.) *And finally, keep in mind the most important aspect of this proposal.*

(Restate action you want the audience to take.) *So let's begin in earnest to develop this closer relationship between ourselves and our clients.*

Summary

Don't try to knock out a report or proposal in a few minutes if you want to keep the audience concentrating on your words. Think through your idea thoroughly before you start to put it together. Be clear on the key idea you want to get across and what it should accomplish and what the audience wants and needs to know.

9.6 REHEARSALS
Practicing Your Delivery

When you shoot from the lip, you risk getting shot down. After you prepare, practice. Don't wing your talk. Practicing reduces panic and almost eliminates flubs. So start rehearsing your delivery.

Knowing how you want to say what you have prepared will keep you from coming unglued. You can gain speaking experience by participating in discussions at committee meetings or talking before small groups such as civic and social clubs and business or professional groups.

With enough successful experiences, you may still get nervous before a talk, but that's just inner excitement that will make you go over well. Psych yourself by thinking that you're simply going to have a conversation about a subject you know better than your audience does.

Start your practice session by converting your talk into bullet reminder points. It is from these bullets that you'll practice rather than to try to memorize your talk. Word-for-word recall can be very difficult if not disastrous.

Strategy

Simulate the conditions under which you'll give your talk. Picture the room and the people. See the audience you have to capture. Practice with any props you'll use. Listen to a recording of your voice.

Steps

1. Practice the way you imagine it will be. Speak out loud in your full voice. Don't try to mimic anyone. You have information others want to hear, so practice enjoying your talk and letting the real you come through. Let the audience feel your confidence, enthusiasm, and animation. Create the conditions you expect with a pretend mike, lectern, or by standing behind your chair. Stand straight with feet a little apart to avoid swaying. Move naturally because you make the audience uneasy if you're glued to one spot. Walk briskly to your place with a pleasant smile and wait for quiet before you start. Don't try to compete with noise or talking.

2. Practice the way you'll involve the audience. Smiling and constant eye contact spells instant confidence and says you're anxious to communicate. Visualize your audience. Move your head from side to side, stopping for a few seconds at each face. What questions could you toss out? What common experience or goals do you share? What visual aids might increase their interest? If you're going to be drawing on the blackboard or flipping a chart on an easel or playing a recording, practice the motions you'll be using.

3. Review and critique practice sessions. If possible, have a friend video tape your practice performance. Short of professional training, this is the best way for you to see and hear how you come across. Watch the tape with someone whose opinion you trust. If you can't arrange a video, practice with an audio recording and listen intently to your voice. You especially want to eliminate a droning monotone, a shrill pitch, long-winded explanations, choppy and erratic rhythm, voice dropping at the end or rising when there's no question, mumbling, slurring, and running your words together. Alter your pace so that you're not too fast or too slow, but do go slower and lower to emphasize a point. Also practice by talking in front of a mirror to improve your facial expressions.

4. Decide details in advance. Get rid of pesky little choices well before the time you're going to speak. You don't want to worry if the tie you picked has a spot on it or if a lock of hair will drop in your eyes. Get your hair trimmed and examine your clothes ahead of time. Arrive early to check out such items as chairs, mike, lectern, displays, blackout for film, and electric wiring for video.

Summary

The experienced speaker, who talks about the same subject time after time, doesn't need to rehearse. But if this is the first time you're speaking about a particular topic, practicing at home will help you get favorable attention. Few people can get away with memorizing a talk without losing naturalness and spontaneity. Instead, list the points you want to bring out and reduce these to one or two-word bullet reminders. Practice giving your talk from your reminder notes. But do memorize your opening and closing. That's what you want your audience to remember and where you can score the greatest impact.

9.7 BODY LANGUAGE
Aligning Unspoken with Spoken Messages

Sometimes without saying a word you create excitement when you communicate. Body language can send potent messages.

"He couldn't look me in the eye and say that" is an example of attitudes and prejudices showing up in body language. If you're not completely sold on what you're saying, you can't hide it because your motions, gestures, and facial expressions give away your thoughts and emotions. So convince yourself before you try to convince others. And make sure the body language you transmit is in synch with your spoken words.

Interpreting body language is not an exact science. One person crossing his arms over his chest signifies a protective shield; another does this simply because she's chilled. Unless someone yawns during your talk, one signal by itself doesn't tell you too much. Collectively, however, these signals are a general guide to how others are reacting to what you're saying.

Strategy

Watch for unspoken signals in yourself and others. Closer observation will enable you to better respond to body language. Send the same body language message as your verbal message. Look for the words people aren't expressing.

Steps

1. Be alert to positive signals. Here are some signs that you are giving or getting a favorable response.

HEAD	small nod to agree or signal you understand; facing the other directly
FACE	returning a friendly smile; brighten, approving expression
EYES	constant unflinching contact, confident, wide open; little blinking; looking up, trying to remember
MOUTH	relaxed, opened slightly, moistens lips
ARMS	relaxed, dangling naturally at the side when standing, over arms of the chair when seated
POSTURE	erect, head high, neither stiff nor slouched
WALKING	brisk and purposeful, but unhurried
SITTING	straight or leaning slightly forward
GESTURES	slow, small, natural, relaxed without any quick, jerky moves
HANDSHAKE	warm, firm grip, no rush to pull away

2. Recognize negative signs. Body language often indicates when people are annoyed, defensive, tense, nervous, bored, and uncomfortable. More careful observation can help you spot when you're not having the desired effect upon others. Here are common signals.

HEAD	shaking head back and forth; forced nods; turning so as not to face the other directly
FACE	sedate, cheerless, no smile; smiles are untimely
FOREHEAD	wrinkled; finger pushing up forehead
EYES	looks away or down to avoid contact; blinking frequently or for a long time; lids narrow
MOUTH	tight, clenching teeth, biting lips; clearing throat or forcing a cough
JAW	tightened muscles; chin to the chest

ARMS	folded, especially if high across chest
HANDS	rigid moves; folding hands in front; clenched fist; tight grip on arms of chair; holds side or back of head, tugs at ear; handshake quick and short
FINGERS	drums table, twiddles thumbs, laces fingers; points finger at you
POSTURE	stiff or slouching; head down
SITTING	rigid, legs uncrossed flat on floor; leans far back in chair; shifts away from you
GESTURES	doodles, fidgets, squirms, plays with buttons, strand of hair or items on desk; jerky moves; sneaks looks or wants to be caught looking at a watch; jerks glasses on and off

3. Clarify mixed signals. It's perplexing to try to read unclear signs. Those sending these messages probably are not sure themselves how they feel. When you observe the following signals, stop and make the intention clear. Give additional information or reasons.

- nodding yes, but sounding opposed
- tilting head to one side
- frowning abruptly, either disagreeing or confused
- stroking chin, rubbing face
- hesitating, gazing into space
- scratching head

Summary

Body language creates interest and excitement. Just be sure the signals you send mesh with the words you say. By carefully observing the body language of others, you get a better idea of how you're coming across. Should the signals seem out of kilter, clarify before you proceed.

9.8 COMEBACKS

Capitalizing on Heckling or Critical Questions

Hecklers can be nerve shattering when you're giving a talk or presentation. They ask questions not to get more information from you but to steal attention for themselves. Some get their kicks from teasing and some are hostile. If they can goad you into losing your cool, they've succeeded.

Other questioners who hit you with critical remarks may simply have an honest disagreement. Without ulterior motive, they want to point up the causes of a problem.

Whatever the intent, you can learn to enjoy and profit from the exchange. If you evade or stall instead of giving a direct answer, you lose your credibility. However, you're not at the mercy of detractors. You can anticipate most of the charges, identify most of your opponents, and prepare to seize the opportunity. With additional facts at your fingertips, you'll regain control of your audience.

Strategy

Convert the beefs into benefits. Turn the cheap shots around by beefing up your position with prepared comebacks.

Steps

1. Try to neutralize opposition in advance. If you know from past experience that someone will try to destroy your presentation by interrupting with derogatory remarks, be ready with a statement that will allow you to finish. When you suspect opponents will pull apart a certain point, beat them to the punch. Bringing it up yourself and answering the charge dilutes the force of an attack. When possible, beforehand line up persuasive colleagues who will openly support your views. Sometimes you can talk to an opponent in advance of your talk to narrow down the areas of disagreement.

2. Go along with a joke. Let teasers and hecklers have their little fun getting a moment's attention from the audience. If possible, tell a joke on yourself, but don't worry about being clever. Show you're a good sport and move quickly to the next comment.

3. Restate a hostile question. If the attack is personal, rephrase the question to the issue level. Take a moment to collect your thoughts, then grab control. Acknowledge any aspect where you agree with the critic and, without stomping on anyone's ego, fire back the facts. Being specific will increase your credibility.

4. Admit a mistake. When you're caught in the embarrassing situation of having your error held up to the whole group, admit your mistake (or that of your unit or department), apologize, and quickly tell how you're correcting the situation. Give the pertinent facts, then move on to the next question.

5. Be honest when you don't know. Bluffing will get you into trouble or you may find yourself in a quibbling contest. Just promise to find out the answer and inform the group later. If you're asked hypothetical (What if . . .) questions, say there are so many variables, you can't speculate.

Script

(Beat opposition to the punch.) *I imagine some of you might be thinking that we can't afford to go this route, but actually the opposite is true.*

(Agree where you can with a critic.) *What you say has merit. However, the latest studies have shown a new direction. You can see from this chart that maps the trend over the past three months . . .*

(Correct outdated information or misinformation.) *I can see how you came to that conclusion, but the fact is . . .*

(Get your apology out of the way quickly and move on.) *Yes, I did underestimate the time, and I'm truly sorry if that misled you. However, I've notified all the parties involved and they've agreed to . . .*

(When you don't know the answer) *Those figures won't be out before Thursday. I'll get back to you at that time.*

Summary

After you've practiced your presentation, write the toughest questions you can imagine. Keep asking yourself what this group will be concerned about. Then spell out the answers. During the talk, you may get a question you hadn't anticipated, but you can still go in feeling confident. You know you can come back in strong, simple language to almost anything critics throw at you. Should you ask for questions and get no takers, volunteer by posing one or two ("I'm often asked about . . . "). Or have a few plants in the audience.

10

---

*A*TTRACTING *F*AVORABLE
*N*OTICE BY *W*RITING
AND *C*ALLING

The impressions others get from listening to you on the phone and reading your memos, letters, reports, and proposals, as well as what others write about you, affects how you're rated as a rising star.

Review the ways you are getting your ideas across to sharpen your writing and phoning skills. One essential ingredient is being aware at all times of who will be reading or listening to you and why. Be clear on what you hope to accomplish and what's in it for those you're trying to reach.

Many people release their anger and frustration by putting their thoughts down on paper or picking up the phone. Uncorking bottled up emotion is good for you, but remember to tear up your words after you've written them. And refrain from calling until you calm down. Burn into your brain this admonition not to write or say anything that could embarrass you if anyone else were to see or hear about it. That will save you a lot of grief later on.

10.1 BREVITY

Shrinking Your Words to Expand Your Impact

Fill a mug on your desk with a dozen sharp red pencils. That's to remind you that rambling wordiness is a cardinal sin you can't afford to commit. Nobody has time or patience to wade through your verbiage. You leave people jeering instead of cheering when you haven't learned to edit yourself down to essentials. When saying too much, you tend to stray or editorialize. This takes the focus away from the message you're trying to send.

On paper, you have time to go back, delete the excess, and punch up your writing. The telephone requires advance preparation and self-discipline. You zip your lips and think before you speak.

With a little practice, you can master most of the techniques advocated by communications specialists. Brevity properly handled speeds reader and listener comprehension.

Strategy

Boil down your thoughts or information to the essence. Stick to the point you're making.

Steps

1. Apply the So What? test. Strike extra words not needed for clarity. Ask yourself, "Is this word necessary? Is this point truly relevant?" You don't need four examples to clarify a point when one will do. Or a clever anecdote if it doesn't exactly fit. Red pencil every word and phrase that doesn't earn its keep. But don't get so carried away when you're cutting that you leave people confused or jumping to incorrect assumptions.

2. Condense long sentences and paragraphs. Vary the lengths and break them up if there's more than one key thought. If you are citing a few supporting points or statistics, you may be able to list them as bullets. Use contractions. That's how we speak, and it's shorter.

3. Separate back-up data. Remove charts, statistics, and other details or background from the main body because this clutters and dilutes the strength of your message. Attaching this information, to be referred to as needed, enables you to keep your letters and memos to one page and to top your reports and proposals with a one-page executive summary or highlights. Even technical writing can be simplified with fewer words and an informal tone.

Script

Achieve greater impact by:

- deleting nonessentials

  unless needed for the sense of the sentence, strike every "the," "that," "of," and "in order to."

- watching for overuse

  of "very," "and/or," "that is," "it's a good idea to," "as it were."

- shortening phrases

  "take into consideration" to "consider"

  "held a meeting" to "met"

  "at the present time" to "now"

  "of the opinion that" to "believe"

  "in view of the above" to "since"

  "due to the fact that" to "because"

  "will you please arrange to attend" to "please attend"

  As for "needless to say," don't say it!

- avoiding phrases that can be insulting

  "as you know" may be interpreted as "you stupid fool, you should have known about this policy." If it's known, why repeat it? If you're not sure, say "you may know."

Summary

Rising stars can express their thoughts in a succinct message. They don't cram the most words into the smallest idea. When you compress, condense, and write tight, others have an easier time understanding you. Your words carry more weight when not weighted down by excess language. The only caution is not to cut so close to the bone that the meaning is scrapped. When you've written an inspired potent phrase that isn't really needed, it feels as if you're cutting off your right arm to delete it. Ease your pain by saving it to use later, when there'll be a better fit.

10.2 CRITICAL POINTS ———————————————

Stressing Accuracy, Clarity, and Emphasis

You gain notice when everyone you work with knows the factual information you present can be counted on for accuracy. Slipping in unverified data is misleading, and you go down a few points in credibility. If your work looks neat, but has sloppy spelling (especially misspelled names or mismatched names and titles), your bright star loses some more twinkle. Ditto for grammatical errors that can cause confusion and misunderstanding.

Adding to confusion is gobbledygook, a murky mixture of jargon and vagueness, often intentionally obscure and manipulative. If you deliberately use such unintelligible camouflage, the perception is you're trying to disguise your inadequacy or ignorance. When you play hide and seek, making your reader search for the meaning, deduct some more points.

Unless you emphasize what readers want to know and what you want them to know, your purpose is buried in unbroken or repetitive narrative. If your writing's difficult to absorb, much less retain, readers miss the message or give up trying to find it.

Strategy

Check and double check your writing before turning it in or mailing it out. If there's any way for readers to misunderstand what you're saying, they'll find it. And if you don't accent what you feel is essential, they may overlook it.

Steps

1. Verify your information. Don't assume something is correct because it sounds right or a little familiar. Addresses and phone numbers change. Positions in companies change. A misspelled name can lose a customer. Last year's statistics (even last week's) may be outdated. Conditions fluctuate, so make sure your position on an issue still holds up.

2. Constantly consult your dictionary. Don't guess if you're not sure about spelling or meaning. Be particularly careful about words that sound alike but have different meanings. If you can't find a word because you don't know how to spell it, a synonym will probably have your word in its definition. Take the time to select a better word choice, a shade closer to the idea you want to convey. It's okay to repeat a word if a synonym doesn't quite fit. Sometimes you want to use repetition for impact.

3. Use abbreviations and acronyms appropriately. Spell out the full form before using only the initials. For example, the first mention would be, "Economic Commission for Latin America (ECLA)" and after that, just ECLA. Strike abbreviations that may not be known throughout the office, such as "return EBD Friday" for End of Business Day. Better to say "return by 5 P.M. Friday."

4. Be specific to avoid ambiguity. Simplify and clarify. Delete jargon or inner circle terminology among those who can't decipher it. Generalities sound evasive, as if you're trying to talk around a subject or keep the boss from finding out something. Don't keep talking office equipment when you really mean computers. Specific facts, numbers, examples, and descriptions not only clarify your meaning but also build your credibility.

5. Place vital information strategically. Catch the readers' interest in the first sentence and keep the first paragraph short or they may not read any more. Words at the beginning and end of a sentence, and sentences at the beginning and end of a paragraph carry more weight. So does repeating a significant word, phrase, or dynamic slogan.

6. Keep paragraphs short and vary sentence length. Chop up complicated structure by listening to yourself read aloud. Strive for a smooth rhythm with your own beat. Add bridging words (on the other hand, in fact, furthermore) to link your paragraphs. To keep readers from getting lost in a maze of unending paragraphs, after the general statement separate the several points, listing one under the other using bullets, numbers, or asterisks.

7. Highlight mechanically what you want remembered. Use headings, subheadings, **bold** print, or *italics* or underlining, or words in ALL CAPS.

Indent an entire paragraph with extra wide margins.

> Box in especially important information.

Script

(Look up words that sound alike to be sure you're using them correctly.) *Of course, I won't elicit (induce) contributions by illicit* (unlawful) *means.*
Use office stationery (letterhead) *to make known your stationary* (fixed) *positions.*

(Eliminate gobbledygook.) *A question about which there has been evidence of considerable differences of opinion vehemently espoused by both sides,* which, uncloaked, becomes a mere *controversial issue.*

(Avoid grammatical confusion.) *Mary's supervisor said she was opposed to the restriction.* (Misuse of personal pronoun—who was opposed, Mary or her supervisor?)

Summary

Your bosses, colleagues, and workers have to know they can depend on you for accurate information. Don't guess. Don't assume. Check it out. Make yourself perfectly clear. If something doesn't sound quite right, double check. Go back over your writing to eliminate incorrect spelling and grammar and confusing gobbledygook. Review your work to be sure you've put stress in all the right places.

10.3 HOOKS

Reeling in Readers

It can't be said too often. When readers pick up your writing, something has to click into place to snag their attention. How do you bait the hook? With their interests. The impersonal word is seldom heard.

Giving your work an intriguing title is the first hook. The second hook is in your opening line and first paragraph. Tell your readers instantly what this has to do with them. How will they benefit from or suffer without this information?

To develop your message, start by defining your purpose. In one sentence, write down exactly what you want to etch on the minds of the readers. Then put yourself in their shoes. Mull over how this information will be received from their vantage point. What is it they want to know and why?

Your closing remarks serve as the third hook. Restate your message. If you're requesting action, say why it should be done and by when. If you're giving information, ask what else you can do to help.

Strategy

Put the needs and interests of the readers first. Know what you want to accomplish, but remember that the hook is in what they want.

Steps

1. Get a good title for memos, reports, and proposals. Pretend you're a headline writer. Pull in the reader by creating something short, snappy, and eye catching. Try to center the title on the action you're advocating. On your memos, go beyond the subject and add the purpose. This will draw in the reader and also help you keep your message short and focused.

2. Find a strong lead. It's easy to get stalled when your mind goes blank worrying about coming up with a clever lead before you can proceed. Just start writing as a warm-up exercise. Talk about your purpose and the reader's needs. Now examine your writing to see if you, like many others, take two long paragraphs before you get to what the reader wants to know. When paragraph three begins with "Therefore," that's a tip off. Your lead sentence is probably at the start of paragraph three (without the "therefore") and is usually something easy for the reader to grasp. Another technique to use if the lead doesn't come to you right away is to develop the body of your writing first and then come back to write the opening.

3. Start with a positive, understanding tone. To get good results, the message to be received is not what you want, but what the recipients want. If you're annoyed or angry, scolding won't accomplish anything but develop a turn-off. And the fear tactic may create so much tension that your readers will stop concentrating on the message and dwell only on the fear. Respect the thinking and talent of your readers. To persuade them, they have to see the importance and relevance of what you have to say. Show readers how they can achieve their desire, ambition, or objective by cooperating.

4. Nudge action or tell what you're going to do. To find the closing, look back at your lead and restate your purpose. Or emphasize what you want remembered or acted upon. Or consider starting a story at the beginning, stopping it as you go through the body, and then concluding your piece with the end of the story.

Script

(Put purpose in the memo's title.) *New order forms—a real time saver*

(Put a hook in your opening.) *I heard you're planning to expand your division and I have some ideas you might find useful.*
We're interested in enlisting intelligent people like you to help our leaders analyze . . .

(Change an intimidating, self-centered tone.) *Frankly, we're concerned. Twice we contacted you and haven't received a response.*
(What does the writer want?) *It occurred to me you may be interested in learning a little more about . . .*

(Use a closing hook.) *I hope you'll find this cost-cutting idea useful. If you'd like more information or details, call me at . . .*

Summary

An exciting lead sets the mood. Aim to be a little provocative. Look for the hook, something that will intrigue readers and make them curious enough to read on. You might start with a stimulating question, or any of the openers discussed in verbal presentations. Close with another hook, retelling what you want and how that affects the readers or why they should be moved to act.

10.4 REPORTS AND PROPOSALS
Preparing Impressive Presentations

There are two kinds of reports and proposals that can help you appear to be a rising star. One is taking the initiative yourself by spotting a need, then investigating it. The result would be a report of your findings with recommended action or a proposal offering a solution to a situation that needs improvement.

The other kind originates from an assignment to gather information and report back. Getting advance clarification on the kind of report expected as well as the time frame will enable you to prepare a paper the boss really wants and will appreciate.

Even if you're not required to submit progress reports on extended projects, it's in your best interest to keep the boss aware of you and your work. Here, too, data collection isn't enough. If you want to be perceived as valuable, you have to take the initiative and present a little more than was asked of you, such as pointing out danger signals and suggesting remedies.

Strategy

Prepare reports and proposals that go beyond amassing facts. Working from a base of your understanding of the need or purpose, present an interpretation of the information. Write in a form that will be most useful as well as attractive.

Steps

1. Start by getting the purpose on paper. Clarify the need if it hasn't been spelled out for you. This will save you a lot of time and heartache later. Just in case you were on the wrong track, the boss can correct you in the early stages.

2. Let your ideas flow before you buff and polish. Don't worry about grammar or style until you get your ideas down. With the purpose as your focus, sort and categorize your notes into major segments. Eliminate anything that doesn't fit well into your general outline. Correct spelling and grammar and enliven with shorter sentences and paragraphs. As you substitute synonyms, select words for impact and that talk your boss's language. Use terms the boss says all the time. Achieve a lighter, conversational tone by reading your paper out loud.

3. Use a cover sheet. Title the proposal across the top of the page. Then write a subheading, "Highlights" or "Executive Summary." Everyone reading your report will appreciate information boiled own to its essence. In three paragraphs or less, making every single word count, write a hard-hitting summation of your recommendations or conclusions resulting from your investigation or activities. Include in your summary a brief recap of the problem and purpose of the report. At the bottom right, put your name. If you are chairing a committee, put your name as chairperson and list the members (alphabetically) who helped write the report.

4. Package your work attractively. Neatness does count and so does easy referencing. For a long document, separate the segments. You may need a table of contents, with such headings as Introduction, Methods, Results, Recommendations, and Appendices. Consider sectional tabs, or even a different color paper for each section. Be consistent with the way you handle margins, headings, capitalizing, italics, underscoring, double and single spacing, and block or indented paragraphs. Break up long paragraphs with subheadings and more blank space. Take nonessential details and background data out of the body of the report and use them as attachments or appendices.

5. Proofread again and again. Sometimes you don't "see" an error the first time, so proof your paper two or three different times. You might ask a cohort to proof it for you also.

6. Add a personal touch. Clip a one- or two-line, enthusiastic, confident, handwritten note to your report.

Script

(Clarify the reason for the report.) *Boss, it's my understanding that the purpose of this report is to determine the value of this new equipment and that the information could include . . .*

(Talk the boss's language.) *We can achieve more impact if we . . . We can curtail protracted negotiations by . . .*

(Call attention with a handwritten note.) *I found the subject fascinating. I'd be happy to answer any questions you have about this report.*

Summary

Take the risk and show some initiative when writing reports and proposals. Think long and hard about the purpose of the paper, then analyze the information you've collected. Go beyond organizing the data. Give your recommendation, even if it wasn't asked for. People don't know how valuable you are unless you show them.

10.5 LETTERS
Nudging Action or Desired Results

Before you write one word, change hats. For the moment become your readers. What would they think about this situation or information? Jot down what you imagine would be their viewpoint, concerns, needs, wants. If they were sitting across from you, what questions would they ask you?

Next, think about the message you want to send. Define in one sentence what you want the letter to do. Determine how you can tie your message to your readers' interests. Why would the readers want to know this?

Tell them immediately. Treat your first sentence as a headline. Stress what they'd be interested in, not what you want. We all resent having to go through a whole letter before the writer gets to the point. Just make sure you make that point in the first sentence and that it in some way concerns the readers. You have to grab the reader's attention. So right off, you tell them what you're writing about and why they'd want to hear it.

Strategy

Write a letter as though you're talking face to face with the reader. Immediately link your message to reader interest and close with the action you want taken.

Steps

1. Send your letter to a real person with a name. Go to the trouble of calling up to learn the name of the director of the department or the president of the company, or whomever you're writing. "Dear Sir, Madam, or Ms." is an immediate turn-off. Call the person's office or look up his or her name in the business directory in your library. A name is the most personal possession each of us has. We want to be called by our name, our correct name, correctly spelled. Also check that names and titles coincide.

2. Observe old-fashioned courtesy. What you consider friendly, others regard as presumptuous. Call strangers Mr. or Ms. unless you're invited to call them by their first names. (This applies especially to your boss.) Acknowledge titles (Professor Jones, Judge Smith, Dr. Brown). That's their title. They earned it. Why risk offending them?

3. Project a positive, understanding tone. Inject a light touch, professional but friendly without being cute. Even if you're taking an opposing stand, you can be pleasant and respectful of everyone's right to an opinion. Use softening phrases to take the edge off your bite.

4. Take the starch out of your style. Write the way you speak—cordial and conversational. If you're being natural, the letter will sound like you when you read it aloud. Remove jargon and jarring phrases. Write tightly, red-penciling extra words, phrases, and even paragraphs.

5. Be clear, concise, and correct. Double check for accuracy and correct grammar. Make sure days and dates are correct and coincide. If what you're stating sounds like fact but is really opinion, say so. Keep sentences and paragraphs short with sharp points clearly visible. Delete long descriptions by using more nouns and action verbs and fewer adjectives. To remain straightforward without exaggerating or rambling, hone generalities into pertinent specifics. Make every effort to keep your letter to one page. Factual data weighing it down can be put on a separate sheet and attached.

6. Conclude with the desired action. Include in the last paragraph whatever you want the reader to do or what you intend to do. You may want to restate the opening paragraph. If you're requesting action, give a deadline. When asking a favor, mention that you'll be checking back in a few days. Avoid the presumptuous "Thanking you in advance," which comes across as either arrogant or too lazy to say thanks when the request is granted.

7. Save time and be more effective answering mail. As you read through your stack of mail, circle essential information or underline or highlight important points. Make notes in the margin, a 1, 2, 3, 4 outline for your response. Refer to your notes and to the date of the letter as you reply or dictate a draft. If you have to write the same kind of letter frequently, develop a form letter that you can personalize.

Script

(Convey a positive, understanding tone.) *We understand this has been difficult for you.* (rather than the unfriendly *it is understood that . . .* or a critical *your undated letter . . .*)

(Separate weighty data and attach.) *You'll find attached a breakdown of the costs.*

(Be more concise by changing stuffy, longer terms into word shrinkers.) *Verification* to *proof, promulgate* to *issue, modification* to *change, ameliorate* to *improve, ascertain* to *learn.*

(Instead of thanking in advance) *Thank you for your consideration. I'll call your secretary to learn when it will be convenient for you to meet with me.*

Summary

You are representing your office with every letter you write. Use these letters to make friends for your company or department or project. Even when answering a complaint, make friends. Use an understanding tone, acknowledging the other person's position. Then in a polite, friendly manner explain yours. Do this, and you're calling positive attention to yourself.

10.6 MEMOS AND NOTES
Making Yourself Perfectly Clear

To impress your boss, peers, and workers with your memos and notes, keep them simple and uncomplicated. Use informal notes to uplift morale, thank your boss, or congratulate a colleague.

Memos serve to announce, confirm, and inform. Interpret trends affecting the company. Circulate correct information to stop false rumors. Request help from colleagues or staff as well as to share data with them. But play it smart. Sending too many memos is like talking too much during staff meetings. Pretty soon people stop paying attention. Conserve memos for a specific purpose, not to keep advertising your existence. And alphabetize your distribution list or you'll stomp on somebody's ego.

Also, refrain from using memos and notes to tackle a controversy. Negotiation or consensus needs the back-and-forth discussion of face-to-face confrontation. Delete digs from your notes or they'll haunt you later. And beware of being set up by an unscrupulous colleague who, knowing you're opposed to a new system, will try to get your thoughts in writing to use against you. Talk it out instead.

Strategy

Write more and better memos and notes. Win friends and gain attention with the personal note, which has practically gone out of style. When you send a few lines of recognition, you stand out and your thoughtfulness is remembered. If your memos are sharp, short, and purposeful, people will read them.

Steps

1. Title your memos. Use the subject heading to entice people to read the rest. Expand the brief subject ("Deferred Compensation") to something that affects the reader ("A New Plan to Increase Your Retirement Income.")

2. Boil memos down to a crisp one page. Busy bosses appreciate your saving them time. They also know only those who have mastered a subject can write succinctly. If the memo's a report, begin with your "Recommendation." Squeeze this into one or two sentences. Divide the rest into sections, giving each a headline. Attach detailed data as "Background Information" in the event the boss wants to know more.

3. Cut out wastefulness. Some memos can be handled faster and cheaper with a 30-second phone call. Most offices have floor to ceiling files filled with useless trivia. Don't make unnecessary copies. When you won't need to refer back to the memo, but it requires a response (to "Can we meet on the 17th?"), jot a note right on the same memo, or on a small self-stick note, and send it back. You'll look decisive and efficient.

4. Develop the congratulatory or thank you note habit. Send an excited note of appreciation to the boss for the new assignment. Think how good your worker will feel receiving your written pat on the back. Or how pleased your cohorts will be when you say how well they handled a project. Send notes to anyone in the office who's been recognized for anything—a promotion, a civic award, a contest winner. A handwritten note is particularly distinguishable from the mountain of typed and printed paper crossing everyone's desk. The eye is drawn to it.

5. Invest in subtle self-promotion. Order an unusual color paper for your memos or notes. Everyone in the office will react with instant recognition and attention ("Oh, here's something from Bob") without even picking it up. Or, as a time saver, you may want to use different colored memos for different purposes. Be sure to initial and date your memos to get credit for your work now, and later to save time and guessing when they were prepared.

Script

(Calm down before sending angry notes.) *Tony, I do appreciate everything you've done for my division in the past, but I'm troubled about your decision in the Lakes matter. I'm sure you didn't intend the potential consequences that I foresee. Are you free to discuss this on Friday at 3?*

(Make the purpose clear, for example, to inform.) *Initial tests show some deterioration. Therefore, we want to take extra precautions when . . .* (or to ask for help) *Since our costs are sky-rocketing, we're going to need your help to keep our heads above water* (or to confirm—no ideas, details, or negotiations here, you'll give them at the meeting) *Tuesday, Feb. 18, will be fine. We'll probably want to discuss (1), (2), and (3).*

(Express feelings in a quick note.) *Boss, I'm really excited about the new project and I look forward to the challenge. Thanks again. Alex, great work, keep it up!*

(Win friends with thank-you notes.) *Our talk this afternoon was so stimulating, a slew of new ideas have popped into my head. I am most grateful for your time, counsel, and encouragement.*

Summary

As with reports and letters, think through your notes and memos before you write. It is more difficult to be clear when you're being concise because every word is important. If the subject of your memo is involved, outline it first and put your points in logical order before you start. Keep your writing professional, but light and conversational, using simpler, more informal terms. When appropriate, end with the action you want, or ask readers to call you for more information. Make better use of the note and memo to win friends, gain attention, and be seen as a rising star.

10.7 WRITING TIPS
A Guide for Keeping Attention

You have leeway to develop your own style when writing reports, proposals, letters, memos, and notes. Artists who have studied fine art know precisely the distortional liberties they take with their abstract paintings. In the same way, you may occasionally want to break usage rules. For example, instead of a complete sentence, you may decide to use only a word or two. Nothing more. Just for effect.

Write in a style that's natural to you, keeping in mind that grammatical mistakes will detract from your effectiveness. Deduct points if you confuse the nominative and objective cases (writing "from my partner and I" when it should be "from my partner and me"). And even if your paper's grammatically correct, you lose more points if you lose your readers by burying your message.

Work from a sketchy general plan or outline before you begin. Many writers use $3'' \times 5''$ index cards, putting each point on a separate card. Then they make stacks—about three or four piles for a report—of closely related ideas, which are then shuffled so that one thought flows easily to the next.

Strategy

Make your writing more appealing to your readers. Review the following reminders.

Steps

1. Search for more effective words. Use your dictionary and thesaurus to find more accurate and better tints of meaning. Forget cute, you're after comprehension and favorable attention. Seek more active verbs and substitute the weak "to be" verbs. Pick adjectives and adverbs so colorful that the reader can visualize what you describe. Choose the simpler over the fancy words. Delete unnecessary or overdone phrases.

2. Create effective sentences. Vary the length to produce an interesting rhythm. Insert linking words (moreover, in fact, conversely, for example, however, as a result, similarly, therefore, finally) to slide from one point to the next. Choose the energetic active voice over the dull life-sapping passive voice. When you trim the fat in quest of conciseness, leave the meat. Cutting too deeply obscures the meaning.

3. Make your paragraphs readable. Break up long, involved ones. Keep paragraphs short, just a few sentences. Aim for a solid unit. Open with the main idea, then the supportive or explanatory ideas in logical order, with major emphasis on the first and last sentences. Link one paragraph to the next by a bridging word or by repeating a key word from the end of the preceding paragraph.

4. Lighten and tighten. No one wants to plow through rigor mortis material. If you sound starchy stiff, you lose attention. Don't get technical unless you're writing for technicians. To sound conversational, write the way you speak and make it sound like you. Relate your subject to real live people even if you're discussing inanimate objects. If you're talking equipment, people will be using it, or perhaps the equipment will be replacing people.

5. Discipline yourself not to stray from the point. Whatever is not directly related to the key idea is a digression. You may feel great distress in cutting out a beautiful paragraph that doesn't exactly support or emphasize your point. Delete and file. You'll use it more appropriately someplace else, some other time. The reader's attention span is limited. The more you confine your subject, the greater the chance for impact.

Script

(Substitute more active verbs.) *Surge* instead of *sudden increase. The meeting spawned innovative plans* rather than *the meeting was productive.*

(Change passive to active voice.) *It was suggested by the boss that consideration be given to* to *the boss suggested we consider.*

(Choose the simpler word.) *Face* rather than *countenance, expand* for *maximize.*

(Strike trite expressions.) *Cut the mustard, between a rock and a hard place* (and unnecessary phrases) *the project sounded good in terms of a quick return* can be shortened to *the project's quick return sounded good.*

(Remove the starch.) *Attached is . . .* instead of *attached hereto please find . . .* (Do you know anybody who talks that way? Why write that way?)

(Link paragraphs, for example, by repeating a key word from the preceding paragraph. If paragraph ends . . . *to come up with a plan,* use the key word, "plan," to start next paragraph) *The plan, however, could not be enacted . . .*

Summary

Writing style is personal. Develop one with which you feel comfortable. To keep the readers' attention, however, keep it light and close to the way you talk naturally. Go easy on adjectives, adverbs, and personal opinions. You're more effective when you're objective. Stick to facts and eliminate unsubstantiated, judgmental comments.

10.8 TELEPHONE TIPS
A Guide for Improving Telephone Techniques

There's no way to break this to you gently. Your call is an interruption. An intrusion. Whenever you call anyone, you are causing that person to stop whatever he or she is doing in order to talk to you.

Sometimes people are delighted to do so. Sometimes they just can't talk to you at that moment. The only courteous thing to do when you want more than a minute's conversation is to ask, after identifying yourself, "Do you have (however many minutes you need) to talk to me now?"

You make friends or lose friends on the phone. Especially irritating is the person who screeches, talks too loudly, or mumbles. You can't speak distinctly if you have food, gum, a cigarette, or a pipe in your mouth. Hold the transmitter about 3/4" from your lips to achieve a more natural tone.

Strategy

Mind your manners and sharpen your message. You may not be aware of how well or poorly you're coming across. Or that you're saying something on the phone you really didn't want repeated (and it will be). The following tips are offered as a reminder.

Steps

1. Jot down points ahead of time. An abbreviated script allows you to sound spontaneous as you rattle off point after point in logical order. Determine in advance how to phrase a sensitive matter and practice saying it a few times so as not to sound as if you're reading. Notes will keep you from rambling or having to call back because you forgot to say something. When the other person is talking, give a verbal nod that you're paying attention.

2. Prepare a "Talk-to Reminder" Form. Divide a single sheet of paper into blocks for an easy, useful technique. Head each block with a different name, the people you check with daily. As a thought occurs to you ("I have to talk to Charlie about the new ruling"), jot it down in the appropriate block (under Charlie, "check new ruling"). Also, keep notes during talks to remember what was agreed upon. You'll find it saves time to cluster calls you return during a period you've set aside, and let your people know the times you like to be called.

3. Begin your calls with consideration. After exchanging hellos, immediately identify yourself. No one has time for guessing games. Then find out if the listener has time to talk now, and if not, ask for a good time to call back. Smiling before dialing comes across the line like a warm handshake. So does dialing your own calls and treating others as though they're as important as you are. Answering your own phone, besides saving everyone's time, lets you gain contacts, information, insight, and suggestions. It also alerts you to problems and motivates your subordinates.

4. Answer the phone with consideration. Pretend the company president is calling you. "Hello" isn't informative. Give your name and unit or program in a friendly tone. Try to pick up on the first or second ring. Explain delays; it's rude to keep people hanging on without comment or to hold the receiver while you finish a conversation with someone else. It's also rude to keep interrupting an important discussion to answer your phone and carry on a conversation. Instead, arrange for your calls to be held or meet somewhere out of your office. And if you're taking a message for someone else, don't pry.

5. Hook your listeners after the courtesies. Get right to the point. Busy people don't tolerate ramblers. Within thirty seconds, state why you're calling and why you're calling that particular person. Visualize the listener. Either you need some information from that person or you want to impart some. Be prepared with concise, specific answers if queried. And don't let a secretary put you on hold. Interrupt with a request that you be called back as soon as the boss's other conversation is concluded.

6. Hang up gently. End your conversation gracefully without either of you prolonging the goodbyes after business is finished. Carefully replace the phone in its cradle. Slamming down a receiver is like slamming the door in someone's face.

7. Instruct the message taker. If your calls are to be screened, agree on a tactful approach. If you'll be away, have the message taker know when or where you can be reached or if someone is pinch-hitting for you. If you are making the call, rather than leaving your name and waiting to be called, ask the secretary's name and the best time to call back.

8. Handle the boss who won't return your calls. Are you trying to discuss a problem the boss wants to avoid? The boss knows what you want, but may not be ready to act. Perhaps your suggestion is logically correct, but politically stupid, and the boss doesn't want to explain. Rather than keep pestering, stop calling. Switch to nonpreachy, factual, daily written updates on a worsening condition. Or question the boss about priorities. Once you do your part and put your warning in writing, back off or you could suffer the consequences. It's the boss's decision to make, right or wrong, not yours. If you can't get a straight answer and you're empowered to act, move and then let the boss know what you did. If you can't act and the boss wants still more information, try to deliver it personally.

Script

(Signal that you're listening.) *Really, then what happened?*
Oh, certainly, I can understand that.

(Explain delays.) *It will take a few minutes to look that up. May I call you right back?* or *I won't know that until this afternoon, may I call you back about 3?*

(Hook the listener immediately.) *I'd like to meet with you to discuss some marketing procedures I believe would help us both.*
I trust your judgment and I'd appreciate being able to kick around a couple of ideas I have.
Our mutual friend, Mark Workman, suggested I call you.

(Don't prolong goodbyes.) *Thanks again for your help. Goodbye.*
I'm sorry we weren't able to help you. Perhaps next time. Goodbye.
I'd like to go into that, but I'm due at a meeting in a few minutes. We'll talk soon. Goodbye.

(Take messages without prying.) *May I have James call you back as soon as he returns?*
Julie's away from her desk. May I tell her who called?

(When you're not available) *I'm sorry Ms. Hamilton, but Mr. Brown is away for the afternoon. However, Ms. Smith is handling his calls. Would you like to speak to her?* or *Mr. Brown will be in a conference until 10. May I ask him to call you back then?*

Summary

Tape record yourself during a few telephone conversations to hear how you sound to others when you're being spontaneous. Pay particular attention to your pace, tone, volume, pitch, rhythm, and enunciation. To warm up your vocal cords in the morning, read something out loud for a couple of minutes. Remember that a sharp, considerate message wins attention.

11

KNOWING HOW TO GET AND USE INFORMATION

How can you be seen as a rising star if you feel as if you fade into the furniture and your real value to the company is underestimated? The answer is to gain attention by making others more aware of your existence.

Work harder on discovering and routing information. By keeping alert, you pick up useful news floating around. You hear of policy changes about to be implemented, who will be heading the new project, how the boss really rates your performance, where there'll be a job opening.

Of course, when information spreads mouth to mouth, it gets both filtered and embroidered. When it's important, check it out by going right to the source. And don't stop with listening. Feed in information about yourself that you want spread, both orally and in writing. Be ready to get information by you and about you funnelled through both channels.

11.1 OUTSIDE THE LOOP
Plugging Gaps When You're the Last to Know

You didn't hear about the opening in a branch office until the job had been filled. Had you known, you would have applied. But you're left out of the information loop. Nobody bothers to tell you what's going on.

Exchanging information is a two-way street. Whether intentionally or unaware, perhaps you appear distant or unfriendly, if not downright frigid. Maybe it's just your reserved nature. Regardless, you can't afford to learn accidentally or incidentally about changes affecting your job. You can't afford to close yourself off from the network that sends information and ideas from person to person.

You say you pride yourself in staying out of office politics, which you consider malicious and dangerous? Office politics doesn't have to be devious. You can avoid negative aspects by the way you act. Be honest but tactful about your beliefs instead of playing games you think might preserve your job. Office politics can be the path to promotion, which sometimes goes to the most politically adept instead of to the most qualified. Be friends with everyone. You never know who says what to whom about you.

Strategy

Get into office politics. Staying clear damages you two ways: (1) You lose the benefit of shaping what others say about you. Simply because you're there, people are going to talk about you, whether or not you indulge. (2) You shut yourself off from an important information source. News of changes, appointments, openings, and opportunities spread throughout the grapevine faster than the speed of light. In addition, office politics can inspire teamwork and spark innovations.

Steps

1. Cultivate sources directly connected to the information loop. Listen more carefully to what the boss is saying to you privately and to the whole staff at meetings. Read executive orders, memos, and company newsletters for between-the-lines meaning. Utilize open-ended questions to extract opinions and comments from others about what they've written. Supply information that will make your boss look good. Prepare periodic updates to keep open the lines of communication. If you're asked to respond to a top executive's special request, put your name on your work.

2. Get news from below. Make friends at every level. If you reward initiative and good performance and encourage questions, you'll learn what your workers are thinking and worrying about. This sets the stage for getting their good suggestions as well as the latest talk that's circulating. They'll talk more freely if you express your concern for them. Try simple things, like letting them know their suggestions worked or arranging a car pool to an office function knowing many people hate to walk in alone.

3. Warm up if people say you're hard to get to know. Exchange small favors or shifts, take phone messages, stop to chat a minute before going directly to your desk or while waiting for the elevator. Have coffee or lunch with colleagues a few times a week. You don't have to be best friends, just friendly. Tune into the mood of the office, the norms for your particular organization, and you'll be hearing a lot more of the latest news.

Script

(Don't miss the boss's meaning.) *Did you get the same impression as I did when the boss was talking about the proposed alliance at the meeting this morning?*

(Encourage others to talk to you.) *That was an insightful report you did on merger potential. I'd be interested to hear your opinion on another matter. What do you think about . . . ?*

(Track down job openings.) *Iris, rumor has it that you were offered a promotion along with a transfer to our main office. I'm not trying to pry if you haven't made a decision, but if you have, I'd like to know because I'm interested in applying . . .*

Summary

Take your head out of the sand and observe. If you feel people are withholding information from you, you are probably failing to raise your antennae to receive the news. Become more alert as you observe, listen, and read. Warm up and ask better questions. Pay attention to who's talking to whom. Analyze rumors you hear. Bits and pieces of information you collect won't complete the jigsaw puzzle, but you'll probably get the general picture.

11.2 GRAPEVINE
Feeding in News You Want to Be Spread

If you've deliberately chopped down the grapevine because you find gossip repulsive, you may have shot yourself in the foot you need for climbing up. Not only do you miss out on getting news, you're also cutting yourself off from an important channel for spreading word about your effectiveness.

The informal grapevine is a pipeline, instantly propelling messages you want others to know. Because it is often accurate, many depend on it to get information they need. It offers a subtle, or not so subtle, way to toot your own horn and pump in information.

Much gossip is innocent fun poking with strands of the latest events mixed in. Yes, sometimes it turns ugly, with damaging character assassination. In that case, ask the carrier for verification. Disagree if you know the truth. Help nip wild or explosive rumors. But stay tuned so that you can beat the drums to spread your own news and lead others to regard you as a rising star.

Strategy

Use the grapevine to publicize your thinking and activities. Feed the network and it will get back to the boss what you did to make the boss look good. Use it to let your peers and subordinates know you appreciate their help and to share credit with them.

Steps

1. Share bits of news, gossip, and your interpretations. When you give, you receive. Discuss how the new administrative order will affect everyone. Explain the importance of what you're currently working on to your department.

2. Create circumstances to use your information. Use the grapevine for some subtle boasting and to accept the praise you deserve. Don't toss away compliments out of false modesty. Also correct any misinformation being circulated.

3. Control information that flows through bulletin boards. Bulletin boards are often neglected or haphazard, so messy no one can find useful information. Volunteer to maintain the bulletin boards. Post articles from newspapers, journals, magazines, and newsletters. Be on the lookout for good cartoons, mount and add your own succinct comment. Color code for instant reference; for example, green for personnel news of openings or scheduling, red for new executive orders, blue for new product/service information. People will notice your efforts and seek you out.

Script

(Join in innocent gossip.) *Did you hear that Lisa will be starting maternity leave on Friday?*
Is it true that Frank's going back to production?

(Offer interpretations.) *I think the new procedure has two flaws we're going to have to work on . . .*

(Toot your horn.) *Have you seen the monthly report yet? I was surprised and excited that my team was able to increase production by . . . Boy, that's a great bunch to work with.* (Don't reject earned compliments with *Joy did all the important work.*)

(Stop malicious rumor.) *I'm really surprised to hear you say that about Arthur. I've worked with him for seven years, and I've never had reason to question his integrity. Where did you hear this story and how do you know it's accurate?*

Summary

Rethink your attitude about office gossip if you've been trying desperately to avoid it. The grapevine can bear fruit as a positive channel for planting news you want spread. Feed it regularly to produce positive attention.

11.3 REAL ANSWERS

Asking the Right Questions

To be regarded as a rising star, you don't need to know the answers. You just have to know how to get them. If you're greeted with one-word grunts or a shrug of the shoulders instead of a response, look again at your questions. You can't get useful answers unless your questions are penetrating.

"What can we do to improve conditions?" is a non-question. It invites scattergun replies because it sweeps across the entire surface without any focus. You have to dig deeper: "What policies and procedures need to be changed to increase productivity?" That would be a starting point, the basic comprehensive question, the first of a cluster of questions that will lead to the core of the issue.

"Why has productivity declined?" "When did we start experiencing a down trend?" "What new policies, procedures, or conditions occurred at that time?" "How did employees react to the change?" The basic who, what, when, where, why, and how questions are the tools to keep a discussion relevant and productive.

Strategy

Lead your group in reflective thinking to call attention to yourself in a positive way. At your staff meetings and other such gatherings, ask the questions that make everyone ponder the problem, sifting and relating ideas, gathering and interpreting the evidence, until you arrive at a solution.

Steps

1. Initiate questions that elicit ideas and opinions. This is far different from knowing the answer and arguing your case which you will do on other occasions. When you're exploring, ramming through your opinion stifles creative thought. If you know a given topic is on the agenda, prepare yourself to lead the discussion even though you're not the titled leader. Work on the basic question to toss out for others to interpret for its various implications.

2. Ask questions to test opinions and challenge incorrect factual statements. Prepare in advance a cluster of follow-up questions, both analytical and factual. Jump in with soft and polite challenges, asking for verification when something doesn't sound right to you. Rephrase a question to ask it again and to learn if there's general agreement.

3. Keep the discussion to the issue. Listen carefully to the ideas that are thrown out to find those worthy of closer examination. Suggest delving into tangential issues only after you finish the current one. Questions you pose should be short, clear, and specific.

Script

(Supply the basic question.) *In discussing how to speed up delivery, why don't we start by asking what's causing the back-up?*

(Challenge misinformation.) *Alice, would you mind telling us where you found that information? I have a commission report here with conflicting data that you may want to compare with yours.*

(Avoid going off course.) *Bob, that sounds like an interesting idea with a lot of potential. We really should explore it, after we finish discussing . . .*

Summary

If you can concentrate and coordinate, you can be a tremendous asset to your organization. Once you can see how pieces relate to one another and help develop the thought pattern among the people you work with, attention and recognition will follow.

11.4 FACE TO FACE
Talking in Person to Net More Information

When you need to discuss a touchy subject, do it in person. Observation improves communication. You can tell a lot by looking at people. They send you messages by their posture and walk, how they dress and accessorize, their grooming, and of course, by their gestures and other body language.

Face to face gives you another advantage. You get an additional indicator by viewing reactions. You see as well as hear or read. You can watch for conscious, intentional signs to match the implications you think were in the words.

Arrange a meeting to talk in person if you're convinced your boss thinks you're a mind reader. Meet with your workers as well. They need opportunities to be seen and heard on their views. To feel pride in their jobs, they want to look at you and know you understand what they need. They like when you level with them—face to face.

Strategy

Talk in person when you need to settle any situation. Instead of relying on phone calls or memos, use your observations from face to face meetings to supply missing bits of information vital to getting attention.

Steps

1. Arrange to meet when issues are sticky or complex. Phone calls are fine for short discussions, not for involved ones. And angry remarks you put into writing come back to plague you. Watch the whole picture.

Observe if the actions match the words. If not, use tactful questions to get to reality.

2. Handle the boss's silent treatment. Don't take lack of communication as a personal rejection or worry unnecessarily. Instead of asking if you did something wrong, go after the information you need to know. When your crystal ball doesn't help you pin down the boss to a decisive reply, remember the boss may be under some pressure that's holding up a decision. If you have done something that's annoyed the boss, however, you want to know that, too. In the meantime, you're getting behind in your work. You need a face to face discussion.

3. Put your ego on hold. For the moment you're trying to settle a question. Don't create walls by getting your feelings hurt in the discussion. Try to listen and watch unemotionally and professionally, keeping your mind on the issue and off your feelings.

4. Use humor or a smile. Ease the tension with a friendly gesture. Try to tell a little joke on yourself.

Script

(Handle touchy situations in person.) *Bill, are you free for me to come over right now? I have something we need to discuss that's important to both of us.* (If he refuses) *May I come over after your meeting? This is* important.

(Nudge the unresponsive boss in person.) *Boss, I'm wondering if you need any more information on the proposal I submitted? Or do you just need more time to evaluate it?*

(Meet in person to ease tension.) *Okay, I agree, that wasn't the best idea. Now, let's get back to the issue we're trying to settle.*

Summary

Phone calls and memos are fine for ordinary, simple communication. But when the issue is complex or sensitive, you need the advantage of looking at each other face to face. Above all, don't put your anger in writing. Wait until you calm down, then go settle the matter in person. A rising star keeps fences mended.

11.5 FEEDBACK ————————————————————
Opening Clogged Communication

Clogged communication is like a clogged drainpipe. Very little gets through. In an office, this obstruction causes workers to throw up their hands feeling helpless.

You want your boss to tell you what's going on and how you're doing. And you wish you were allowed to have more of a say so you could feel you have a stake in the success of your company. How do you get the boss to tell you the vital information you need to know to do your work right? How can you pull out priorities, directions, and opinions?

Consider how the boss benefits when the information flows up as well as down. Think how you profit from an exchange with your subordinates. Then propose an easy method to set the feedback process in motion.

If you're not getting the kind of feedback you need from your boss, you can't sit around waiting until a bad evaluation falls on your head. Ask! And if you're not giving to and getting from your workers the kind of feedback you both need, make changes right now.

Strategy

Arrange for specific, constructive feedback. Make contact soon after the start of a new assignment, and establish a set procedure for frequent and periodic feedback after that.

Steps

1. Give your boss a reason and a way. Suggest a system to regularly exchange feedback. When you're on a lower level, you need a way to question high ups and actually get some answers. Somebody has to bother to tell you information that affects your job. Your boss needs to hear opposing views or new suggestions; so when you're proposing, concentrate on consequences. Explain the need and mutual benefits from a regular, definite time to get together each week or month to review the work and plan ahead. Clarify objectives by restating them in your own words, using a common vocabulary.

2. Give effective feedback to your own subordinates. The flip side is how you speak to your workers. In a reassuring tone, express your confidence and let them know you're depending on their abilities. Coach them with suggestions for achieving objectives or making improvements or adjustments. They have to hear from you that their good work is admired. They need praise, encouragement, security and recognition. They want to know their ideas are being considered, if not implemented.

   3. Beware of feedback stumbling blocks. Good feedback means specific, tactful, and nonthreatening remarks and trust in the accuracy of the information given. When comments are critical without being constructive, that's dousing enthusiasm with ice water. Another error is in assuming you know how someone else feels. Unless they tell you, you really don't know. It's also important to limit the amount of information to how much can be digested at one time. If you talk too much, workers get overly anxious about every detail and end up making more mistakes. When you give too little, they're unaware that they keep on repeating the same errors.

Script

   (Ask for the feedback you need and are not getting.) *Boss, I think it'd be very helpful to both of us if we could review the work of my unit on a regular basis. I want to be sure I'm on target, and I know how important it is to you to meet our objectives. Could you spare ten minutes first thing on Tuesday mornings?*

   (Put objectives and priorities into your own words.) *Let me be sure I understand what we're trying to accomplish. You feel this new procedure would increase the number of customers by a third. Is it more important for us to concentrate first on the telephone or on the mail contact?*

   (Give encouraging, specific feedback.) *Joan, the approach you're using is good, but I believe if you and your team put your heads together, you could come up with something even better. I suggest you concentrate your efforts on a tighter background check. I know I can depend on you to come through.*

Summary

   Bosses as well as workers need to give and get information from above and below. It's mutually advantageous. Take the initiative and arrange an exchange. Suggest a regular time for periodic and frequent feedback. Keep tuned to keep attention.

11.6 INTERPRETATION
Introducing Your Company to the Community

If you can link your project—in any way—to a public benefit, you've latched on to another way to gain attention for yourself and free publicity for your company. Maybe the packaging of your product helps the environment. Perhaps you had a video taped as you supervised college student interns. Or you're in charge of hiring the disadvantaged or training unskilled labor in an assembly operation.

When your company expresses a social responsibility by forming partnerships with government agencies and private institutions, both company and community benefit. If you help with this work and then spread the word about it, you benefit too. Keep alert for projects that can produce results and impact.

Businesses have long recognized the sponsorship of special sports events as a means of self promotion and building goodwill for the company while entertaining the public. Some organizations publish and offer to the community booklets with specialized information. Some sponsor training, workshops, and conferences.

Strategy

Suggest a public interest or public event project to develop a dialogue between your company and the community. Then offer to coordinate the effort for your office.

Steps

1. Look into sponsoring communitywide workshops. Spot a need and find the experts for workshops or seminars. It's amazing how much local talent is available. You want to emerge as the company spokesperson for this community service.

2. Look into sponsoring printed information. Checklists, fact sheets, brochures, or audio or visual tapes can be produced "as a public service." Think about some facts that the public needs to know or about important how to's they'd be interested in knowing more about.

3. Translate your profession's technical jargon into plain English. Explain proposed laws to the business community. This could lead to the formation of a study group, which you might be able to chair and then be in position to announce the recommendations.

4. Seek media coverage. Your project merits media attention if it benefits or will have a significant effect on the community. If there is a visual story to tell, contact TV stations; if not, the newspapers. Keep in mind that human interest and exceptions to the rule (unique, first time) spark interest, as does information the public needs to meet a crisis or conflict.

Script

(Suggest sponsoring a community project.) *I'd like to volunteer my services, Boss, on behalf of the company, to launch a communitywide effort to promote volunteerism. If we can focus on a project such as refurbishing a children's center, this would get media coverage and do a tremendous amount of good at the same time.*

(Suggest sponsoring a workshop.) *Boss, I'd like to suggest that our company sponsor a tax legislation workshop open to the community. With that new tax proposal now being debated, there's a great need and sudden interest in receiving more information. It would be received as an important public service.*

(Suggest sponsoring printed information.) *With the current water shortage crisis, we could offer an important service by printing and distributing a booklet with tips on conserving water.*

(Suggest sponsoring interpretive data.) *The newest government regulations are so full of gobbledygook I literally translated them into English. What if our company offered something like this to our local trade association?*

Summary

Answering a community need not only helps people in the community, it also builds good will for the company. Be on the lookout for projects, workshops, or printed matter that your company could sponsor. Offer to coordinate the activity, and you and your company can receive well-deserved attention.

11.7 PUBLICIZING ———————————————————
Getting Your Story Told

You did a fantastic job and nobody even said thanks. Nobody knew. To be perceived as a rising star, get your accomplishments publicized. This takes three things:

(1) The result has to be important, significant, or of widespread interest to a particular group or the general public. Company newsletters, professional journals, and trade magazines are receptive to all aspects of the work, especially task-force recommendations or divisional findings. Radio, television, and newspapers focus on items relevant to the whole community or that contain good human interest.

(2) Contact channels appropriate for that particular story. Within the daily newspaper, for example, decide if you want to talk to city desk, or financial, sports, religion, medical, travel, or consumer news. Or maybe you want to submit a provocative letter to the editor or give your views in an article for the op-ed page.

(3) Present your material or yourself in an effective way. Put printed information into a form the media can use: fact sheets kept current, press releases, articles, audio and video tapes, pamphlets, and brochures. Prepare for phone contact with busy editors. Understand the time restraints of broadcast interviews. Narrow your message for talk shows.

Strategy

Analyze all your activities to find aspects to publicize. Consider which ones would appeal to company, business and professional, community, or national media.

Steps

1. Check with your boss. Each organization has its own rules (or no rules) about media contact. Tell the boss the significance of the proposed story and get the go-ahead.

2. Alert the media that you have a story. With accurate, concise, and condensed information, call appropriate editors to determine interest. For TV/radio news coverage of a company event, send a brief fact sheet (they consider press releases antiquated junk mail) to the assignment editor a week ahead and call late afternoon for airing the next day. Immediately go to the point of your call, answer any questions, and ask if they need anything else to cover the story. For a newspaper release, write in a reverse pyramid with the basics on top so your story can be cut from the bottom to meet space demands.

3. Prepare for TV/radio news interview. Don't be surprised if everything you said is edited down to a ten-second sound bite. To influence what's included, develop and keep honing one main point until you can chop it down to ten seconds. Memorize this (only this to sound spontaneous). In case there's more time, list the questions you can anticipate—not only the basics, but how you feel about something happening in your company. For complicated issues, provide a simplified fact sheet. Listen intently to be sure you understand the question before you respond. Be prepared for follow-up questions to explain your reply.

4. Prepare for TV/radio talk shows. Make your most important point first, rather than leading up to it. Keep it simple and straightforward, with three or four points to support your message. You're educating the interviewer as well as the public. Mention your company and your boss whenever you can slide this in gracefully. But focus on issues to avoid sounding self-serving. At the end of the program, repeat your message.

5. Look good on TV. The audience needs only a few seconds to judge you. Dress simply. Keep the attention on your words, not on a flashy tie or jangling jewelry. Don't wear anything new, but something you've always felt comfortable in. To emphasize, lean toward the interviewer. Don't look away, bounce in your chair, or lean way back. Forget the camera and look at the interviewer. If there are other guests, look at the person talking.

6. Sound conversational and in control. You're there because you know more about your subject than most people do. Act in command; don't just respond. Sound enthusiastic, smile, nod, show you're at ease with your remarks. Be careful not to lose your temper, just disagree politely. Forget it's TV and enjoy your conversation with one person who knows little or nothing about your business or project.

Script

(Get the boss's okay.) *Boss, if you have no objection, I'd like to submit an article to our national journal about the success we've had with this method. If they print it, it'd be great publicity for the company.*

(Call your journal editor.) *Would you be interested in a story about a cost-cutting method that's often overlooked? . . . Great, I'd be glad to submit an article for your consideration.*

(Call your company editor.) *I have a story that might interest you. Our accounting department has developed a time-slashing system for busy directors that . . .*

(Call newspaper, TV, or radio editors.) *We have an answer to the public's demand for more information about . . . Would you be interested in hearing about it?* (Keep voice friendly and animated.)

(Prepare a ten-second sound bite.) *We're elated with results from Greentree Corporation's new team-management approach. Our quality is up, our costs are down, and our service is better than ever.*

Summary

Submit a letter to the editor or an op ed article when you have an answer to a problem. If it's within the company, contact the editor of your newsletter; for the trade, your journal; affecting the whole community, your local newspaper, radio, or TV. If your project has significant results, such as a new procedure that could benefit others, report it to the appropriate media. Review all you do to find some aspect worthy of media attention, and consequently, of more attention to you.

11.8 A GUIDE FOR DEALING WITH DIFFICULT MEDIA

A reporter calls, and you hold your breath. You don't know what's coming at you. Even seasoned politicians are scared of media traps.

Whether the request is for a radio, TV, or print interview or for you to respond to a few questions over the phone, stop and think before you say a word. You can't allow yourself to be pushed into talking off the top of your head just because somebody else has a deadline to meet.

Be as accommodating and friendly as you can. You may simply be asked to confirm factual data or public record. Maybe they only want background information on your two employees who were in an accident this morning. Just don't be rushed into making mistakes that will be highly publicized. Reporters come prepared to ask the questions they've carefully thought out. You must take similar steps. If you want to sound good, you need a little time to get ready.

Strategy

Grab control by insisting on the time you're available to talk to the media. Just because a reporter throws a question at you doesn't mean you must answer instantaneously. For a simple issue, explain you can't talk now but will call right back. When the matter is complicated, arrange a meeting a few hours later to give yourself a chance to review the issues.

Steps

1. Be clear on the company position. When setting up the meeting, ask what topics are to be covered and how your organization fits into the story. If this is a controversial or sensitive matter, discuss with your boss points that should be stressed. Write down what you hope to accomplish as a result of the interview.

2. Anticipate the questions. With a couple of trusted colleagues, you can figure out most of the queries and kick around answers that best fit the message you want to get across. If this is for TV or radio, prepare a ten-twenty-second summary of that message. A news story will probably be thirty seconds or less (even a major story is covered in ninety seconds), so get to the point immediately and keep all answers short and simple. Anticipate a "why?" response, to which you can then explain your previous remark.

3. Tell the truth. The evasive "no comment" makes you appear guilty. While most reporters are honorable, don't depend on confidentiality. Don't even ask for it with "That's off the record." If you refuse to see reporters, they'll probably get the information somewhere else, and you will have blown your chance to tell your side.

4. Be ready for troublesome types. Some reporters have a sneaky way of going after the quote they want from you. When you find yourself sandbagged, keep calm. Move smoothly and quickly to something positive. If you lose your temper on camera, the audience can be unforgiving. Below are sample responses to attack queries.

Script

(When a reporter's call catches you off guard.) *May I call you right back?* (Write out a sentence or two, edit for accuracy, brevity, and quotability before returning the call.)

(When a reporter requests an interview.) *What subject will we be discussing? And if you'll tell me the type of information you need, I'll have it ready for you.*

(Explain when you can't comment.) *I'd like to talk to you, but the case is pending and the court won't allow us to say anything about it for now. I'll get back to you as soon as I can.*

Handling troublesome reporters

NEEDLERS try to stir up a little excitement at your expense. They goad you, puncturing your ego, just to get a reaction from you. Don't bite their bait. However, you can't let the implication stand. Take the offense, being particularly friendly and factual.

Q You were appointed just to fill an affirmative action quota, weren't you?

A I've been with the company six years. (smile) Check my background and achievements, Mike, and it will be crystal clear I was brought in and stayed on because I'm competent.

JUGULARS try to cut your throat by getting you to admit to poor planning or poor policy. Ignore the attack and shift attention to a positive action you've taken or are planning to take. Let the public see you're in the midst of solving a problem.

Q The large number of complaints about your service started when you hired a new manager. Are you planning to replace Paul Cross with a more competent manager?

A The Superior Company's only concern is to provide the best possible service for our customers. In all past performances, Paul Cross has proved very competent. Upon learning of complaints, we appointed a team to investigate. Just as soon as we have the complete report on Friday, I can tell you the exact action we'll take. (If an error is found, accept the blame, repent, and say how the mistake will be corrected.)

TRAPPERS throw out bait, hoping to lure unsuspecting you into admitting a blunder. They try to get you to contradict something previously stated by you or your company.

Q Now, really, you're not saying you expect a turnaround by next month, are you?

A Yes, I am, Liz. That's exactly what I am saying, and, furthermore, we're planning to . . . (Go on to the next point.)

PROSECUTORS try to trip you up with tricky interrogation. You'll recognize the Have you stopped beating your wife? type of question because no matter how you answer, you lose.

Q You haven't stopped fighting their attempts to get the hiring policy changed? You don't deny that, do you?

A (Don't touch the question in that form—rephrase.) Dan, if you're asking me whether I believe in equal pay for equal work, of course I do.

ICEMEN just stand there saying nothing after your comment. This manipulative freeze is designed to pressure you to keep on talking because they hope you'll blurt out some secret to fill the awful silence. Fool them. Don't be intimidated and don't speak without thinking about your answer. If you have nothing to add, just smile. If you're ready to make another point, then leap in.

A In addition, I'd like to point to the success we've had with . . .

MUTILATERS mean well, but have a problem. They get everything mixed up. When they butcher the facts, gently straighten them out.

Q I understand you're handling 125 percent more cases than last year?

A Let me explain, John. We are handling 125 more cases than last year. That increase of 15 percent enables us to apply . . .

SUPPOSERS always have a hazardous hypothetical question. Usually, to answer it would mean committing yourself to an action you haven't completely thought through. Steer clear.

Q What if the board rules that you can't continue providing that type of service?

A Peter, there are so many variables, I can't even make a good guess at a response to that. However, I can tell that all our efforts and energies are aimed at providing . . .

Summary

Take the time to think before you speak. If you haven't faced the media before, of course you're going to be scared. But you need the experience. The only remedy for getting over your fright is preparation, thinking through the probable questions and the best responses. You can have a few reminder notes, but don't memorize anything except your ten-second message. You don't want to seem stiff or anxious. Instead keep your basic message firmly in mind and your answers will flow from that. When you can speak effectively to the public for your organization, your star is rising.

12

POLISHING FAVORABLE
PERSONALITY TRAITS

In a highly competitive climate, the closer we come to unrealized aims, the more frustrated we get. When discrimination's not a factor, you wonder what's holding you back. The restraint may be an invisible net of perceptions held by people you work for and with. If so, what can you do without the power to change anyone but yourself?

Therein lies the key. You *can* change yourself. You change perceptions by changing the way *you* act. It works like this: Act the way you want to be, and eventually you stop pretending and become the way you act. Your actions alter your attitude and, in turn, change the way others see you.

Actions and attitudes grow out of habits, which are formed by conscious choice. When a choice is satisfying, the brain stores that decision and uses it repeatedly as the same situation arises until the act is automatic. When an action no longer serves you, you have the power to change the habit and, in doing so, to improve the opinion others have about you.

12.1 EYE OPENER
Deciphering How Others Perceive You

In ranking qualities, bosses often give top rating to getting along with others and motivating them to work better. Some say these skills are 80 percent of the job. So how others regard you becomes increasingly important in your quest to be judged a rising star.

But unless people tell you, how can you know what they're feeling? You don't know; however, you can make a good guess by becoming more observant. You can learn to peek behind the mask of those who put up a good front. Study their body language, listen more closely to the meaning of thier words, clarify their inferences, and question suspected hidden meanings.

Still, it's difficult to see yourself as others see you. To assess perceptions, you also need a strategy, planning, and good records.

Strategy

Devise your own perception-watch plan. Work from a checklist and keep a diary. These tools will help you transform attitudes about you and your work from neutral and negative to needed and positive. As you enhance perceptions of your value, you protect your position and attract attention for your future.

Steps

1. Define your weak spots. We all have vulnerable areas. Mark yours on the following checklist of negative personality traits. You know deep down the ones that you are going to have to change. This is just for you. Nobody's watching. So be excruciatingly honest with yourself.

COMMON NEGATIVE TRAITS

_____ abrasive, harsh, rubs others the wrong way

_____ aloof, unsociable, disinterested

_____ arrogant, haughty, know it all, unearned superiority

_____ backbiting, highly critical, judges others severely

_____ bickering, griping, haggling, petty

_____ blocking, obstructing, prevents action

_____ boring, repetitious

_____ complaining, nagging, whining, acts like a martyr

_____ careless, negligent, inattentive, does slipshod work

_____ exaggerating, magnifying, makes empty boasts

_____ gossipy, prying, snoopy

_____ harassing, heckling, needling, provoking, goading

_____ indecisive, wishy-washy, changeable, inconsistent

_____ indifferent, uncaring, clock-watching

_____ inflexible, unbending, stubborn, pigheaded

_____ insensitive, inconsiderate, imposing

_____ insincere, hypocritical, two-faced, steals credit

_____ interrupting, pestering

_____ loud, blustering

_____ opinionated, domineering, preachy, runs roughshod

_____ pessimistic, sees perpetual doom and gloom

_____ pompous, pretentious, self-important

_____ procrastinating, stalling

_____ pushy, presumptuous, bossy, takes over

_____ ridicules, finds fault, dumps blame on you

_____ rude, insolent, curt, abrupt

_____ vain, conceited

_____ undependable, unreliable, can't be trusted to perform

2. *Write a daily, crisp narrative of relevant and significant interactions.* You now know what signals you are looking for. In a small notebook, list the few traits you're trying to improve. Every day by each trait, state whatever relevant reactions you observed and heard. Get conversations and discussions going by tossing out some questions, then later record the responses.

3. *Evaluate responses over a two-week period.* Using a scale of 1 to 5, with 1 being little positive reaction and 5 the maximum, draw a chart to show your progress and detect areas that still need improvement. You gain insight by treating a subjective evaluation in an objective manner. By charting you can see if you're being consistent, treating people in the same improved way day after day.

Sample Diary Notes

Trait to change: Boring, repetitious

2/10   Martha started to agree with me, but Jake interrupted, as usual.

2/12   I was about to tell a long, involved story, but caught myself and made it brief. Pat and Jim paid attention and asked me questions.

2/13   Had lunch with the gang. I was trying to tell about a phone call I received. Carl yelled for me to get to the point. Everyone joined in. Back to square one.

2/17   At the meeting I gave the one-minute report I rehearsed at home. Jake tried to interrupt me, but I ignored him. I think I did very well. The boss nodded approval.

2/20   We had a discussion about which equipment to order. I offered an explanation of the technical language, and they seemed bored, so I shut up.

EVALUATION CHART									
(1 = minimum positive reaction; 5 = maximum positive reaction)									
TRAIT:	2/10	2/11	2/12	2/13	2/14	2/17	2/18	2/19	2/20	2/21
boring, repetitious	2		5	1		5			4	

Summary

Your ultimate goal is to feel good about the way you act and how you treat the people around you. Becoming more alert to what turns others off and charting your efforts over a few weeks period will help you achieve that aim.

12.2 TURN AROUND
Reversing Exasperating Personality Traits

Once you get a bad reputation it's difficult—but not impossible—to change the flaws that cause people to ignore you. Psychologists tell us we can alter our lives by altering our attitudes. You have the essential potential to correct impressions that detract from your value. Only you can do this. And the only one you can count on changing is yourself.

The modifications you achieve show through in your mannerisms, posture, and an air of self-confidence that says you're worth paying attention to. When you think, feel, and act differently, others sense it and change their reactions and responses to you.

By working on the negative traits you listed previously, you're already on the way to becoming the image of yourself that you visualize. Now substitute more effective and positive habits for the ones you are displacing.

Strategy

Emphasize positive traits that will replace the negative habits holding you back. Begin every day with fresh resolve to work on the new habits. Bolster your efforts by visualization and affirmations. Look intently for opportunities to act out your resolve. Start making friends without waiting for others to come to you.

Steps

1. Define your goals. Recognize certain habits that once gave you satisfaction but no longer do. Analyze the situation and how you've changed. Accept yourself as you are today with the new objectives you've developed. Today's desires will motivate you to spell out your current aims, replacing old habits with new, more satisfying ones.

2. List positive traits you want to substitute for old habits. Examples of positive traits to replace negative ones:

diplomatic	confrontational
focused, centered	ambiguous, unclear on issues
friendly, warm	unsociable, aloof, distant
gracious	insolent, vain
good listener	opinionated, dogmatic
helpful	arrogant
honest, sincere, straightforward	slippery, manipulative, phony
modest, unpretentious	pompous, self-important
outgoing, happy for others	self-centered, indifferent
persistent	pestering
polite, well-mannered	rude, brash, impolite
quiet confidence	loud, blustering
realistic, legitimate	exaggerating
respectful, noninterfering	busybody, unasked-for adviser
tactful, sensitive	prying, butting in

3. Refine your remarks. Become more concerned with how you may be offending people unintentionally. Refrain from petty sniping. Others hearing it will fear you'll be spreading stories about them as well. Try to be less emotional when giving your opinions. Yours is not the only reasoning that may be right. Be careful about interrupting, and listen more intently to what's being said. Admit your mistakes; don't try to alibi out of them.

Script

(Disagree professionally.) *We seem to have different figures on that. I'll be glad to double-check and get back to you this afternoon, okay?*

(Start with a quality you admire or a point of agreement.) *I've always regarded you as straightforward, and I know you believe those allegations to be true, however . . .*

(Don't tell people what they're thinking or feeling.) *What you really want is . . .* can be rephrased to *please tell me in your own words what it is that you really want.*

(The sin is not in erring, but in covering up. *A mistake was made* is evasive and arrogant. Tell what experience has taught you.) *Yes, we should have been better prepared. From now on, we are taking the added precaution of . . .*

Summary

Getting rid of negative personality traits requires taking a good, long look at the way you've been acting. After you've pinpointed the troublespots, define the positive traits you want to develop to replace them. Be especially concerned about protecting other people's feelings and they'll pay more attention to you.

12.3 RAPPORT
Making Each Person Feel Special

It may be nice to be nice, and being considerate is polite. But much more is at stake—your own best interest. People pay attention to and want to work with those who try to meet their needs in small as well as major ways.

You let them finish their thoughts without interrupting. You talk about the lessons to be learned from their mistakes. You let them save face instead of backing them into a corner. You help them succeed and feel good about their work. You encourage them to tell you about their little successes.

In doing this you stand apart because most people are so busy, so wrapped up in themselves, so intent on impressing everybody, that they often ignore the people they work with every day. Your motives may be pure, but by treating every person as important, by showing interest in each one as someone special, you are building a devoted following. You'll have a vigorous cheering section.

Strategy

Make people matter. Establish in your office a cordial, caring relationship with as many people as you can, at every level. Aim for mutual support and improvement.

Steps

1. Enhance another's self-image when you request or order. Explain to others how they will realize their goals or gain approval or achieve a competitive edge by doing what you want done. Consult them for suggestions in their areas of expertise. Fire up enthusiasm by showing a sincere concern. And call them by their right names. Don't say "Lenny" if Lenny prefers "Leonard."

2. Be a good listener. Let others unwind when their feelings run high. Allow them to finish presenting an idea without your butting in. Use questions to coach or guide rather than superimposing your thoughts as the gospel. Pull their ideas out of them and help them express themselves more clearly.

3. Be more generous with compliments. Instead of hogging all the credit for yourself, share it with others who played a part. Tell teammates or workers how essential their performance is to meeting the goals of your unit. Express your confidence in their abilities.

4. Make others feel good about your criticism. Convey the message that you know they're trying hard to do good work and your comments are meant to help them get where they want to go. Scolding and embarrassing destroys ego and initiative and builds resentment. Let others make their own mistakes, then help them convert the mistake into a positive lesson.

5. *Fight for the rights of your workers.* Back up your subordinates when an unfair directive comes down. Do what's right, keep the faith, and you'll gain their respect and everlasting loyalty.

Script

(Applaud another's competence.) *Ted, you know so much more about machines than I do. Would you please take a look at this and tell me . . .*

(Show people they're special by helping them get where they want to go.) *I'd like to see you get ahead. If your aim is to become an assistant manager, what do you think you would have to learn to accomplish this? . . . I think you're on the right track. Let's work out a little plan that can keep you going in that direction.*

(Give compliments that are sincere.) *I am impressed with the work you did while I was away. It was a difficult job and you really came through. Thanks so much.*

(Give criticism that's constructive.) *I know how much time you've devoted to this. It's good, but you could make it even better. You're relying so heavily on harsh reality that you're overlooking benefits. People need to hear the former, but they want to hear the latter.*

Summary

People aren't robots. They need to be treated with genuine regard and concern. Let them know somebody thinks they're worthwhile. Pick up on bits of personal stories so that you can ask about their interests. Questions help you establish rapport and get others to open up. Tell your workers how proud you are of their performance and how essential they are to the total operation. Given this sense of belonging, they'll feel the security they need and repay you by singing your praises.

12.4 LEADERSHIP ————————————————————

Providing Vision and Positive Direction

When it comes to leadership, a title isn't vital. Whatever your position, if yours is an influential voice in response to perplexing situations, you're noticed as a leader.

Adhere to a solid core of principles and you can grasp what's needed. The actions you suggest put principle into practice. You might believe, for example, that everyone should be treated fairly and suggest an incentive bonus as equity for effort. By placing people above procedures, you establish mutual dependency and trust. This cooperation improves morale and increases production.

Start by having basic company policies etched in your mind. Know why they were formulated. Then you can display intelligent foresight because what you say will flow from your understanding of the background. That, along with your personal set of beliefs, enables you to articulate a deep conviction that your company should move in a given direction. As you offer vision and a sense of direction, you are perceived as a leader.

Strategy

Dare to speak up and reveal your vision for the company and your ideas on making that vision a reality. Use a knowledge of your company's history and policies along with a belief in your own set of principles to respond to problems.

Steps

1. Convert negatives to positives. You can't achieve a goal that's stated as being against something. By reshaping the idea into what you *do* want, you can develop strategy and tactics to achieve the objective. Look to your principles and company policies as your guidelines and you'll appear confident, definite, decisive, organized, and in control.

2. Conceptualize, then analyze. Let your thoughts flow without judging them. Play with the ridiculous. Maybe there's a kernel of value there from which a realistic concept can emerge. Now examine your creative thinking in realistic terms until you can articulate your concept in clear, concise language, along with the plan to achieve it. Be assertive when you've figured a better way to accomplish something.

3. Take calculated risks in areas you control. Top management is looking for innovative thinking, but first investigate your ideas so as not to go off half-cocked. See if there are sufficient resources and know-how to carry them out. Enjoy the debate instead of dreading it by knowing, before you present the idea, how probable objections can be met. Be willing to compromise after listening to your people or your customers, as long as you don't sacrifice your principles.

Script

(Restate negative as positive.) *We all seem to be saying that we can't suffer the decreased output. In other words, what changes do we have to make to increase the output, how much, and by when?*

(Take the initiative.) *There may be a better way to accomplish that. I'd like to help explore the possibility of increasing output by . . .*

(Present a positive approach to an impossible assignment.) *I'd be glad to supervise the computer operators even though I don't know too much about computers. However, the university offers a one-day workshop teaching this kind of management. That would be a good investment for us.*

(Give definite, decisive, relevant directions.) *If we're going to beat the competition, this has to be completed by 3 P.M., and mailed out this afternoon* rather than *This has to be completed soon.*

Summary

First you focalize, then you vocalize. People pay attention when you can articulate your vision and provide direction. Dig deeply for the real issue or important principle involved. Look to play a cohesive role, suggesting ways to mesh divergent views. Think through probable consequences before you speak up, being careful not to knee jerk when there's a problem. Take the time to explore the available options and don't (accidentally or purposely) usurp the boss's authority.

12.5 TRUST
Exuding Confidence and Inspiring Loyalty

Bosses look for people they can depend on to understand what's needed and to act decisively. You're not much better than a robot if you aren't willing to move within the bounds of your authority. Keep going back to the boss, asking that approval be programmed before you take a step, and you're regarded as a milquetoast.

If you want your boss to trust you, take a chance even though you may make a mistake. As long as your act is reasonable and not reckless, you'll gain both the boss's respect and your own self-confidence.

To build confidence and loyalty among your subordinates, make their errors seem easy to correct. Keep the criticism impersonal. Treat them as trustworthy instead of hog-tying them, demanding a dozen sign-offs before they can act. When you trust them enough to let them learn from a challenge, they grow in the process.

Strategy

Win trust from your boss, colleagues, and workers by acting with resolve, keeping your word, and showing that mistakes are a learning experience. A rising star inspires confidence.

Steps

1. Develop a decisive work style. When you're faced with a dilemma and can't decide which alternative is worse, broaden your choices. Look for other options. Try hard to work it out yourself before running to the boss to decide.

2. Keep your promises. Dependable work habits build trust, and acting responsibly earns you a good reputation. Listen to a request in its entirety before you make any promises. Give yourself a little leeway on deadlines, then deliver ahead of schedule. Send timely reminders to help others keep their promises to you when you're dependent on them for segments of work you have to turn in on time. Build that same safety margin into assignments you give your workers.

3. Treat mistakes in a positive way. When you make a mistake, admit it instantly, apologize, and state what corrective action you're taking. If one of your peers blunders, help bring the group together with suggested action rather than let the group continue attacking the offender. Express your trust and confidence in your workers. Treat their mistakes as learning experiences so that they don't spend half the day documenting approval and writing memos to justify their decisions.

4. Understand confidentiality procedures. Know the rules for your particular office or, if you're the boss, set the rules you want followed. If you're new, ask before you blunder by poking your nose into material that's off limits.

Script

(Build trust by showing your self-confidence. Brainstorm by yourself or with colleagues to come up with more options instead of bothering the boss.) *I've run into a brick wall. How else can I get the information I need? Who might be able to help me?*

(Show you can be counted on by acting responsibly.) *Kay, something unforeseen happened with the printer that may cause a delay with the report. Would it be all right if you receive it tomorrow morning instead of this afternoon?*

(Follow confidentiality rules.) *What's the procedure here about opening mail marked 'private' or 'confidential'? Are we free to take files off the boss's desk or out of the drawer?*

Summary

Being trusted is a privilege earned over a period of time. When you try hard, see the broad picture, move decisively, and get results, others are drawn to you. Create trust and confidence by acting as if you know what you're supposed to be doing and you're determined to get it done.

12.6 MAGNETS
Pulling People Toward You

An exhilarated person gets attention. You feel the magnetic attraction as energy flows from one to another. A simple and sincere smile can be your magnet because it makes you look as if you're succeeding, and most of us like to be with successful people. The smile also says you're reaching out, trying to make others feel comfortable to be with you.

If those around you seem indifferent, maybe you need to give them a little encouragement by being friendlier. Perhaps you have to amass information that's more interesting, items you can all get excited about. When you know enough about a subject to develop some strong convictions, your own enthusiasm comes through. Or maybe the thrill is gone now that you've worked your way up, and you have to find a way to get back some of the old zest.

You can't will your workers to be enthusiastic. You have to feel it yourself before you can instill it in others. But you can generate excitement by giving people the freedom to work out details for themselves as well as carefully explaining your incentive program.

Strategy

Become more animated to attract favorable attention. Increase your energy, search for ideas that create excitement, and improve the manner in which you get your message out. Rekindle the spark you used to feel when using skills you're no longer practicing.

Steps

1. Recharge your energy. Eat right, get enough sleep and exercise, and enjoy some form of recreation to produce the energy you need to go back to work. When something's troubling you, once you decide how you're going to resolve the difficulty, you'll feel renewed energy. Learn how to ease off and let go when matters are out of your control. There's no point in tearing yourself apart, you're only draining your energy.

2. Allow yourself to be innovative. You don't have to be a creative genius to practice adaptation. When you read or hear about a good idea being used in another field or another company, think how that idea could be applied to your work. Maybe it can stand alone, maybe it's the way to expand your current project. Once you've worked out the puzzle, enthusiastically present it to your staff meeting.

3. Use the sharpened skills you used to enjoy. Forget the job description and assume responsibility for making your assignment more interesting. If you can't work your prized skill into your current job, offer to teach it to other employees who could use the training. And if that doesn't work out, look at an after-hours activity. If, for example, you enjoy public speaking but it's no longer part of your job, join the speakers' bureau of your favorite civic or charitable organization. If you like to train, a community school could use your talent once a week.

4. Study how you come across. Go through your photo albums and examine the expressions on your face. Do you look pleasant, animated, and are you smiling? Listen to tape recordings you've made to hear if there's life to your voice. When you get assignments, do you sound eager, and when you give assignments, do you make them sound interesting? To renew your excitement, try rewarding yourself after you complete each stage of your project or win a new account.

Script

(Show your enthusiasm by adapting ideas.) *There's a great article in this month's journal that's right on target for us. It describes how to improve the delivery system. I've made copies for each of you so that we can discuss the ideas more fully.*

(Show your eagerness to take training.) *Boss, I really am grateful for the chance to learn new skills.*

(Recharge your spirit by teaching others.) *Boss, you know I was a salesperson before I came to work here. I'd be glad to coach our other managers in selling skills for those times when they have to approach directors about . . .*

Summary

There's an air of excitement about a rising star. The enthusiasm and animation are contagious. Rising stars are not afraid to be creative, to suggest something a little unusual, or to try a new approach adapted from someone else's idea. Rising stars find ways to keep recharging their energy and stimulating others around them.

12.7 ENJOYMENT ―――――――――――――――――――――
Promoting a Spirit of Fun and Good Humor

There is no eleventh commandment "Thou shalt find no pleasure in thy work." Why can't you be serious about your commitment and still enjoy being in your office and, at times, actually having fun or a few good laughs? Maybe you can't transform the whole staid organization, but you certainly can influence, if not control, the climate in your own bailiwick.

If you're in charge, you decide if the atmosphere will be relaxed or rigid. You set the tone, choosing to use persuasion or coercion. You can encourage creativity by involving your workers in decisions affecting their work rather than by being dictatorial. You can sense when to pick up the pace or slow it down if the group is exhausted.

But you don't have to be the boss to turn up the thermostat. You can find ways to pep up your meetings. Slavery to meeting routine leaves everyone bushed, bored, or floored. Add a little excitement by being prepared for a debate on an urgent issue. Vary your report from the standard presentation. And certainly one of the best ways to bring enjoyment to the office is by constantly finding excuses to celebrate.

Strategy

Appoint yourself a committee of one to break the tension. Act as a cohesive force, helping your cohorts band together. Point out the humor in situations. Initiate celebrations. And let yourself be happy for other people.

Steps

1. Present information in an interesting way. Invite experts as guest speakers to your staff meetings. Show a video tape to give an in-depth picture. Play an audio tape of an interview with customers. Encourage team competition to come up with the best answers.

2. See the opportunity. Instead of complaining about a tough assignment, see it as a challenge to improve a skill. Pick up the gauntlet when it's a job you never tried before but are qualified to learn how to do.

3. Exhibit your excitement when others achieve. Share in the joy of their victory. Be happy for them without feeling jealousy or resentment. Your time will come. You don't have to go one better with a story about what you did that tops their accomplishment or news. Relax and help them savor the moment.

4. Celebrate little successes as a unit. Encourage team spirit. Make your department or project one that works together and commemorates a good try as well as a win. Add a little hoopla. You don't have to break out into a chorus of the company song when you land a new account or your team breaks a record and comes in ahead of schedule. But celebrate in some fashion—by bringing in a diet-defying cake or awarding pins, buttons, badges, framed certificates, or gag gifts.

5. Use peer pressure to motivate your workers. An even better celebration is the presentation of cash bonuses for each member of a winning team. It is more motivating and effective to award teams rather than individuals. As the team pulls together, it leans on each member to produce. Teams, usually limited to ten each, give each worker a greater chance to win and avoids pitting worker against worker, with possible petty but bitter rivalry.

Script

(When you're too scared to show excitement about a new assignment.) *Boss, I'm really looking forward to my new job and I'd like to prepare for it. I've studied your requirements and the recommendations from the previous director. I have a few questions* . . . (Write down what's upsetting you. If you can't work out a solution or evolve a plan, maybe you misunderstood aspects you need clarified.)

(Be generous in spirit.) *Jeff, what wonderful news! I am so happy for you. You certainly deserve the award and it couldn't happen to a nicer guy.*

(Get others excited by showing your own excitement.) *Do you realize how far-reaching this is? Answers to the problem they gave our team to solve could spill over and affect every department. We could be real heros besides collecting the prize.*

Summary

Find ways to make your work place a more pleasant place to work. You don't have to be the boss to bring in some fun and excitement or help get people working together. Nor do you have to score wins to celebrate. When you acknowledge good attempts, you're depositing positive attention to your account.

12.8 ETHICS
A Guide for Matching Means and Ends

Getting and keeping attention means you're selling yourself. Now selling yourself and your message is an honorable endeavor as long as you don't sell your soul in the process. You can promote yourself and persuade others without resorting to the creation of false images.

Good ends can't justify bad means. If you're thinking, "As long as the record looks good, what's the difference?" think again. Devious methods (deliberately lying, cheating, shortchanging, disrupting, backstabbing, stealing credit) may get you an instant goal, but you risk losing many supporters. The real you shows through when you try to hide beneath false colors, and you gain only disapproval by exploiting the people you work with (or anyone else for that matter).

Any manipulating you do should be to yourself—getting yourself to act better, strive harder. The really tough question is what to do when two rights conflict. Or when something is legally right, but morally wrong. And how do you make a decision when there are no company guidelines?

Strategy

Request that rules be enforced and that clear guidelines be established for your organization where none exist. Policy has to be defined when company, worker, and customer rights are in conflict.

Steps

1. Eliminate bad acts that achieve good results. The easy decisions are when right and wrong are perfectly clear. For example, an elementary school principal craved national achievement awards so badly that he cheated by elevating the test scores he reported. The children, teachers, and parents were all highly motivated as a result of the awards—until word of fraud leaked out and there was a full-scale investigation. Abuses needn't be that dramatic; they can start small and grow. From the top on down, the message must be clear that breaking the law will not be tolerated.

2. Establish guidelines for ethical employee behavior. At other times, there may be no violation but there may be the appearance or perception of wrongdoing. Suppose, for instance, you are offered gifts by people receiving orders from your company. Are you allowed to accept? If so, is there a limit on the value? You need a clear and stated policy.

3. Establish procedure when rights are in conflict. Even more difficult are times when company rights, employee rights, and customer rights go head to head. You promised to give employees accurate and truthful information, but you're afraid the company can't stand a plunge in morale. You've always shown compassion for those who deal with you, but now you have to call in accounts that are overextended. The answers will take protracted soul-searching and reexamination of the company's mission.

Script

(A little cheating is still cheating.) *Jane, will you punch in for me while I run across the street and pick up some Danish?* (on the surface, no problem until a habit is formed and the requests mushroom.)

Jane, please punch me out when you leave. I need a few hours off this afternoon to attend to personal business.
(Give Jane the backing she needs to refuse.) *Oh, George, I'm sorry I can't do that. You know they're strictly enforcing the time card rule now, and everyone has to punch his or her own card—or else.*

(Set a firm policy when there's no clear right or wrong behavior.) *Boss, I don't know what to do about this expensive pen set I was given by the Briber Company. I can't find the appropriate response spelled out any place. And I certainly don't want to cause an incident that could blow up in our faces.*

(Establish procedure when rights are in conflict.) *If we reduce the time, we reduce the quality, and we've always promised top quality. But if we don't reduce the time, we cut our profit and can't survive in the business. Why don't we study a few of the cases we have to deal with, exploring the implications and consequences openly and freely? Only after reviewing our obligations to the public, our workers, and the company will we be able to state a clear, concise policy.*

Summary

Most people want to do the honorable thing and look for ethical leadership. Rising stars accept responsibility for their own actions. Morally, what's the difference between petty theft and major theft? Stealing supplies from the office is stealing, just as is digging into the cash register or changing records to skim money for yourself. When there's no stated policy and no clear right or wrong action, ask that a policy be established and written in clear, no-nonsense language. If rights are in conflict, suggest that discussion groups or training sessions explore the ramifications and come up with a concisely stated policy.

PART IV

RESPECT

BEING PERCEIVED AS A PRIZED PART OF THE COMPANY

You can't settle for less. It's your birthright. Every individual deserves respect as a fellow human being. You should want more than mere courtesy if people have been underestimating your value to the company.

When you feel you make a difference and you've *earned* your good reputation, you move up to a level of high self-esteem and secure self-confidence. Then you can afford to be generous and cooperative in helping others, your organization, and in the process, in helping yourself.

If you go around thinking, "I get no respect around here," it's time to change the way you're coming across. Plan the actions and responses you are going to make. Take a risk by taking credit for your work. You're already accepting blame for your mistakes. Now grab the glory when you do something good. Take a risk by showing initiative. People can't know what you're capable of doing if you don't show them how well and fast you get things done. And take a risk by speaking up for yourself, or your rights will continue to be trampled upon.

13

SHEDDING A DOORMAT IMAGE

If you don't like being berated, ignored, or dumped on, then stop letting people walk all over you. Roll up that doormat image and spell out how you do expect to be treated. Otherwise you're bestowing upon your boss, peers, and workers the right to wrap you in chains of inferiority.

When people annoy you, tell them. If they talk when you have the floor, stop and wait for quiet. If they're late for appointments, leave. If your good work isn't recognized, point out your accomplishments. If an issue is important to you, get support for it. If the workload is unfair, ask that the system be adjusted.

Change the way you act, and you change the way others react to you. Take control by appreciating your own worth. Remember that organizations are looking for innovative thinking. If you disagree with your boss because you see a better way, say so. It's within easy grasp to earn self-esteem and the esteem of others by making them aware that you deserve respect. Respect, however, is mutual, giving and getting. Reexamine how you handle your workers who take advantage, put down, disparage, and discriminate. Then question if you accord subordinates the same respect you give your boss.

13.1 BOORS

Demanding Courtesy—Even from Your Boss

You can't bargain for courteous treatment. You give it; you get it because everyone is entitled to it. If bullies sense you're intimidated, you'll never earn their respect. They keep perceiving you as their victim.

While you may have no control over what is said to you, you do have a choice in how you respond. Even when your boss bellows across the room instead of correcting you privately. Even when your colleague hurls a nasty charge to your face or behind your back. Even when your valued worker goes into a prima donna dance.

When you're being treated uncivilly, resist the counterpunch. Remain polite as you explain your feelings or your position. You can stand up for yourself without threatening the boss's authority or stomping on the egos of others.

Perfect the ability to toss out questions, a potent weapon for speaking up and speaking out. Accepting rude behavior without comment is not being tough. It's being weak.

Strategy

Make others realize they're treating you badly. Throw rude people off guard by being polite yet firm.

Steps

1. Allow offenders to feel important. The rude and crude may lack self-esteem, using boorish behavior to call attention to themselves and fight their insecurity. If honest acknowledgment doesn't work, end the conversation.

2. Gently tease the offender. This tells the boor you're self-confident about your work and refuse to let accidental or intentional remarks intimidate you.

3. Dare to disagree. When you, personally, are knocked down along with your suggestion, get back up and defend your position. Be unemotionally and quietly aggressive. Question a charge or objection. Request an explanation. If your boss riddles your proposal, ask precisely, specifically, what is needed or ask to redefine priorities.

4. Insist on being treated courteously If someone persists in sweeping the floor with your feelings, take away the broom. Leave.

Script

(Begin with honest praise.) *Generally, you show clear thinking, but in this case you're off the mark.*

(Tease to ease tension and restore courtesy.) *Boss, if you want to act like Alexander the Great, barking orders and attacking my performance, that's your right. You're in charge and I salute you. But attacking my feelings or motives or sanity isn't part of the game plan. Let's get back to what you want done.*

(Firm, strong, polite response to *that's a stupid idea.*) *I disagree, boss. I think this is a good idea since it allows us to accomplish our objective at a reduced cost.*

(Don't stand there allowing yourself to be kicked.) *Look, Larry, if you don't like this plan, fine. We can iron out our differences. But we can't get anywhere with name calling.* (Refuse to stoop to that level.) *Either we agree to speak respectfully to each other or I'm leaving right now.*

Summary

Show you can't be intimidated by personal attacks. Without rising to the bait, keep displaying your good humor, untiring energy, great ideas, willingness to learn, and skills in handling people. Challenge hurtful remarks by questioning the attacker instead of letting your anger fester. Choosing a constructive way to redirect your anger lets you protect your dignity while the offender saves face. Respect begins with courtesy.

13.2 VACILLATORS
When the Wishy-washy Waste Your Time

When indecisive bosses keep you hanging on vital issues, unable to make a decision, they are devaluating your worth. You can't proceed without the boss's okay or decision. Your assignment needs are ignored, and no one's telling you why you're being kept waiting or when you'll get an answer.

When peers are consistently late with their segment of work on your joint project, you feel responsible yet powerless to regain respect. They procrastinate, ignoring completion dates you both agreed upon, making you late with your own deadlines. You resent their irresponsibility, absentmindedness or inconsideration. Your work suffers because they are remiss.

And when your subordinates sit on an assignment, not sure how to proceed but not telling you they need help, your first thought is that you have a bunch of disrespectful deadbeats who are taking advantage of your good nature.

It's past time for you to regain control of your time and stop letting vacillators steal respect you are due.

Strategy

Help vacillators focus on the consequences. When choices must be made, assist them in looking at which alternatives rank higher in importance to the outcome.

Steps

1. Distill the information you present. Give a vacillating boss solutions instead of problems. Simplify terms and limit the options to consider. Offer some guidelines for making the decision. Or prepare a short summary of highlights, spelling out the few decisions and considerations.

2. Control the flow. Present the most urgent questions first to prevent the boss from getting hung up on less significant matters. Don't criticize the boss's indecisiveness to anyone. It will eventually get back to the boss. Keep a calendar indicating the lead time you need for getting the boss's okay.

3. Talk mutual interests to tardy peers. If the behavior doesn't improve and you can't get cooperation, then ask the boss to review the procedure and unlock the gridlock.

4. Get subordinates to restate the assignment. Once you're sure the assignment is clear, ask them to tell you the anticipated consequences if work continues to be late. Then enforce your agreement.

Script

(Instead of asking the vacillating boss *what should we do about it?* narrow the choices you offer.) *Boss, we could do x or we could do y, and x seems to be better for the department because . . . Do you agree?*

(Give stated objectives as the guideline.) *We've said our main concern this year is to maintain our standard of quality. If that's our priority, this plan allows us to . . .*

(When you can't convince colleagues to follow the agreed deadlines.) *Boss, on the Smithson project that Ellen and I are jointly heading, we've run into a problem that requires your intervention. We could keep a better time schedule if we were to reorganize along the lines of . . .*

(Move the stalling subordinate.) *Jerry, I know you take great pride in your work, but I must have that report by 4:00 or we'll lose the deal. Turn in your draft now and you can put on the finishing touches later.*

Summary

Make it easier for stallers to decide or act. They don't comprehend that everyday decisions that can be corrected easily and inexpensively ought to be made quickly. Whether their vacillating is due to fear that they won't meet their own high standards or fear that they'll make a mistake, or whether its a way to get even with you, you have too stop them from pulling you down and lessening your value to the organization.

13.3 DEPENDENTS
Refusing to Do Another's Work

You weren't hired as a mother hen or father confessor. It's fine to be a team player who pitches in and helps out, but you're not helping anybody if you continue to assume another's responsibility.

Your peers ask for your help, and you do practically all of their difficult assignments for them. Or your colleagues use your good ideas without acknowledging your part or giving you credit. You may feel unappreciated by these thankless ingrates, but what's worse, think how you come across. How can you earn respect when you don't demand respect for yourself?

Instead of standing up to advantage takers, you keep your resentment bottled up. Yet, even though you say nothing, your suppressed hostility comes through. They know you don't really want to help them, that you're only trying to buy their friendship or approval. And they're laughing at you behind your back.

Don't help others for the wrong reasons. You can show concern and still demand they do their own work and credit you for your efforts. Show you care by appreciating their need to grow. Suggest, and let them work it out. That's the kind of help they need while you increase your self-respect and the respect others show you.

Strategy

Help steer the boat, but allow others to do their own rowing. Remove yourself as the oarsman and let dependents learn to sail on their own. No struggle, no progress for them, and no respect for you.

Steps

1. Turn the requests around. Limit your part to making suggestions. Tactfully refuse pleas that lead to your doing your peer's work for them. Make them accept their responsibility.

2. Identify yourself as a contributor. Instead of freely doling out ideas your peers capitalize on, be part of the presentation. Or sign on as a co-author to the report.

Script

(Tactfully refuse.) *Yes, I agree, Mr. Royce is difficult to deal with, but you're never going to learn how to handle that type if I keep making the calls for you. I'll give you a few pointers, but you have to do it yourself. I know you can pull it off.*

(Insist on acknowledgment when you play a part.) *Look, guys, if you want my help in writing the proposal, then my name has to be listed as one of the submitters.* Or *Before I help you with the presentation, is it clearly understood that I'll be one of the presenters?*

Summary

It's bad enough that you're not helping others when you don't allow them to learn by making their own mistakes, but you are also hurting yourself. Colleagues who get you to do their work for them not only get out of the work, they also think of you as a pushover. You don't have their respect and you don't respect yourself, and nobody else knows the value of the work you're able to contribute. Stop being a crutch for them and start standing up for yourself.

13.4 INTERRUPTERS

Curbing Delays and Interference

Interrupters usually don't realize that when they barge in, they're showing little esteem for the value of your work. They display scant regard for your precious productive time.

In many offices you have to manufacture the time to work without interruption. If your desk chair faces an open door or popular passageway, move the furniture. Keep the passerby from catching your eye. Remove the help-yourself snacks from your desk. Pile reports on empty chairs to discourage colleagues from plopping down. Arrange for your phone to be answered while you close your door and concentrate on a report. Or escape to an empty conference room.

You have to take the action necessary to get the courtesy you deserve, even standing up to a boss who permits constant interruptions during your scheduled private review sessions or when impatient people interrupt you and you're unable to finish expressing your thought. Stop allowing yourself to be mistreated and plan ways to be shown more respect.

Strategy

Take a two-pronged approach. Gently and tactfully stop the interrupter, and also arrange for changes in procedure or conditions to minimize future interruptions.

Steps

1. Designate specific times for both interruptions and no interruptions. If you need an hour a day to concentrate and plan, exchange with a co-worker to take each other's calls during that set period. Or close your door and post a sign ("available after 10:30") or move your work to a conference room or the library. Tell your workers the times you're available for them to drop by. Ask your boss for a time when you can talk without interruption.

2. Meet outside your office. If you go to your colleague's office, you can get up and leave. It's harder in your office to get rid of the colleague who keeps on talking after business is completed.

3. Hold your own against interruptions at meetings. When you're giving reports or making suggestions and rude colleagues break in before you can finish, interrupt the interrupter and finish what you want to say. Avoid interruptions by avoiding preambles. Make your point before you start explaining it and shorten your remarks. Maintain eye contact and don't read a report or give out copies in advance.

Script

(When someone plops in uninvited, you don't have to talk.) *Could it wait till afternoon? I'm really swamped now.*

(Interrupt the interrupter.) *Excuse me, Carol, I'm in the midst of making a point. Please let me finish.*

(When they interrupt your talk.) *Yes, and as I was saying . . .* (restating and continuing your point) or *I'd like to respond to that, but first, I want to say . . .* (Don't let them keep you from expressing your thoughts.)

Summary

Many interrupters simply don't realize they're being disrespectful, cutting into your time or disturbing your thought process just when you're really rolling along. They don't know, and you have to tell them—gently and tactfully—that you can't be interrupted at this time. More than that, to avoid much interruption, take control and alter procedures or ask for specific changes.

13.5 IMPOSERS

Preventing People from Taking Advantage

Sometimes advantage taking is unintentional. The system may be to blame. In a large organization employees can be so smothered by rules that they're confused over who's supposed to do what. In smaller settings there may be a memo issued each time there's a crisis. With no codified regulations and without clearly written policies and procedures, people interpret (and misinterpret) for themselves. Emphasis is on red tape. People do something because it's a rule even if that rule doesn't relate the activity to the company's purpose.

Imposers, on the other hand, take advantage on purpose. They plan to manipulate. All that matters is that they achieve their own goals. They don't care if you're hurt or inconvenienced or if your importance is played down.

Your boss decides you're a good worker who never complains and deliberately overloads you. Your cohorts "borrow" your staff without asking or dump their work on you. Sometimes boss and peers gang up, making deals that affect your work but not including you in the discussion. You allow this to happen by keeping still. Now you have to undo it because your perceived value is tied to the respect you get.

Strategy

Speak up for yourself. Whether the system needs to be corrected or the advantage takers need to be stopped, you have to change how you're being treated to feel self-respect and to be respected by others.

Steps

1. Suggest ways to correct poor procedures. If you're being overworked, ask for priorities. If rules are confusing or there's too much emphasis on trivia, offer to codify the regulations. If lines of responsibility and authority are muddied, request clarification.

2. Assert yourself without crushing other egos. No need for a confrontation or a personal attack. An easy way to say no is to suggest alternatives. The other person is more interested in seeing that something gets done than in your doing it.

3. Hold your own without apologizing. When others take advantage of you, stop saying you're sorry. You have to stop them. "Sorry, I can't" is really all that's necessary.

Script

(Offer to clarify.) *In the past few years our rule book has grown like Topsy, with some of the later decisions cancelling out former ones. I'd be glad to get a group together to organize them.*

(Offer alternatives instead of *Why are you doing this to me.*) *Boss, I know you want me to handle top priority items. To prevent a backlog, I'd suggest we expand the secretaries' responsibilities by training them to handle these less important, routine matters.*

(You owe the imposer no explanation or apology.) *I'm sorry I can't help you, David. Maybe Marla has time.*

Summary

When you're being imposed upon, either the system is poor or people are manipulating you. Unless you speak up, you will continue to be victimized as your perceived worth is diminished.

13.6 UNASKED FOR ADVISERS
Ending Assumptions That You Must Agree

Another form of disrespect comes from opinionated colleagues who are convinced they know how to do everything better than you do, including how you do your own job. And they don't mind cramming their advice down your throat even though you don't want it.

Some are usually right on target and take for granted you'll welcome and agree with what they're proposing. The gods have spoken. No room for discussion or disagreement. With absolute conviction of their omnipotence, they wear you down and make you feel stupid.

Whether or not they mean it this way, the implication is that you're incapable of thinking for yourself. While they're instilling these thoughts in you, they're causing others to infer that you're not doing your job well.

You have to find a way to stop these advisers from minding your business with their unsolicited opinions.

Strategy

Prepare and confront. Being as polite and unemotional as you can manage, let the opinionated speak before you refuse the offering. Swallow your pride if you hear something useful.

Steps

1. Convince yourself you're on solid ground. Do your homework. Arm to the teeth with questions that can bring out the issues you want. Questions are helpful to get others to see alternative positions without directly challenging these advisors.

2. Show your competence. Have your facts at your fingertips. That gives you the confidence to say, in effect, that you can run your own show.

Script

(Use questions to point up options.) *How would that improve the condition? What advantages are there over the old way? What if we were to . . . ?*

(Tactful refusal) *I appreciate that you want to help, but this is my responsibility and I'm handling it.* Or *Thank you for your interest, but I've had a lot of experience in these matters and I can take care of it.*

Summary

Be well prepared with your information so that you can stop unasked-for advisers either with questions or by refusing the advice. Express appreciation for their concern (try to sound sincere because you don't want to make new enemies), but let them know you're capable of thinking for yourself and carrying out your assignment. Expect respect.

13.7 DEAF EARS
When Workers Ignore Your Agreements

You thought your expectations in quality and quantity were clearly understood. Now your workers are ignoring their promises to you. Deadlines are not observed. The finished product is falling short. They ignore your posted schedules. How do you maintain your high standards and still get work turned out or turned in on time?

While the level of performance is affected by many factors, one of the chief ones is the manner in which you motivate your workers. Showing them more respect results in the need for less control. You can start by letting your subordinates play a role in setting their own goals.

If you acknowledge that subordinates can think for themselves and are capable of doing the work, then there's no need to insult them by requiring approval and disapproval at every step. If they're careless, and you certainly can't allow your unit to turn in sloppy work, send it back.

Making the corrections yourself gets you farther away from your goal of a productive unit. Why should they try? You're going to do it anyway. If you want respect from your workers, allow them to learn by forcing them to stretch.

Strategy

Gain subordinate respect by being tough and soft at the same time. Tough is making it crystal clear you're not backing down from your high standards. Soft is showing concern for the individual as well as for the product.

Steps

1. Build your team. Make each player feel that he or she is part of a group pulling together to get the job done. Not "my" or "mine," but "our." Respect them as team members by interpreting and sharing management goals. Help them think the way those at the top do, weighing a decision on whether it will help the company (and, in turn, themselves).

2. Confront the duds and deadbeats. Start with whatever they're doing well, then discuss what's worrying you. Present examples of their work, showing exactly what's wrong and the specific changes that need to be made. *Have them tell you* how they can improve and regulate themselves before you offer your opinion.

3. Show small, caring, personal consideration. Don't assume you know what someone else is thinking or feeling. Get them to tell you. Make them feel comfortable about asking for your help before you decide to take over. Respect individual personalities and working styles. Some people, for example, need detailed plans; others like to work out the plan themselves.

Script

(Relate work to management goals.) *Joe, you're a good worker and I want to help you advance. How do you think your unit can move us closer to the goals I've laid out?*

(Demanding quality gains respect.) *I've reviewed your work and you're showing good insight. But I've marked the places that are sloppy—misspelled words, incorrect grammar, non sequiturs. How do you plan to check yourself in the future to improve the quality of your papers?*

(Showing concern) *I noticed you fell behind schedule this month. Is there some problem you need to discuss with me?*

Summary

Review goals and rules and provide the tools. Then don't accept below-standard performance from your workers or try to fix the work yourself. Send it back until they get it right. Win respect from your subordinates by respecting their ability to work without your constant checking up, but still showing consideration for their thinking and caring about their well being.

13.8 DEMANDERS
When Workers Abuse Your Tolerance

Some workers have their own agenda, and it has nothing to do with company needs. The lazy and manipulative drag their feet, constantly forgetting, stalling, or acting helpless until someone else does their work. Others keep nagging for prima donna privileges. Or they steal time the company pays for by conducting personal business all day long.

Some subordinates use company business as a basis for self-promotion. They ignore your directives, telling you they thought the end justified the means. ("I just couldn't pass up this great opportunity. There wasn't time to find you and get your approval, so I went ahead without it.")

The best managing is coaching. Help your workers achieve, but convey that they are responsible for their own performance. You have to stop them from taking advantage of your easygoing style. Unless you hold fast to your rules, subordinates will bend those rules until they break. And all respect for you will evaporate under these potentially dangerous conditions. Your standing depends on their effectiveness.

Strategy

Regain control by regaining respect. Enforce your rules with consistency; explain the need and how the rules actually help the workers. Make clear the consequences when rules aren't obeyed.

Steps

1. Clarify your directives and expectations. In addition to written rules, there are the unwritten and unspoken rules. Instead of letting your workers pick these up haphazardly, review difficult areas before they become a problem for you and your team. New workers especially need this type of discussion.

2. Agree that a problem exists. Subordinates have to understand why something is a problem that has to be corrected and the consequences if it is not.

3. Identify specific behavior that must be modified. Pull out of your subordinates what must be done to change the consequences and why it's in their best interest to do so. Get them to accept responsibility and tell you possible solutions. After you agree on a plan, follow up with frequent, specific, and constructive feedback. Lavishly praise good work.

Script

(Explain the need to adhere.) *Luanne, do you understand that the rule was made to protect you, me, and the whole office? I do appreciate your eagerness, but what will be the consequences if your action proves inaccurate?*

(Coach rather than tell.) *Neal, I've been concerned lately about getting a better-balanced workload. Frankly, you're not honoring our agreement, and we're going to have to make some changes. How do you propose we solve this problem . . . ?*

(Place responsibility where it belongs.) *Allen, tell me what happens when you tie up the phone all day with personal calls and clients can't get through? . . . That's right, our client needs come first, so what options do you think I have?*

Summary

Be consistent about your rules. Make sure your subordinates understand the need for the rules, the consequences of breaking them, and how they are personally affected. Discuss solutions until you reach agreement on a plan, getting subordinates to restate the proposed action in their own words. Your reputation depends on their good work. To bring this about, gain their respect by enforcing your rules.

14

CURTAILING DISCRIMINATION

It's now more beneficial for workers who feel they suffer indignities because of race, sex, age, religion, national origin, or disability to sue and for lawyers to help them sue. But the goal is still to decrease discrimination. This means being able to recognize it, deciding when to fight and when to let go, and knowing how to stand up for your rights.

The significance of the Civil Rights Act of 1991, which bars discriminatory hiring, firing, pay, or promotion, is that it shifts the burden of proof from employees to employers. It gives employees the right to have their cases heard by juries and to sue for punitive as well as compensatory damages, such as back pay. The Americans with Disabilities Act of 1992 protects qualified disabled workers, starting with companies employing 25 or more.

Activists hope that employees, bolstered by important added legal protection, will feel more self confident dealing with perceived unfair treatment. Experts anticipate a better work environment, but warn of higher costs passed along to the consumer, along with increases in litigation, paperwork, and bureaucracy. Because there's so much at risk for both employee and company, every positive alternative should be tried first in your efforts to get the respect you deserve.

14.1 REAL THING

Separating Discrimination from Making Excuses

Antagonistic, glaring, overt discriminatory actions are easy to recognize. Subtle prejudicial actions are harder to deal with and protest against. For example, from the *assumption* that qualified women workers don't want to travel because it disrupts their family life, bosses give these high profile, promotable assignment gems to males instead.

Offenders see the groups they target as a threat to the status quo and their jobs. The Labor Department says women and minorities trapped in lower and middle management plateaus bump up against a glass ceiling. They lack access to development programs and corporate mentors. Stereotyping prevents advancement. People over 50 can be undercut simply for looking old even though they may be more energetic and knowledgeable than younger workers.

Whatever your complaint, there are issues you must separate before you take any action. Only you can say if you're really being held down and held back or if you're using discrimination as an excuse for not getting where you want to go. Reexamine to decide if the problem is your inability, your lack of initiative, or somebody else's prejudice.

Strategy

Investigate if there's real discrimination and, if so, take remedial steps. Begin by raising awareness that a problem exists and how eventually everyone in the company will be affected if it isn't remedied.

Steps

1. Determine if there's an intimidating or coercive environment. For example, in sexual harassment situations the "reasonable woman standard" is now being applied; that is, how would a reasonable woman interpret these actions?

2. Eliminate rationalization. Targets of alleged discrimination have to look deep inside and ask if they have a chip on their shoulders. Are you blaming every problem you have on people "who have it in for us"? Are you really qualified, or as qualified, as the one who did get advanced? Are you challenging stereotypes, for example, by daring to venture into nontraditional assignments?

3. Make your objections known and seek a remedy. Before you even think about litigation, first try to improve the climate. Ask for anti-discriminatory educational training. Request that more women and minorities be included in special projects and actively solicited for job openings.

Script

(Check out conditions by talking to co-workers.) *I'd like to know if any of you have ever had an experience like I ran into today. I'm wondering if this attitude is pervasive or directed only at me?*

(Show determination not to be excluded because of stereotyping.) *Yes, boss, I know it's unusual that I'm requesting this assignment, but I know I can do it, and all I'm asking for is the chance to prove it to you.*

(Suggest remedial action.) *Boss, we have to protect the company against these actions by uninformed employees. We need to add a segment to our regular supervisory training on how to recognize and deal with discrimination and harassment.*

Summary

If you feel you've been discriminated against, whether the attitude is widespread or directed only at you, make your objections known. You're not after reverence, just common courtesy. Suggest how conditions may be remedied. If you're complaining about lack of opportunity, express a willingness to take risks into new directions.

14.2 FEDERAL LAW

Seeking Advice About Violations

In the midst of a difficult economy, new social legislation increased protection for the disabled, older workers, women, and minorities, and also put increasing pressures on business. Media news and televised congressional hearings made employees more aware of their rights under new anti-job-discrimination laws. The growing number of lawsuits attests to this awareness—a situation that's forced many employers to review their personnel policies to reduce litigation and consequent costs.

Specifically, the Civil Rights Act of 1991 bars discrimination in hiring, firing, pay, or promotion based on race, sex, age, religion, and national origin. It shifts the burden of proof from employee to employer, permits jury trials, and allows punitive and compensatory damages, such as back pay. Damages are capped on a sliding scale. The law broadens the grounds for lawsuits and expands the class of those who can take legal recourse.

Effective July 26, 1992, the Americans with Disabilities Act bars employers of 25 workers or more from discriminating against qualified disabled in hiring, firing, pay, and promotion; and in July 1994 this applies to employers of 15 to 24 workers. Also, recent Supreme Court rulings on age bias encourages pursuit for age-discrimination claims.

Strategy

Understand your rights. Whether or not you find yourself on either side of a lawsuit, you should become familiar with your rights under federal law. Then, despite the risks, you can better decide if and when enough is enough.

Steps

1. Study your rights. Get full information from the U.S. Equal Employment Opportunity Commission (EEOC). Get advice from support groups. Ask how to form a task force to study and recommend procedural changes, how to update personnel office hirings, and how to take action on perceived bias.

2. Tell your company what it needs to do. Make your problem known in a strong, calm, factual voice. Many companies don't realize their obligation unless confronted with the danger of ignoring it. When it's explained how discriminatory practices are hurting the company, it makes sense to adhere to the law before violations are reported.

3. Collect evidence. Preserve copies of discriminatory memos and any other tangible items that could back up your word. Keep a diary with dates, witnesses, and notes of conversations you found offensive. Discuss the disturbing problem with friends. If you decide to file with a government agency, you'll need to spell out specifically why you found the conduct to be offensive.

Script

(Explain your problem.) *Boss, my being confined to a wheelchair will cause some difficulty when my office is moved next month. Would you consider installing an electric door so I'll be able to maneuver in and out by myself?*

(Explain benefits to the company.) *Some managers don't yet realize their discriminatory jokes that once got them laughs can now get them dismissed. We can't afford to lose our managers, and we can't afford the toll those slurs are taking on our workers. We need seminars to review personnel practices and update supervisory training.*

(Quietly collect evidence from co-workers.) *Did you experience a similar problem, not being assigned to the front office because of your accent? . . . We ought to form a task force, and if there's a record of discrimination, we can make some strong recommendations.*

Summary

Today it may be more beneficial for an employee to sue, but litigation is an extremely serious step. This is one of the most difficult decisions you'll ever have to face because so much is at risk. Even if you're not fired, there are subtle ways you could be denied a raise or passed over for a promotion or isolated as a troublemaker. If you leave after complaining, in some industries you could find yourself blackballed. So examine all aspects and exhaust all positive approaches to being shown respect before you decide on a lawsuit.

14.3 BATTLEFIELDS ———————————————

Choosing Your Fights Conserves Your Strength

Pick your battles. Don't dilute your energy and the power of your arguments by fighting over every issue. Save your fights for what's really important to you, like equal pay for equal work and getting a deserved raise or promotion. If you complain about everything or spread yourself too thin by fighting on too many fronts at once, you weaken your attack and people stop listening.

Don't assume that every male is a chauvinist. Don't assume every female is after your job. Don't assume every white thinks you're stupid.

Don't assume every boss thinks you're automatically over the hill at 50. Yes, there's plenty of discrimination out there, but stop wrapping everybody in the same blanket.

First, try to take the fun away from your offenders. If the remarks aren't really harmful, laugh and let them roll off your back. If the insults are mean and harm your reputation and career future, take action. You can't let feelings fester inside.

Strategy

Seek a resolution or at least an improvement in current conditions. Consider the pros and cons of all your options before you do anything. And remember, you do have recourse under federal law.

Steps

1. Seek help from support groups. Prioritize your concerns. Once you hit the glass ceiling, discrimination is less obvious, federal laws are less useful and, in some industries, fighting could lead to your being blackballed or to more subtle harassment. Attend professional association meetings and programs. Find groups and agencies (for example, Commissions on the Status of Women) where you can get concrete tips on how to stand up for yourself without provoking retaliation and how to utilize contacts and build a stronger network. Should you consider leaving the company to go on your own, these groups offer seminars on securing capital and getting new business.

2. Seek help within your company. Try to sensitize your boss to your feelings. Make your point, politely, without jabbing it in. Let your boss know you want to move up so badly you're willing to take risks, work extra hours, live with tension. You're not asking for special treatment, but you're ready to pay the same price as those do who advance. Search for a mentor, not only to help you develop skills and make contacts, but who could also explain to your boss how discriminatory actions hurt the company and lose good workers.

3. Ask that a diversified task force be appointed. Request that the group study hiring patterns and bias and make recommendations. If refused, gather several cohorts to compile complaints giving evidence that job openings aren't posted and the offended can't get training or plug into the management pipeline.

4. Consider the grievance route. Is there a grievance committee or ombudsman to whom you could speak anonymously? Request a confidential investigation and disciplinary action if necessary. Be prepared for being hit with countercharges attacking your credibility and having to prove your charges. If you're not satisfied with the type of investigation and you wish to proceed with your complaint, file your charges with the EEOC. There may also be state and local government agencies to assist you.

5. Consider: Are you better off resigning without protest? Filing a complaint is a decision you have to make for yourself, depending on how strongly you feel about being victimized. Find out the estimated waiting time before your case would be settled, including an appeal if you win. In your case, do you risk being drummed out of the industry? If economically and emotionally you can't afford the fight, consider leaving on good terms with a fine letter of recommendation. This won't correct the wrongs, but it would let you move on to a workplace with less discrimination. Your choice depends on your priorities.

Script

(Laugh off the inconsequential.) *You can't be serious.* (Walk away to fight another day.)

(Some people don't realize they're discriminating.) *Boss, I want to talk to you about the European assignment you gave to Keith. You said you knew I wouldn't want to be away from my family for a few weeks. Since I was never asked how I felt about that, I want to make my position perfectly clear. It's have bag, will travel. I am ready, willing, able, and anxious to do any job the guys do. So please, don't count me out.*

(Seek help from your mentor.) *Paul, my boss has such a high regard for your thinking, would you be willing to talk to him? The atmosphere in our division is getting worse every day. I'm not the only one troubled. I'm afraid discriminatory slurs are going to result in lawsuits, and several of our best workers are totally demoralized. Potential costs alone are enough reason to stop this behavior.*

Summary

Decide what's really important to you. You sap your strength if you fight over every slight. But when you're told you don't need as much money as the men because you have a husband to support you, or you see evidence that you and other highly qualified minorities are skipped over for promotion, or every day you have to dodge discriminatory slings and arrows, it's time to weigh your options and seek some remedies.

14.4 BELITTLERS
Objecting to Religious, Racial, and Sexual Slurs

Telling crude jokes at work ceases to be funny when discriminatory slurs are called illegal and companies must protect themselves against lawsuits. Offenders say they didn't mean to hurt anyone, but intent isn't at issue. It's the effect upon the victim. Yesterday sneaking disparaging messages into your mailbox was blinked at. Today it's cause for the culprit's pink slip because companies fear litigation.

Haters excuse their hatred by pointing to undesirable traits. Others exercise prejudice by not allowing time off during holy religious holidays. Or they'll claim older workers can't learn new skills even when reports show they bring more expertise to the job. Skill and knowledge are overlooked as you overhear "Can't I pick 'em? She really has big ones" or "Let Lucus carry that, his kind are stronger." The victim thinks that's discrimination, but can't be sure. Coworkers know the slurs are offensive, but keep still or go along with the "joke."

If you don't take a stand, you are accepting these conditions. People fear retaliation, knowing they have to keep working with the offenders, and they may deny it's happening or refuse to file on the slurs.

Strategy

Sensitize offenders and take steps to improve the work environment. Keep telling yourself the belittler is the person with the problem—not you. Try to reduce insults by reducing hostility. Stress the loss to the company if slurs go unchecked.

Steps

1. Seek an expression of repulsion at discriminatory practices. Explain how nondiscriminatory policies help the boss and help the company. Suggest the need for educating officials and co-workers. Object every time a colleague tells racist, sexist, or ethnic jokes. Speak out, or your silence perpetuates this cruelty. You and your peers are the real force for change. But you have to accept the challenge each time, every time. Even offenders respect you for saying what you believe.

2. Examine the messages you send out. This doesn't excuse the offender, but it might improve the climate. For example, women can go easy on smiling and constant offers of help, which can be misinterpreted as weakness. Minorities, inadvertently perpetuating discrimination, can stop unconsciously sending signs that they perceive their status lower than others.

3. Try to overcome the offenders' resentment. Belittlers need to raise their self-image to overcome their own feelings of inferiority. Show them the recognition and appreciation they deserve. Ask for their opinions about your work and thank them for their suggestions.

4. Tell offenders how the slurs make you feel. Invite your boss to lunch where, in a nonconfrontational manner, you can talk over the problem. Show the courage of your convictions by being strong, factual, calm, and courteous.

5. Use company procedures for complaints. If the existing system doesn't work, move to establish a mechanism for quickly investigating complaints and harshly punishing offenders. Ask for strongly worded policies prominently posted and for training sessions for every worker, not just management. With tougher laws, costs of lawsuits, and possible damages hanging over their heads, bosses are more apt to comply.

6. Keep records and gather evidence. If your complaint to the company isn't investigated sufficiently or facts are twisted to discredit you, see 14.2, Federal Law, Step (3).

Script

(Show disapproval.) *That really bothers me when you talk about Willie like that. I know you mean that to be funny, but I want to tell you that I find it offensive. Please don't say that again around me.*

(Point up benefits and consequences.) *If we can reduce discriminatory practices, we'll increase our productivity. Workers who are offended are not doing their best work, they're absent more or they leave the company, and we have to train others. Or they go to lawyers and our costs skyrocket. We face jury verdicts and damaging publicity.*

(Elevate awareness.) *We need to expand training to include new ways to handle these problems. An example to increase sensitivity is to change to nonsexist expressions, such as: "man hours" to "work hours," "manpower" to "personnel," "she thinks like a man" to "she thinks logically like a good manager."*

(Explain your feelings.) *Boss, I know you don't realize how I feel when you say "That's a darn good job for a black." You intend it as a compliment, but if you think about it, you'll see it's really degrading.*

Summary

Recent federal laws give you more protection, prohibiting your being fired if you complain about discrimination. But some advocates say the well intentioned law lacks real teeth, and the risk is that you may be harassed in more subtle ways, such as being isolated after being branded a troublemaker. Until your company shows more dedication to enforcing an antidiscriminatory policy, point out the costs. Besides obvious litigation costs, the hidden costs are when energies are drained away from work and morale and productivity sink, even if complaints never reach the courtroom.

14.5 INEQUITY ————————————————————

Earning Less for the Exact Same Work

You're a victim of gender bias, irrational discrimination based on a person's sex. You do the same work but receive less pay because "You don't have to give her a raise, she's making a lot for a woman."

You're not well represented in policy making positions. As a professional, you earn lower fees than your male counterpart. If you're a manager, you probably earn half the salary that men do. Some studies show an important factor in inequity occurs when women take off several years or enter the work force late in order to raise children.

While the earnings gap between the sexes has narrowed so that women now earn 72 cents to the men's dollar, for millions of women over 50 the figure is 64 cents. Most of them never trained for higher paying positions. If you're stuck in a lower paying job you may have been denied assignments that would have shown you're qualified to move up.

Strategy

Educate management on the dangers of gender bias. Until management is willing to recognize the existence of discrimination and prejudice in the workplace, the treatment will be perpetuated.

Steps

1. Do a salary check to establish inequity. Confirm your perceptions. Perhaps others have longer tenure, entitling them to more pay? Are they actually the same assignment, responsibility, and authority as on your job? Form a task force to check records and prepare a chart of your findings. List assignments not offered to the qualified that would have led to promotions. If applicable, point out deals made at private clubs from which you're excluded. Now you and your task force can take your findings to the boss.

2. Request procedural changes. Suggest regular educational programs on current laws. Develop materials that can be used in supervisory training sessions. Ask that job openings be posted before they are filled so that every qualified worker can apply.

3. Separate your raise from company profits. Profits may be down, but you can increase your pay without getting a raise. Ask when you achieve special accomplishments that this be acknowledged with a cash bonus. A nonthreatening approach for getting a raise is to change your present job by developing new responsibilities or identifying the need for a new job. The boss may not know your capabilities if you don't speak up.

4. Take advantage of any training opportunities. There's no guarantee you'll earn the same, but consider moving into the fastest growing occupations and into nontraditional jobs in fields dominated by men where the pay is higher. You can't always play it safe, but it should be your choice if the job is too dangerous for a woman. Sometimes you want to chance assignments that are more important to the company. Sometimes it's more important for you to head a project than to keep playing a supporting role.

Script

(Using the evidence you compiled.) *Boss, the six of us have acted as an unofficial task force, gathering information about salary distribution. We know you'll be interested in studying our findings and recommendations.*

As these figures confirm, it costs the company a tremendous amount to lose trained, competent workers. If a woman leaves for maternity leave and then goes elsewhere because no part time is available, the company again must pay training costs to replace her.

The company also loses out when valuable talent goes unrecognized. When jobs are filled before openings are announced, when training is limited to a selected few, when women aren't represented on the management committee, it's not only unfair and illegal, but also you're not taking advantage of your valuable resources.

Summary

The stamping-out-inequity process starts with a commitment from the top. If you get management to care about making changes, even if only to protect its financial hide, at least it's a first step. But inactivity remains unless and until you set something in motion. Just gathering and presenting your factual evidence can, in itself, be enough said to start corrective measures.

14.6 OVERLOOKED
When Your Peer Got "Your" Raise

You worked harder, but your colleague with the right connections got the raise. You feel your interests were ignored in the name of expediency or politics. But were they? Before you go any further, ask yourself: Have you been willing to commit, to pay the price, to take the risk?

Salary depends on your value to the company and the current rate in the job market for your type of service. You can work very hard without increasing company profits and productivity. And without increasing your pay, your boss can recognize your efforts, for instance, by changing your title.

To judge if your company is willing to let you advance on your merit alone or if your moving up depends on the boss's approval, consider the last time you changed titles. Did it increase your responsibility, authority, salary, and staff? Were you given training that would help you get the next job opening? Or are you basically at the same level with a fancier title? In your company are executive minorities and women just window dressing or are they responsible for heading major projects, and are they included in behind-the-scenes policy making?

Strategy

Go after a raise by creating a reason. If you didn't get the raise you feel you deserved, try negotiating an increase. Also study company news releases and reports to pick up on the direction in which the organization is moving. Then propose a project, that you direct, that could increase company profit or improve the product or contribute to goodwill.

Steps

1. Prepare to negotiate. If you feel you really earned the raise and it's not forthcoming, document market salaries and trends. Know how your salary compares and if you're making at least the minimum amount you can earn elsewhere. If you're told money is tight, the company really may not have money or it may be a sign they're willing to bargain. Consider what else you can ask for, such as adjusting your working hours or receiving a percentage increase in a stated number of months.

2. Practice your request. Document your accomplishments, the amount of money you saved the company, your contribution to increased income or improved product. Instead of asking for "a raise," be specific, with definite numbers. Make yourself one-word reminder notes to serve as a script. Rehearse at home so that your voice is strong, firm, and unemotional. Be ready with answers to objections, such as low profits and continued layoffs, that you can anticipate.

3. Seek out opportunities. Don't wait for the knock. You may be bypassed because your boss doesn't know what you can do. You may not have to compete for a raise if you can propose a new way to meet a company need.

Script

Boss, I know this is still a difficult time for the company, but I'm sure you understand the importance of motivating workers like me who produce the results you need. For example, in the past six months, I was able to . . . Don't you agree that a 15 percent increase is reasonable and in keeping with the current market?

Well, if the money is tight now, perhaps we can agree on some other form of compensation. I would be willing to accept instead a conditional cash bonus in three months based on . . .

(Proposing a new project that you wish to manage.) *In line with our company priorities, I'd like to show you my proposal for increasing our revenue by linking two segments . . .*

Summary

When you didn't get the raise or new responsibility you were expecting, ask yourself if you're still on track, headed in the right direction. Keep trying to position yourself on a path that leads to a higher level, where your worth will be recognized. Don't be pacified by a change in title if you can't look forward to a promotion later on. Aggressively seek new opportunities.

14.7 PERSISTENCE

Maintaining Positive Professionalism

Targets of alleged discrimination may misinterpret signs they receive. A boss, assuming workers move well on their own, fails to give feedback, and this is misread as disapproval. Or the targets themselves misinterpret responses after they continually step on others with no regard for the welfare of the group. They make enemies by their own actions. Their race, sex, or age has nothing to do with it.

Other targets may inadvertently send misleading signals. Those with a happy, smiling personality can be perceived as pushovers. If you're a 24-hour smiler, know you can persist and persevere without offending. And unless you don a serious expression during discussions, you're not taken seriously. Standing firm with dogged resolve to achieve a goal or reverse a bad practice earns you the respect of your adversaries. The tough and tenacious professional is pleasantly polite—courteous and respectful, but not perceived as a fawning bootlicker.

Another mistaken signal comes from sensitive people who want to include others when decisions affect the latter's work. Instead of motivation by arm twisting, these leaders hold steadfast to the principle of active involvement. In the face of snickering opposition, they eventually earn respect by their willful insistence that a purpose be realized.

Strategy

Pick up and send the right signals. Don't blame discrimination if the problem is a troublesome personality trait. Know your mission, your sense of direction, so that you can develop a tough inner strength and not have to constantly seek approval or praise from your boss or colleagues.

Steps

1. Let your body language reflect the seriousness of your message. Don't send a mixed message, smiling, trying not to offend, when you want to make a sobering point.

2. Examine your rejection. If you experience similar reactions outside the office, the problem may be something you are doing rather than a personal attack because of your sex, race, or religion.

3. Study before you speak. Before jumping in to decry discrimination, contemplate the issues facing the company. Be able to describe the specific procedures that have to be altered, substituted, or eliminated.

4. Avoid personal attacks. Present the problem as your problem or a company problem without firing both barrels at your boss. Your aim is for positive resolution. Expound the benefits of cooperation.

Script

There has been a series of incidents and several remarks made to me that I regard as slurs. I have a list here of what has occurred, along with my suggestions for ways in which we might improve . . .

I know you agree that this can be a serious problem for the company. It is my understanding that I'm not the only target of discrimination. I've come to you first to ask you what we can do about it.

If we can find a way to reduce the antagonism, we can continue without disrupting the quality of our work. Would you agree to hosting a special program that's being offered by . . .

Summary

Be sure the problem is really discrimination before you give it the title. Sometimes the wrong signals are sent and received. If discrimination is the problem, be clear on your specific charges and how you would like to see the situation remedied.

14.8 STANDARD SETTER

Establishing a Model on Your Own Turf

Somebody has to show the way. Ideally, the word comes down from the top that discrimination will not be tolerated and that offenders will be dealt with harshly. But while you're waiting for that to happen, at least start something within your own bailiwick. Set a standard that can be copied.

Maybe you can't control the hiring process in the personnel department. Maybe promotions also are out of your hands. But as long as you are supervising people, you can make certain that each person is treated with respect.

People need to work together without being polarized into subgroups (male/female, black/white/Hispanic, older/younger) continually fighting each other for more control. Within your own unit, you can be the cohesive force. You don't even have to be the head of your unit to be a unifying agent and help establish a standard of fair and courteous treatment to everyone. You just have to be willing to try.

Strategy

Produce an incentive plan. Create a desire for real sharing and teamwork within your own unit.

1. Recognize the needs of the players. If more pay is their priority, negotiate an agreement that if the team can produce X widgets in Y time, they'll receive a cash bonus to be evenly divided among each member. A team approach creates a greater awareness of the need for equality and the important role each one plays in contributing to the group.

2. Recognize the future concerns. See the trend and prepare for it. Employees are being asked to take greater responsibility for planning their own careers, training and retirement. Ban together to get the needed training. Call in the experts to give advice on protecting pensions and securing retirement.

Script

(Determine group priorities.) *I'm taking a little survey among our group. How would you rank these items in order of your priorities?*

(Band together for protection.) *We need advice on how to protect ourselves in the future and would like to have training courses set up that would help us plan . . .*

Summary

One of the best ways to stop bickering is to unite behind a cause everyone can get excited about, especially one that meets a personal need. You may not be able to control the personnel policies of your company, but you can take a leading part in setting an example of fairness, respect, and teamwork in your own unit.

15

REDUCING PUTDOWNS

Putdowns range from an insensitive "even Jim can do it" to deliberately cruel stabs that weaken one's career. You might expect tyrannical bosses to be the chief offenders, but co-workers who are overly ambitious can be vicious. And even subordinates may cut you down with disguised sniping.

Chalk up some pulverizing put-downs to today's breakdown in business manners. Despite its advantages, the participatory management trend has led to more informality that, at times, has been transformed to more crudeness and rudeness.

Nevertheless, when someone keeps getting you angry, you can't simply suppress your hostility or you'll get sick. Some people get off kilter emotionally, resorting to sabotage at the office or raging anger at home. So you have to find ways to overcome your fear of speaking up to a ridiculing boss, to deal with empire building colleagues, and to stop subordinates you suspect are undermining your efforts.

When you surmise a putdown, aim to solve the problem rather than point the finger. First question to determine if you interpreted correctly. If so, talk up or you give abusers silent approval to keep on hassling you.

15.1 TORMENTORS

Replying to Harsh or Cruel Comments

Put down artists play a game of confrontation. To win in their game, learn to release your anger without unleashing retaliatory hostility. Keep your eye on what you want—respect and recognition—and don't submit to intimidation.

These offenders want to make you feel insignificant, as though you're excess baggage. Your work, your opinions, your suggestions are totally unimportant. There's no courtesy. No sensitivity. No consideration. They stretch out your emotions on a torture rack.

Some use not-so-subtle jokes ("Well, I see you got here before noon today.") Others prefer cruel, sadistic, and harsh comments to get a rise out of you. Another technique is to purposely call you by the wrong name or to pretend they can't remember your name. Whatever the preferred method, you're in for total disregard for your feelings.

Find out why you're being picked on and stand up to these offenders or you will continue to be treated with no respect.

Strategy

Appear to be in control by countering disrespect with courtesy. These offenders are trying to solve a problem by attacking you. They need help with that problem and are going about getting it the wrong way. Use a tactful, pleasant confrontation to try to solve a matter evidently of concern to them.

Steps

1. Accept the emotions you're feeling. If you're so mad you could strangle the boss, admit to yourself you've been hurt. That will keep the tension from building up. Next, figure out what you really want to happen as a result of this encounter. Be clear about your aims. Decide if you're able to treat the insults as impersonal suggestions rather than as direct personal threats.

2. Confront the offender. Aim to control the outcome and discuss the situation as unemotionally as possible. Learn what the real problem is. If you made a mistake, apologize without counterpunching and don't dwell on the apology. Then act confident by restating what's wrong, turning it around into a positive objective to be reached.

3. Negotiate. Suggest a clear statement of your mutual goals and try to work together generating options. Offer to do something beyond your job description that your tormentor boss needs done.

Script

(Be sure you understand the problem.) *Am I correct in assuming that . . . ? Was that in some report? What brought you to that conclusion?*

(Sensitize rather than counteraccuse.) *Boss, I'm sure you didn't realize how trapped I felt when you told me that you wanted to hire a statistician but your boss made you fill the opening by hiring me for my managerial skills. Nevertheless, I'm going to make you glad I'm here. I see some areas where I can help you . . .*

(Respond to cutting jokes.) *Boss, if you're angry about the way I've handled something, please be more direct with me in the future so that we can resolve the problem . . .* (suggesting a solution) *I understand you're upset and you certainly have a right to criticize my performance. However, that Anderson account is still ours if we move fast.*

(When the boss says you're too sensitive.) *Perhaps I am, but you know each of us has different degrees of sensitivity. You feel it's teasing; I feel it's hurtful. So I'd appreciate you not saying that again.*

Summary

Don't be afraid to stand up for yourself, tactfully and professionally. You're not losing control, you're gaining respect. When your boss resorts to putdowns rather than to telling you the problem, use questions to call the boss on it. Try sensitizing your boss about your feelings when your work and opinions are treated as insignificant. If you remain calm and tactful, the two of you can work out the problem.

15.2 SQUELCHERS
When Bosses Enjoy Crushing You

Haughty and condescending, your boss dismisses every suggestion you make. When the boss puts you down in front of an audience of customers or cohorts, that's really hard to take. Leaping in and taking over your job for you makes you appear incompetent. Worse than that, you lose your confidence and everyone else's respect.

Having authority, the boss feels entitled to dominate you and make your decisions. Squelchers are takeover types. Their prime objective is to be in control, thus the constant checking and unwanted assistance. If it's not their plan, it's no good. And when something you've done works well, they take the credit. They believe they're entitled because they're in control.

Faced with disrespectful, domineering, or defamatory supervision, you're left feeling intimidated and alienated.

Strategy

Work around the arrogance. You're not going to change or out-manipulate the boss. But you can change the way you react, improve your relationship, and stimulate interest in your suggestions.

Steps

1. Capitalize on the unwarranted self-importance. Use it, don't fight it. Acknowledge what your boss taught you.

2. Establish a team relationship between the two of you. Move within the framework of your assignment. Consult the boss. Ask the boss's opinion, not permission.

3. Get your ideas considered without antagonizing the boss. Act calm, unemotional, confident. Tactfully remind the boss how good you are, how you are helping achieve what the boss accomplishes. Quantify your contributions.

Script

(Acknowledge your boss's strong points.) *That turned out to be a really great idea you had on handling the delivery delay.*

(Consult, don't ask permission when you have authority to act.) *Boss, I'd like to run something by you. I have decided to deal with our scheduling problem by asking Marty to take over . . . How does that strike you?*

(Toot your horn as a team.) *We really pulled that one off, didn't we? Boss, with your help that makes six new contracts I've signed up this month.*

Summary

When a haughty boss incessantly enjoys deflating your ego, unless you want to look for a transfer, start changing the environment. Stand tall as you work around the boss's problem. Use your energy to get respect instead of wasting it by cowering. You're no sycophant if you give honest acknowledgment. And you go up a notch when you speak of yourself and your boss as a team. Eventually, it will dawn on the boss that you really are valuable if you constantly mention your accomplishments toward achieving the boss's goals.

15.3 BACKBITERS
Facing Down Badmouthing Colleagues

First of all, stop handing a knife to the people who are stabbing you. You're told, after swearing not to reveal your source, that a colleague is about to do you in. Your informant follows up with "But don't dare say anything or he'll know I told you. If you do, I'll deny it."

Now you've handcuffed yourself. You didn't question why the messenger was so anxious to bring you this news. You don't know if it's accurate. And you can't even use the information you received to confront the alleged backstabber and try to avoid a forthcoming attack.

Look first at these deliberately unkind and harsh backbiters. Whether they like you or dislike you is almost incidental. To them you serve a purpose. They ignore your good accomplishments and concentrate on what they decide are your mistakes, twisting the truth to make themselves look good. Misinformed, they don't bother to check out the facts. Often jealous of you, they may harbor strong hidden hostility.

Or if you're too much competition for them, they spread lies and innuendos to undermine your efforts: "Did you hear about Bill? What a shame, I thought he had his drinking problem licked."

Strategy

Refuse to be trapped by a pledge of secrecy. Free yourself to clear the air. Let backstabbers know you've been told about their alleged actions. Control the situation without being abusive in return.

Steps

1. Grill the messenger. Someone who's on your side would want to help you calm the water, not stir up trouble. Refuse to keep secret whatever the informant is about to tell you. Force the issue. If you feel the information is not really consequential, forget it, laugh it off.

2. Confront the potential offender. In a calm, factual manner, state the information that was given you and ask for a response. Don't be surprised if your backbiter denies everything and is stopped cold. If the problem does get on the table, then you can deal with the issue.

3. Discredit the offender's "facts." Start by asking for more specifics about the complaint. Have your facts, explanations, or evidence ready to correct any misinformation. Be positive and tactful. Your aim is to stop the backbiting.

4. Seek possible solutions from the backbiter to resolve the matter. If you contributed to the problem, acknowledge your part. Agree that in the future whenever either of you have difficulty with the other's activities, you will speak directly to each other and not try to go through a third party.

Script

(Confronting the messenger.) *I can't promise you that I'll keep secret whatever you're about to tell me. If there's a problem, I have to be free to discuss it and try to resolve it. Why have you come to me with this information if you don't want to help me prevent an unwarranted attack?*

(Putting the charge before the alleged offender.) *I have been informed that you said I failed to . . . Is that an accurate account of what you actually said?*

(Correcting misinformation.) *Where did you get your information? What do you see as the main problem here? . . . Actually, that wasn't the case, as you can see from these reports . . . How do you feel this situation can be resolved?*

Summary

Since backbiting is criticism said and spread behind your back, you generally learn about it from a third party. Ask yourself why this person is coming to you with the information. Is it to present or prevent trouble?

Don't be snookered into keeping the news secret. Confront the alleged backbiter. You'll clear the air and gain esteem.

15.4 ACCUSERS
Politely Discrediting Troublemakers

You went by the rules. Although you kept trying to make friends, each time you were rebuffed. You may never learn the real reason for an accuser's unrelenting attacks.

There are some people who simply don't like you. The more you try to make friends, the more they think you're a weakling, and the harder they push. And if you complain to the boss, you'll be tagged a wimp or a tattletale.

But let's not talk about revenge. Revenge is a troublesome motive because it's negative, a waste of your energy. It makes you focus on getting back or getting even instead of achieving your goals. So when nice doesn't work with people who push you down to elevate themselves, destroying your reputation in the process, think instead about self-defense. Protect the perception you've tried so hard to build.

Strategy

Develop a plan to ward off future attacks. Send a message to the accusers: Get off my back or else. Stop your underhanded maneuvering to destroy my good name or suffer the consequences. That's the language an accuser respects.

Steps

1. Prepare your campaign to counteract unfair attacks. Determine which options have potential for best mutual benefits and worse personal consequences. Having a plan is energizing because it restores your confidence.

2. Tactfully point up the accuser's misinformation. Respond with accurate facts. Your objective is to get respect, not to get even, so give accusers a way out.

3. Hold the accusers' feet to the fire. When their work negatively affects your assignments, have no compunctions about blowing the whistle on them in a quiet, legitimate way.

Script

(Responding to an unfair attack.) *Bobby, I'd like to know where you got your information.* (Don't deny, but question and then problem solve.) *Do you have any evidence that this is really so? . . . You've raised several points, let's take them one at a time to see if we can straighten this out.* (Remain calm and sound as though you're in command.)

(Make legitimate demands.) *Look, Ken, we don't have to like each other, but we do have to work together. If we can't iron this out, I'm going to the boss with it. You're welcome to come along. If not, I'll go anyway.*

Boss, there's a problem Ken and I have tried to work out by ourselves, but now we find we need your advice . . .

Summary

When you're accused unfairly, you can't continue to do nothing. You find the accuser is getting to you, eating away at your efficiency, eroding your confidence, and destroying your reputation among your cohorts. For all you know, the accuser may have already told the boss how you screwed up. Plan a pleasant confrontation with the accuser to correct misinformation and establish a working relationship. If the attacks don't cease and your work is affected, you have no choice but to go to the boss, preferably with the accuser, for advice. Remain professionally objective and you'll come out okay.

15.5 NEEDLERS
Decreasing Barbs and Backhanded Compliments

Needlers encase their accusations in humor to avoid responsibility for being critical. They often try to grab a little power by making a joke at your expense. It may be innocent goading, but it can be malicious insinuation meant to embarrass you.

When your boss teases you about your performance, assume that's a not-so-subtle hint something's wrong. Don't waste any time checking out what's bugging the boss. If you've done something wrong, you want to correct it immediately. If you're innocent, you want to set the record straight.

When someone else jokingly belittles your performance, if it's of no consequence, don't reveal a reaction to an insult. Smile, laugh, and gently correct, as though you're both in on the joke. Laughing at needlers takes the sting out of the jab and also takes their fun away.

However, if the needler's sting is an unmistakable stab, don't let it go by unchallenged. Turn the tables and needle the needler.

Strategy

Pattern your response by weighing the consequences. Is this a nuisance you can shrug off or a serious threat to the perception others have about you? Will you lose respect if the remark goes unchallenged?

Steps

1. Consider if you have to lighten up. Sometimes needling occurs when you take every little thing so seriously that your co-workers are just trying to get you to relax.

2. Recognize when you're being baited and don't bite. For reasons of their own, some needlers want you to look bad by reacting with anger. Be quiet until you're ready to move. You may decide to wear them down with friendliness, especially if you suspect they're insecure. Or you may decide on counterneedling.

3. Needle the needler. Ask for clarification. Keep asking what the needler means by that, to clarify what's just been clarified, and then to clarify that clarification.

4. Shift the focus. Move away from the personal attack upon you, to the larger issue involved. Select only part of the remark to respond to, ignoring the negative implications.

Script

(After needlers bait you and ask why you're getting so defensive.) *I had no idea I was perceived that way. What makes you say I'm being defensive?*

(Counterneedle.) *Now that you mention it, would you explain the connection? . . . I'm not sure I understand what you're saying . . . Could you clarify that for me?*

(Shift the focus.) *Yes, I did take a two-hour lunch, and boy, was it worth it! I learned from Andy in personnel about some major changes being considered that will affect all of us . . .*

Summary

Whether or not the teasing is intentionally cruel, the joke is meant to be at your expense. Some needlers enjoy getting the straitlaced to unbend. When you're the only one being teased, you may need to lighten up. On the other hand, if you're being baited to make you look bad by blowing up, take a few deep breaths before you respond. If the remark can't hurt your standing, laugh it off. When you feel it does, either needle the needler by asking for more and more clarification or shift the focus away from the personal attack and talk about an issue involved.

15.6 HECKLERS
Responding to Badgering

Hecklers differ from needlers in that they don't attempt to hide their accusations. They're out front and clearly aim to shift attention from you to them. Their humor is hostile. Sometimes it comes out as bitter sarcasm after you've made a presentation, comment, or report at the meeting. It can be an attempt to divert consideration of the point you've just made, which they oppose.

Or they may follow their heckling remark by saying your idea should be referred to a committee where they know it will die from being shunted or shelved. Showing you no respect, they interrupt you again while you're trying to respond.

Hecklers want to promote themselves by devaluating your effectiveness. They keep others from paying attention to your ideas, opinions, and suggestions.

One of the best ways to take back control is to poke a little fun at yourself, the way Abe Lincoln deftly used self-deprecating humor. But whether or not you can use humor, with a little practice you can turn the focus around and actually profit from the heckling.

Strategy

Rephrase the hostile question to remove the sting and regain control. Ask it again your way, then answer it with a point you want to emphasize. Divert attention from the personal attack and move on to something substantive.

Steps

1. Review how you're coming across. Study the body language of the audience. Some heckling comes from not getting right to the point, with the bored group resorting to attacks.

2. Interrupt the interrupter if it's your turn to talk. Hold your hand up in a "stop" signal and don't give the interrupter a chance to take over at your expense. Maintain the attitude that you demand respect.

3. Prepare comebacks for anticipated opposition. In advance, put yourself in the opponent's shoes and you can imagine their comments. Bring up their point before they can get any mileage out of it. Phrase your arguments to show how your audience will benefit.

Script

(Interrupt the heckler.) *Thank you, I'm glad you brought that up. This reminds me to tell you about my proposal for . . .*

(Turning the hostile comment around.) *The comment is why am I asking for your continued support on this proposal when we haven't yet showed a profit. That's a fair question, and the answer is we must continue to avoid the devastating consequences of future layoffs . . .*

(Dealing with negatives before you're attacked.) *Some of you may be thinking this plan is too costly, and I would agree that a lot is at stake here. However, in six month's time, we will start to see such benefits as . . .*

Summary

Hostile humor isn't funny, but treat it at first as though you're going along with the joke. Showing your confidence and control under fire earns you respect. Buy a little thinking time by rephrasing and defanging the attack. Then make your point again, at a higher level. Rather than defending yourself personally, talk about issues. Rechannel the negative put down into a positive solution.

15.7 SNUBBED
Penetrating Tight Circles

Not all putdowns are premeditated. Some peers ignore you because they're thoughtlessly inconsiderate. They disregard your accomplishments and suggestions even though you have the pertinent experience or are more familiar with the task at hand. They don't seek your opinion.

It's not that the snubbers assume you don't have the brains to think for yourself—it's the insensitive manner in which they won't acknowledge you exist and that perhaps you have a better answer. They stare through you without seeing you.

Cliquish in the way they treat outsiders, they make you feel unwanted in their tight impregnable little circle. They fence themselves in when they want to make decisions. They are oblivious to you because they're totally wrapped up in themselves.

And they're a strong influence upon the entire unit. So how can you get them to come to you or seek your opinion when you're not allowed to penetrate the exclusive fortress?

Strategy

Proceed from a plan for tackling one at a time. Stop trying to break through to the whole group and concentrate on winning over single members by tailoring individual appeals.

Steps

1. Set specific campaign objectives. Treat this as seriously as you would a management-by-objectives form. Keep notes on your efforts. Review what worked and what didn't.

2. Study individual hobbies, interests, and backgrounds. Change your thinking from getting through to their group to reaching each one separately. Clip relevant items from articles. Memorize tidbits to talk about. Use questions to start a conversation. Tackle one at a time.

3. Show you're friendly and confident. Take the initiative. Suggest getting coffee or going to lunch. Lead the conversation around to sharing your information, ideas, and beliefs. Solve a problem for them. Offer something they need or lack and would find valuable.

Script

(Prepare your plan of action.) *I'll make three attempts to reach each member of the clique separately. Once a week I'll extend a lunch invitation, then evaluate my progress and note areas for improvement.*

(Use questions to start a conversation.) *What's your secret? Your staff is always so energetic . . . Why don't we continue this talk over lunch?*

(Appeal to individual interests.) *I read in the* Journal *about a recent study that I think might interest you.*

Summary

Break through to an important clique by making friends with each one separately. Appeal to their individual interests. Work from a plan and analyze your progress. Once you break down the wall with a few, you'll get new respect from the group.

15.8 SELF-DEFEATISTS
Refusing Praise Is Cutting Your Own Throat

You're so afraid to sound as if you're bragging that you can't get a simple "thank you" past your lips. But by denying the compliment you deserve, you're not getting the credit that you need and you transmit a negative instead of a positive perception.

It's bad enough when others put you down, but why must you deliberately put yourself down? Graciously accept the compliments you've earned. If others had a part in the success, they should be included as you accept and share the praise. But don't toss out your part altogether, claiming modestly that they were the ones who made the project succeed.

You need recognition and respect not only to be promoted, but just to survive in the job market. Rejecting the compliment is also rejecting the person who extends it. When you say, "Oh, it was really nothing," you're implying the compliment giver can't tell good from bad. And that's no way to make friends or win respect.

Strategy

Determine to accept every compliment graciously. Good manners demand an appreciative, courteous response. It's false modesty or begging for reassurance to protest a compliment.

Steps

1. Show your confidence and belief in yourself. Answering a compliment by looking away, blushing, and apologizing for your efforts says "I don't think I'm any good, and I can't imagine why you do." Bite your tongue before you let any self-putdown remarks escape from your mouth.

2. Accept a compliment without rejecting the complimenter. Change "Oh, it was nothing" to a few words of appreciation so that you don't offend people who are being kind. If you don't agree with the compliment, don't protest or depreciate it. According to that person's judgment, right or wrong, you earned the praise. So just smile and say thanks.

3. Accept a compliment without begging for more. Some people refuse compliments as a way to beg for more and more reassurance. Say they do well, and they'll tell you how badly they're doing. Don't use such emotional blackmail ("You're just saying that to make me feel good") to get others to feed a bottomless pit.

Script

(Accept graciously.) *Thank you. I am a good coordinator. You mentioned the one area I know I excel in.*

(Even though you don't agree.) *Thank you, you're being very kind. And you've certainly made my day.*

(You're never wrong to keep it short and smile.) *Thank you. I appreciate that* (or simply) *Thank you.*

Summary

Allow yourself to accept the credit and recognition you earned and deserve. When rejecting a compliment, your false modesty fools nobody but yourself. Being polite and saying "thank you" is not bragging. It is common courtesy, and to do less is insulting the complimenter. In addition, putting yourself down with a deprecating remark robs you of the respect you're trying so hard to establish.

16

REPAIRING BRIDGES

Oscar Wilde warned us that we can't be too careful in the choice of our enemies. To earn respect and be considered valuable, make it a goal to convert your critics into friends. You can't afford to be undercut. Anyone at any level can cause you heartache when you're trying to hang on or move up.

And stop multiplying your enemy list by placing blame. Of course, if you're responsible for a boner, apologize immediately, say how you'll rectify the error, and move on. But when something goes wrong and you find yourself thinking "The boss is an idiot" or "Marla should have known better" or "Why can't Marcus ever do what I tell him," shift from finding fault to seeking solutions.

Switch, don't fight. Wear the conciliator cap instead of the trouble-maker brand. If you feel impelled to blame something, blame a system you can correct or adjust. Together you and your adversary can examine and extend your options. Together you and your workers can come up with creative solutions.

Resolve your confrontations instead of leaving them up in the air. If you reach out in a professional, mature manner, others will change the perception they have about you. You'll find them meeting you partway and being less critical and more receptive to your efforts.

16.1 BURNOUT

Renewing Your Enthusiasm

You're awfully edgy lately. Instead of your pleasant disposition, you're impatient and impolite. Angry at anyone giving orders and at yourself for putting up with them, and you're still reluctant to delegate.

You have trouble sleeping, are always tired and stressed out, and feel anxiety. You can't seem to get out from under the load dumped on you at work and the pile of unpaid bills at home. With no time for family, friends, or socializing, you find it doesn't take much to get you into an argument.

The worst part about burnout is that the thrill is gone. You were happy working your way up, periodically getting small pay raises and promotions. Now you no longer find job satisfaction. Since the recent merger, when the top brass limited your control over your work, your pride in your product has slipped away.

The first step is to realize that it isn't the job itself that's causing you stress, but how you're looking at the problem.

Strategy

Change conditions in areas that you do control. Take steps to regulate stress. Acknowledge what you can change and stop frustrating yourself over situations you can't. And put some enjoyment back into your life.

Steps

1. Give your own needs a higher priority. Set aside a short period every day to relax, or eventually you'll become physically ill. Long-term stress that builds up, unresolved, can lead to high blood pressure, to heart attacks, and it can reduce resistance to disease. Learn to close your door and close your eyes. Do muscle-relaxing exercises. Meet a friend to go for a long walk. Switch from a working lunch to a relaxing meal. If you've accumulated any leave time, take your vacation now.

2. Initiate changes in your job. List ideas to negotiate with your boss, such as rotating responsibilities or functions with your peers. Take steps to control interruptions. Keep alert for transfer or promotion opportunities. Suggest ways you and your peers can make more of the decisions affecting your work. Offer to represent your unit or department.

3. Acquire a new skill or technique. If you've stopped growing on the job, you're feeling unchallenged. Learn something. Develop something. Look for a new segment that's needed and ask for the responsibility of evolving it from concept to reality.

4. Identify a special skill you used to enjoy that you no longer utilize. Maybe you delegated a task you can take back in exchange for giving your assistant more of your administrative duties. Or you spot a need for a particular skill and volunteer to do this activity again. Use your talent outside of work. Share your knowledge and experience with your network.

5. Yield a little and ease up on your criticism. Resist the temptation to say someone else is wrong, listen to the points being made, and together synthesize your thinking.

Script

(Get your assignments changed.) *Boss, I've read about an exchange program that might work for us since we're shorthanded a lot of times and have to pinch-hit. One person from each unit is sent for one month to learn how another unit operates. According to this article, employees come back fresh and excited, and the company benefits from . . .*

(Develop a project.) *Several customers have been telling me they could use a guide of this type. I'd like to develop one, okay?*

(Learn a new skill.) *How many of you would be interested in having someone here once a week to teach us about records systems?*

Summary

The burnout malady, with its feelings of fatigue and frustration, only gets worse if you don't intervene to change whatever areas you can control. Be kinder to yourself, mainly for your own good health. In addition, when you're suffering burnout you tend to get into arguments you would ordinarily avoid. You can create the perception that you're out of control. And there goes all that respect you've been trying so hard to get.

16.2 DIGNITY

Preserving Pride for Winners and Losers

Complaining is good and good for you. But you have to know how to do it so that you achieve your goals and avoid acquiring additional adversaries.

Get the anger out *before* you have your meeting. Yes, you're upset and you probably have every right to be. But what is the end result you hope will happen? Are you going to throw away your chance to achieve your goal for one moment's satisfaction of telling someone off? Release your hostility to yourself or to a close friend, then take the time to think through a troublesome situation.

After you've figured out your objective, consider the ways it can be achieved. Who has the power or authority to make changes? Exactly how can this situation be resolved or improved?

Now you're ready to talk in a rational, articulate manner. After stating your case, you're calm enough to listen to alternatives proposed by your opponent. If you can work it out, fine. If it just isn't worth the hassle, then express regret and leave. You can disagree but remain on good terms.

Strategy

Solve the problem without attacking your critic. There's nothing that disconcerts your enemies more than your being kind and polite, even offering deserved praise. They want to hate you and you make it terribly difficult for them to do so. Get the discussion back to the issues by examining the facts or the evidence and trying to find some objective that's mutually beneficial.

Steps

1. Begin in a friendly way. Remember the amenities. The handshake, the smile, calling the person by the name or title you usually use. Inquire if this is a good time to talk and, if not, to make an appointment. Be alert to another's emotional state—if very high or very low, delay your talk.

2. Clearly articulate the problem and how you believe it should be solved. When you hear what you believe to be misconception or incorrect facts, let the person finish without your interrupting. Then question instead of stating "You're dead wrong!" With a softer response, ("I can see how you might have concluded . . .") you come across as a reasonable person.

3. Keep attacks impersonal. The ego is fragile, and attacks upon it can cause permanent hurt that won't go away. Don't claim to know someone's motives or feelings, but stick to the issues. Talk about the system or the procedures or the policy that must be instituted or changed. When you're speaking to a subordinate, don't attack the character ("You're the laziest person I've seen!") It's the performance you want improved.

4. Match your body language to your remarks. Don't send mixed signals, for example, nodding your head in agreement and then voicing a protest.

Script

(Watch your timing.) *I can see you're upset. I'll come back this afternoon* or *Is this a good time to talk about the Havilland problem? . . . Would you be free around 11 to discuss it?*

(Avoid denying or excusing and start questioning.) *What led you to think that was my decision? . . . And what kind of report did Ross see?* (Seek evidence.)

(Correct the data.) *I'm afraid you were given some bad information. If that were the case, how do you account for . . . ?* (then supply accurate facts.)

(Show you want to resolve the problem.) *At any rate, it's pretty clear that we're both looking for some of the same results. Do you agree that part of the problem is a backlog in record entry, and if so, what choices do we have?*

Summary

To keep from getting a reputation as a whiner, complain about matters that are really important to you. Brush off the insignificant; it's not worth your time or energy. Attack problems and procedures, not people. Getting your way may prove too costly if you've made an enemy in the process. You can be poles apart and respect each other's abilities. Be a gracious winner, acknowledging the rights of others to their views and thanking them for the discussion. Be a gracious loser, thanking them for their time and expressing your regret.

16.3 GRUDGES

Letting Go of Resentments

If you can't move beyond what's wrong, you're stuck in a rut. There's no way to examine what can be done for improvement unless you change your focus. Grudges are negative and pull you down. Eliminate them.

Harboring bitter, deep-seated ill will, hatred, and resentment over past differences is a heavy weight to tote. The longer you long for revenge, the heavier the load.

You don't ever have to like the person, but you do have to let go of the hurt and anger and other negative emotions the grudgee is causing you. Do it for yourself because it's better for your health, your outlook, your reputation, and maybe ultimately your job.

It's okay to get angry. And it's important to express this anger spontaneously and constructively, but don't let it build up. It's time to stop nursing the old grudge, because it's not doing you any good or earning you the respect and friendships you need. A grudge is a roadblock to getting where you want to go.

Strategy

Plan a pleasant confrontation. Your nemesis may be icy, distant, unforgiving, he or she may turn away when you walk by, refuse to speak directly to you when you're in a crowd—no matter. The old resentment and rancor won't go away without your initiating the effort.

Steps

1. Role play with a friend. Rehearse your approach. Be honest and straightforward and practice talking about the mutual benefits of ending the feud. Your adversary may simply be waiting for you to acknowledge that he or she has done a good job. Offer a legitimate compliment. Be prepared to laugh at yourself or point up the humor in the situation.

2. Stick to your beliefs. You don't have to agree on issues or positions, you just have to be able to discuss them. Show that you're willing to talk, and chances are the other person wants the same thing.

3. Recognize and confront your conflict. Separate the choices, examine the contradictions, and aim for a synthesis. When your opponents must give in, let them save face. If you must give in, be a gracious loser. If you can't work out your differences, at least you know you did your best.

Script

(Practice your talk until you feel comfortable.) *Josh, I've been wanting to talk to you for some time about the problem we had with . . . Although we disagree on basic concepts, I do admire your talent for . . .*

(Stressing mutual benefits.) *I still feel we should be moving in another direction. But since the boss has decided that we have to keep working together, both our jobs will be jeopardized if we don't work this out by ourselves. What do you say?*

Summary

To resolve old conflicts, go in determined that each of you has to win something in the confrontation. Be frank and direct about where you stand, and be willing to give your opponent the same opportunity. If you are willing to face the conflict head on and then let go of your grudge, you may find you've been successful in changing the way the other person acts toward you. You will have converted, or at least neutralized, another critic.

16.4 COMPLAINTS
Accenting the Positive Elevates Criticism

The big trick to successful criticism is making the other person feel happy about hearing what you have to say. Stop fearing criticism or thinking that conflict is bad. It can result in valuable creative effort or an important learning experience. And it can give you a chance to gain control over a touchy situation.

As a supervisor, you often want to give constructive, corrective feedback. The best criticism doesn't sound like a rebuke or a complaint. Your subordinate feels your genuine interest and desire to help and understands that you're suggesting a positive way for everyone to benefit.

But you're treading in troubled waters when you offer unasked for advice to your boss or colleagues. That's usually received as a form of criticism. The price you pay is justifiable resentment. If you must comment without their request on what others are doing, use questions to point out the trouble as you perceive it. Let your queries lead people to draw their own conclusions about the wisdom of their actions.

Strategy

Zero in on issues to be resolved instead of finding fault with individuals. Preserve the self concept. Forget about winning or losing in a contest of wills. Give everyone a way out without humiliation.

Steps

1. Protect the ego. Nobody looks forward to being criticized. But it can be palatable if the recipient feels the comments you are making are the answers they've been looking for. Concentrate on uplifting the spirit instead of deflating it. Use the question technique to avoid nagging or berating. Sandwich your criticism between two layers of positive comments and honest praise about the person's work. If you state the negative first, you risk being tuned out.

2. Impel rather than compel. Keep in mind the reason you're criticizing is to teach your subordinates to become more productive or effective. Be supportive in your remarks. At times you may want to include yourself in accepting some of the blame in order to get the problem on the table to resolve it.

3. Listen carefully. Listen with an open mind, without interrupting. Grant others the same right to contribute ideas. You may hear a partial solution to the problem. Subordinates often have suggestions for improving performance.

4. Deal with specific issues one at a time. Stick to the problem at hand without dredging up an incident that happened a year ago. After identifying mutual goals, discuss how to change or improve the situation. State your opinions frankly, calmly, and professionally.

Script

(Focus on improvement, not on disapproval.) *Sherry, I believe you've been making a good effort, and I know you've been looking for ways to speed up the reports. Along that line, have you identified any new bottlenecks? . . . Have you thought about changing their deadline dates? . . . Let me know next week how you're handling it. I'm sure I can count on you because this is important to all of us.*

(Share the blame to get the matter discussed.) *Jerry, I may not have made myself clear when I gave you the assignment, and if so, I apologize. But now we're faced with a serious problem which I hope we can resolve by putting our heads together.*

(Agree on the problem, goals, and options.) *Am I correct in believing that . . . ? How do you feel about those results? What do you think we should be aiming for?*

Summary

Criticism serves a vital purpose on a much higher plane than does placing blame and voicing condemnation. It can be motivational support when given to help others improve rather than to censure their actions. Concentrate on the desired results, the options, and on keeping everyone's ego intact. Win loyalty and respect for yourself by showing it to others.

16.5 OPPONENTS

Seeking Solutions from Adversaries

You're convinced that a colleague poses a threat to your career, and you feel powerless to fight back. You were sandbagged with an unfair accusation. He twisted reports of your good work into sharp, disparaging criticism. By taking bits and pieces out of context, he produced a lie about the procedures you used. And he never gave you the courtesy of asking for an explanation before he leveled the charge to your boss.

You suspect the motive was grandstanding at your expense. He poses as being vigilant, but he's only trying to make himself appear more important. How can you prove this? You can't. Don't even try. Find another route; not complaining to other colleagues—that will only enlarge the problem. And if you go to the boss without evidence, you'll look like a crybaby.

You're so furious, you see no way to deal directly with your opponent to cut through the web of misinformation you find yourself caught in. Even if he was uninformed or misinformed, he didn't bother to check facts before he attacked. You feel yourself sinking. What can you do?

Strategy

Make friends with your nemesis. Once you admit your anger to yourself, you can find a way to get beyond it. Maybe the attack stemmed from jealousy or hidden hostility, but your opponent may very well be oblivious to you. You just happened to provide a way for him to help himself.

Steps

1. Present the problem as one you both face. Then concentrate on your opponent's needs and the company's goals. Ask questions to make sure you agree on specific facts. State the consequences you foresee. Seek agreement on defining the problem before going on. Stick to issues, without mentioning your hurt feelings.

2. Ask for a possible solution. Acknowledge any part you may have had in creating the problem. Be on the lookout for negative body language as you proceed. Discuss your opponent's ideas realistically and logically. Offer a counterplan, if appropriate, including ways each of you would benefit. Question your opponent's reaction to your plan.

3. Seek a meeting of the minds. If you can't synthesize your ideas, at least you know you handled your anger in a constructive way. And your opponent is less likely to pick on you in the future. Standing up to him earns his respect.

Script

(Your view of the problem.) *Dick, I believe certain misinformation was distributed about my project.* (The passive voice here sounds less hostile than "you distributed.")

(Your view of the consequences.) *If we ask the boss to mediate our differences, we both go down more than a few notches. Do you think we can work this out? I'm willing to give it a try.*

(Admit any part of the blame that was yours.) *Okay, I concede that was an issue I overlooked. However, isn't it true that . . . ? How do you propose we deal with it? . . . What if we were to try . . . Do you see any flaws there?*

Summary

A sneak attack can be devastating. It knocks the props out from under you because you see no way to fight back and to destroy the enemy for ambushing you. That's a war you can't win. Instead, make peace and help yourself. Wait until you calm down, then talk to your opponent. Present the matter as a joint problem, with consequences that will adversely affect you both unless the two of you work out a solution. Your adversary will admire your toughness and avoid attacking you in the future.

16.6 PROBLEM SOLVING

Seeking Solutions from Employees

A growing number of companies are utilizing teamwork and peer pressure to motivate workers. Employee participation techniques, such as quality circle management, have been around for quite a while. Today's version compensates for lack of promotions and raises by offering cash bonuses to teams able to attack a specific problem and improve the quality of the product. Management still can say no to the team's offering, but it's clear they want to hear it.

With or without the bonus, we are looking more to teams for problem solving and morale lifting. With emphasis fading from a traditional star system that rewards the few, supervising small groups takes special skills. Now, more than ever, managers perceived as valuable and respected know how to communicate with subordinates. They inform, interpret, inspire, learn to listen, and elicit solutions.

The specific mechanism for encouraging ideas to bubble up to the top isn't as important as having an effective, follow-up system. Open, informal sessions allow each worker to assume some responsibility for the finished product. Working as part of a team, they no longer feel cut off, but are controlling a segment of their destiny.

Strategy

Use more small group discussions to permit true give and take among workers. Extract the thinking and opinions of subordinates by showing your appreciation of their efforts. Treat them with the consideration you show your customers.

Steps

1. Ask, don't tell. When you want to draw out the thinking of your people, break up into small groups, giving each person a chance to express opinions and ideas. If you start by giving your opinion you make it very hard for them to present a different view. Just ask the questions and gather ideas without voicing your judgment.

2. Promise only that an idea will be considered. Not all ideas are good. Some look good, but to higher ups with a better vantage point they may be impractical and can't be accepted. As a leader, when you know ideas won't fly, express appreciation for the contributions without pulling them apart. Let employees save face or they won't risk rejection again and will stop offering their opinions.

3. Keep your promise. Morale goes up when you say, "We need your thinking." And it plummets when there's no follow-through, never getting back to say if the idea was even considered. Don't promise if you don't intend to keep that promise.

4. Allow criticism of company policies. If you keep trying to protect your job by protecting the status quo, you not only block progress, you also drain enthusiasm. You come across as phony, and you abdicate your real value to the company, presenting a better way.

Script

(Pull out their thinking.) *Ben, you look as if you don't agree with Lisa's point. Tell me how you feel about it.*

(Promise follow up and keep your promise.) *I think there's merit to that suggestion. I'll do my best to argue the points you made at my next staff meeting and get back to you on it next time.*

(Show sensitivity when asked your opinion and you disapprove.) *Henry, you might want to think a little more about the ramifications if we were to do that* (instead of *"it can't work because . . . "*)

Summary

While the debate continues over rewarding individual achievement versus the thinking of the team, more and more companies are looking to teams for improved quality and better solutions. For the team approach to be productive, managers need to instill a sense of purpose and to clarify what's needed. You have to coach, career counsel, give direction, and facilitate. The old days of idle threats are out. Now you collaborate with employees to maintain your high standards and improve the overall system. The team approach works well because *everyone* has ideas and everyone's ideas are respected.

16.7 SURVEYS

Reaching Workers Afraid to Speak Up

You gain respect and value when you can come up with an answer or a way to get the answer. Consider the use of questionnaires and surveys to collect and analyze opinions, information, and suggestions from employees.

These surveys don't pretend to be the results of an exact science. Rather, they're a measure of current feelings as well as a method to gather additional ideas that can help the company improve its quality. Ideally, the answers are sought in such a manner that employees feel free to criticize the system. You're showing some deference to those who do the actual work.

Some more popular types include:

Attitude survey. Though not a precise measurement, it does provide prevailing opinions and eliminates interview bias.

Gallup poll. A form of attitude survey used to determine the current thinking on a given question.

Morale survey. Good for spotting demoralizing influences while they're still small and can be easily corrected. Help control an undercurrent by listing rumored complaints, asking if workers agree or disagree that the items are a problem.

Telephone survey. Serves to take a poll rapidly, for example, to report kinks in a new system. Some workers are reluctant to talk unless they're assured top management really wants to know or if they're guaranteed anonymity.

Suggestion system. Offers rewards (such as cash bonus or time off) when a selected suggestion reduces costs or increases profits. Good for asking workers to provide potential solutions to a stated problem or to find some consensus in dealing with a problem.

Strategy

Go to the people who do the work for their opinions and creative solutions. While surveys and questionnaires create awareness, they need to be carefully worded.

Steps

1. Provide a system for employees to ask questions. If anonymity is a concern, place tear-off forms on bulletin boards for workers to write their comments. Just be sure a mechanism is in place for responding to the comments, such as a column in the company newsletter—or the boss holding 15-minute Q & A informal forums at the work sites.

2. Keep questions on forms short and unambiguous. Eliminate complicated queries and ones that require individual interpretation. Present the possible answers as multiple choices. Go for quick reaction rather than overanalysis.

3. Report results in percentages. Follow with an analysis and your recommendations.

Script

(Word the question to express choice or trade-off.) *Would you rather have A . . . , B . . . , or C . . . ?*

(Telephone survey.) *In your opinion, will the procedure strengthen or weaken . . . ?*
( ) strengthen   ( ) weaken   ( ) undecided

(Morale survey) *Please check the answer that best applies in completing this sentence: It seems to me the most important question we're faced with is . . . ( ) a . . . ( ) b . . . ( ) c . . . ( ) d . . . ( ) e . . .*

Summary

Surveys and questionnaires can be helpful to you in determining how employees feel about given situations and in getting their suggestions for improving the system or the product. But they are equally important in satisfying the employees' need to feel involved and participate in a meaningful way. Use the technique to increase the respect you and your workers feel for each other.

16.8 VELVET GLOVE
Padding the Iron Fist

Some bosses think toughness and concern are at opposite poles and mutually exclusive. Toughness is good when it means making employees responsible for bringing the work up to your high standards, thereby instilling pride in the quality of your product. Toughness counts when you insist that everyone be held accountable for his or her behavior. Toughness is admitting mistakes and getting beyond it. Toughness also needs to be balanced by concern to make the work bearable.

Rather than diminishing the image of strength, caring enhances toughness. Workers will do anything for the tough boss who's not afraid to rephrase an order in a kinder way—the one who expresses appreciation, again and again, without assuming "they know how I feel." Workers don't know, and even if they do, they need to keep hearing that encouragement.

Motivating grows mostly out of mutual respect. When your subordinates are productive and creative, you bask in the glory. And you can put up another gold star for increasing your perceived value to the organization.

Strategy

Coach your workers to come up to your standards. Be tough and don't settle for less. But increase the value of your toughness by showing individual workers that you're concerned with their needs and development.

Steps

1. Develop a sense of mission. You have to know where you think the company should be headed before you can instill excitement in your workers. That's the peg for explaining how each one's job is important and how it fits into the total picture. Establish the marker; then insist on adherence.

2. Keep workers informed. They're entitled to know the truth, to know what's really going on. You have their respect once they know they can trust you to level with them. You have to trust them enough to share the problems and stop the rumors.

3. Direct, don't do. You also have to trust them enough to be an enabler, not an implementer. Give workers precise assignments, then let them figure out for themselves how to carry them out. Subordinates can't learn if you solve all their problems, make their decisions, and direct their staff. Everyone needs breathing room. Ask how you can help without becoming a compulsive checker. Tell them what they're doing right, then your correction. More coaxing, less commanding.

4. Hear their concerns. Be a better listener. If they need to improve skills, offer instructional software packages, suggest courses and seminars, and arrange role playing at problem-solving meetings. Discuss how to plan ahead before they reach a plateau. Help make learning interesting and fun as you assist workers to become more self reliant and assume greater responsibility for planning their careers and retirement.

Script

(Explain your vision.) *There's no doubt that we make the best widgets. Within the next few years, this company will have to expand the number of branches. Ellen, I'd like to you learn enough in your present job to move . . .*

(Be up front.) *Yes, I heard the same rumors you heard. I'll tell you all I can confirm at this point and how you will be affected.*

(Get facts before you accuse, then be tough and caring.) *Suppose you tell me what happened . . . Why? . . . Well, we all make mistakes. Let's review this and see what can be done. I know you do a great job with . . . But I'm unhappy with . . . What are you going to do about . . . ?*

Summary

Before you can be tough about your standards, you need to instill in your workers a feeling that they're part of something greater than their individual jobs. They need to see the relationship between their work and your vision of the company. They enjoy the challenge of working hard when they know you care enough about your subordinates to try to get them to move up to their potential.

In Conclusion

Ten Maxims to Memorize

1. Take more responsibility for managing your career. Betting on yourself is the safest gamble. No matter your organizational level, with so many companies downsizing, realize it's up to you to survive. Take advantage of courses to update and diversify your skills and advance your career. Work from a plan. This puts you in control of yourself, increases your confidence, and reduces risks. You're building a sound structure, and preparing for contingencies, not simply reacting.

2. Aggressively go after what you want. Even if you lose, you learn. Show more initiative by taking calculated risks. Keep current on business in general and your field in particular, as well as on political indications. Express your vision for the company by submitting unsolicited proposals. Team up with your boss to improve the poor climate by stressing benefits to the boss and the company. Watch for line position openings—project directors advance faster than staff support does.

3. Forget your job description and reshape your job to make it more important. Assume more responsibility. Or create a new job that fills a void. Create opportunities by linking your talent to company needs. Know your strengths. Review your past accomplishments to spot a core skill you can expand and market. Find the peg by defining what your company stands for and where it should be heading. What's missing? Relate your plans and proposals to meeting that purpose.

4. Truly believe in quality—you'll separate yourself from the pack. Pledge an unyielding commitment to maintain your high standards even if those around you don't display your passion for excellence. Check and recheck for accuracy and dependability. Compromise can corrupt morals. Make your means as honorable as your ends. All you can and should control are your own thoughts and actions; however, you can keep standards high by coaching your subordinates and asking your customers what they're looking for.

5. You can't change people but you can change their perceptions. Rephrase what you're saying to appeal to their wants and alter their reactions to you. Don't compare yourself or put anyone down, but sell yourself on your own merit. Market yourself via increased visibility and audibility. Tell how you improved productivity or profits, giving specific results you obtained. Let the boss know how you solved tough problems; keep notes for future negotiations. Find channels for spreading news of your accomplishments.

6. Stand up to your boss when your boss is wrong. Companies don't need more bootlickers. They do need innovative thinking and people with vision and a sense of mission willing to speak out for their beliefs—people who can think through a situation and articulate their opinions and ideas. When you suggest a workable plan, it is the boss's decision to accept or reject your views. But don't be afraid to offer. Your clear thinking in itself shows how valuable you are.

7. Develop your workers and mold your team. Your advancement hinges on it. Encourage maximum participation. Elicit the thinking of your troops and use their creativity. You'll increase their pride and improve your product or the system. Allow decisions to be made at as low a level as possible so that workers feel their being there makes a difference. Share your leadership via ad hoc committees, task forces, and teams. Take advantage of your greatest resource by helping proficient workers develop and move up. You'll advance as well.

8. Taste the desired result before you let the words leave your lips. You seldom need to give an instant answer to an unexpected question. If you're not sure, freeze, especially if your emotions are involved. Say you'll call or come right back or that you need a few minutes to consider the question. But do make ordinary decisions quickly. Move; you're probably right, and if not, you can correct these easily. Get a reputation for being quick and decisive. When you speak, get right to the point and stick to it.

9. Choose your battles. Fighting on too many fronts dilutes your message. Create greater impact by concentrating on a few issues. Save your strength for those essential matters truly important to you and let go of the less significant. Stand up factually, unemotionally, and professionally to those who try to walk all over you or who make racial, sexual, ethnic, age, and disability slurs. Debate real issues rather than attack individuals. When you need to find fault, blame the system, not someone's motives or personality traits.

10. Build a base of support. Continually make new friends and convert old critics. Make each person you work with feel that he or she is special in some way. Show your respect and honest admiration. Be gracious with old-fashioned good manners. Tell people you enjoy working with them. Let others save face. Build your own network of supporters inside and outside your organization by sharing information and helping one another. Let go of grudges and concentrate on converting your enemies into friends. You need each one you can get, at every level, to get the praises, raises, and recognition you deserve.

INDEX